EXPLORING COURTROOM DISCOURSE

Law, Language and Communication

Series Editors
Anne Wagner, Université du Littoral Côte d'Opale, France and
Vijay Kumar Bhatia, City University of Hong Kong

This series encourages innovative and integrated perspectives within and across the boundaries of law, language and communication, with particular emphasis on issues of communication in specialized socio-legal and professional contexts. It seeks to bring together a range of diverse yet cumulative research traditions related to these fields in order to identify and encourage interdisciplinary research.

The series welcomes proposals – both edited collections as well as single-authored monographs – emphasizing critical approaches to law, language and communication, identifying and discussing issues, proposing solutions to problems, offering analyses in areas such as legal construction, interpretation, translation and de-codification.

Exploring Courtroom Discourse

The Language of Power and Control

Edited by

ANNE WAGNER
Université du Littoral Côte d'Opale, France

and

LE CHENG
The Hong Kong Polytechnic University, Hong Kong

Routledge
Taylor & Francis Group
LONDON AND NEW YORK

First published 2011 by Ashgate publishing

Published 2016 by Routledge
2 Park Square, Milton Park, Abingdon, Oxfordshire OX14 4RN
711 Third Avenue, New York, NY 10017, USA

First issued in paperback 2016

Routledge is an imprint of the Taylor & Francis Group, an informa business

British Library Cataloguing in Publication Data
Exploring courtroom discourse: the language of power and control. – (Law, language and communication)
1. Semiotics (Law) 2. Forensic oratory. 3. Conduct of court Proceedings –Terminology.
4. Psycholinguistics.
I. Series II. Wagner, Anne, 1968- III. Cheng, Le.
340.1'4-dc22

Library of Congress Cataloging-in-Publication Data
Wagner, Anne, 1968-
Exploring courtroom discourse : the language of power and control / by Anne Wagner and Le Cheng.
p. cm. – (Law, language and communication)
Includes bibliographical references and index.
ISBN 978-1-4094-2347-8 (hardback : alk. paper) – ISBN 978-1-4094-2348-5 (ebook)
1. Law–Language. 2. Conduct of court proceedings–Language. 3. Semantics (Law) 4. Judicial process–Language. 5. Law–Methodology. I. Cheng, Le. II. Title.
K213.W337 2011
347.001'4--dc22

2010052226

ISBN 13: 978-1-138-25687-3 (pbk)
ISBN 13: 978-1-4094-2347-8 (hbk)

Contents

List of Figures and Tables

Figures

Tables

Notes on Contributors

Janet Ainsworth is John D. Eshelman Professor of Law at Seattle University School of Law. Her research interests center on linguistic ideology in legal doctrine and practice, and her work has appeared in notable law reviews, including the *Yale Law Journal* and the *Cornell Law Review*, as well as in linguistics journals. She currently serves as an editorial adviser to the *International Journal of Law and Semiotics* and on the editorial board of Oxford University Press's series *Law and Language*. She has also authored amicus curiae briefs addressing linguistic issues in a variety of legal contexts for cases argued in the United States Supreme Court.

Deborah Cao is a Professor of Griffith University, Australia. She is a linguist and a legal scholar. She has published in many areas involving the study of language and law, including legal theory, legal semiotics, pragmatics and court interpreting. She is a leading writer on legal translation, contributing to many major publications in the field. She has also published major works on the philosophical and linguistic analysis of Chinese law and legal culture. She researches and teaches animal law as well. She is editor of the *International Journal for the Semiotics of Law*. Her books include *Chinese Law: A Language Perspective* (Ashgate, 2004), *Interpretation, Law and the Construction of Meaning* (joint editor, Springer, 2007), *Translating Law* (Multilingual Matters 2007), *Animals Are Not Things* (China Law Press, 2007) and *Animal Law in Australia and New Zealand* (Thomson Reuters, 2010).

Silvia Cavalieri holds a Ph.D in Comparative Languages and Cultures from the University of Modena and Reggio Emilia, Department of Linguistic Studies on Language, Text and Translation. She lectured at the University of Modena and Reggio Emilia, University of Ferrara and University of Parma. Currently she holds a research grant at the University of Milan. Her research interests are focused on courtroom discourse, and in particular on the linguistic strategies used by counsels during the witness examination (that is, reformulations). She has presented her research at international seminars and national conferences. Her publications include "Disadvantage Before the Law: Bleak House," *Textus*, 21(3) (2008), 561–80 (with M. Bondi), "Reformulation and Conflict in Witness Examination: The Case of Public Inquiries," *International Journal for the Semiotics of Law*, 22(2) (2009), 209–21, and "Migration of Forms: Reformulations in Public Inquiry Witness Hearing," in D. Torretta, M. Dossena and A. Sportelli (eds.), *Forms of Migration Migration of Forms: Language Studies*, Proceedings of the 23rd AIA Conference, Bari, September 20–22, 2007 (Progredit, 2009), 417–31.

Le Cheng: Having received his Ph.D in Language and Law, MPhil. in Law, MPhil. in Applied Linguistics and served as a part-time lawyer, Le Cheng is currently a Research Fellow at Hong Kong Polytechnic University and concurrently Research Professor and Associate Director at the Center for Legal Translation, China University of Political Science and Law (CUPL), and Adjunct Professor at NIT, Zhejiang University. He is also a co-editor of *Translated Series on Law and Language* (CUPL Press) and a guest editor of *International Journal for the Semiotics of Law*. His interests and publications are in the areas of legal translation, semiotics, terminology, language and law, languages for specific purposes (LSP) and discourse analysis.

Christine Alice Corcos is Associate Professor of Law at Louisiana State University Law Center, and Associate Professor of Women's and Gender Studies, Louisiana State University A&M, Baton Rouge, Louisiana. She received a BA with High Honor from the Honors College, Michigan State University, where she was inducted into Phi Beta Kappa and Phi Kappa Phi, an MA in history from Michigan State University, and a JD from Case Western Reserve Law School. She has published numerous articles in the areas of speech and privacy rights, European legal history, and law and popular culture, the report *La Politique du Logement aux Etats-Unis: Aspects Juridiques, Economiques et Sociologiques* (with Grimes, Levasseur, Langlois and Ward, PUCA, 1998) and the collection *Law and Magic: A Collection of Essays* (Carolina Academic Press, 2010), and is the co-author of three casebooks, including *The Law of the European Union* (2nd edn., with Alain Levasseur et al., Carolina Academic Press, 2011). She runs several blogs, including the Media Law Prof Blog and the Law and Magic Blog, available at <http://lpcprof.typepad.com/law_and_magic_blog/>.

Maya Khemlani David is professor of linguistics at Malay University and an Honorary Fellow of the Institute of Linguists, United Kingdom. She was awarded the Linguapax Prize (2007) for research conducted on language choice of minority ethnic communities in Malaysia. Her primary research interest is in language in society, and her recent publications include *The Sindhis of Malaysia: A Sociolinguistic Account* (Asean, 2000), *Methodological Issues in Language Maintenance and Shift Studies* (Peter Lang, 2002), *Teaching of English in Second and Foreign Language Settings: Focus on Malaysia* (Peter Lang, 2004), *Language and Human Rights: Focus on Malaysia* (University Putra, 2007) and *Code Switching in Malaysia* (Peter Lang, 2009).

Sarah Dettenwanger is currently a law student pursuing her Juris Doctor at Duke University School of Law. She obtained her BA in Linguistics and MS in Sociolinguistics from Georgetown University in Washington, DC. Her research, abbreviated for this chapter, examined the relationship between power, address terms, reference and jury perception in US courts. Some of her previous language and law research has focused on lawyers' persuasive strategies on direct and cross-examination as a linguistic argument for alternative dispute-resolution. Other research interests include narratives in computer-mediated conversation, synchronic age differences in slang topics, and characteristics for distinguishing authentic versus faked suicide notes.

Flora Di Donato is currently a researcher in Philosophy of Law at the Open University Pegaso (Naples-I). In 2007, she was awarded a Ph.D in Philosophy of Law at the Law Faculty of the University of Naples "Federico" in collaboration with the Faculty of Law of the University of Neuchatel-CH. She also received grants to carry out research and training at the Swiss Institute of Comparative Law (Lausanne-CH), and NYU (School of Law). Her main research topics concern the relationship between *law, culture* and *narrative*, with a focus on the construction of facts inside the trial, as well as the interactions between *lawyer* and *clients* within the framework of the social-legal context. In 2010 she received the *Adam Podgórecki Prize* by the Research Committee on Sociology of Law for the book "La costruzione giudiziaria del fatto. Il ruolo della narrazione nel processo" (Milan 2008).

Gillian Grebler is a cultural and linguistic anthropologist with a special interest in law. Her current research deals with the socio-cultural and human rights implications of false confessions and wrongful convictions. During the 1980s she did law-related research in Israel and England on a range of policy-related issues concerning police, courts and trials, and participated in BBC Television's *Rough Justice* and two BBC documentaries about the interrogations and false confessions of psychologically vulnerable suspects. She contributed a chapter to the *Routledge Handbook of Forensic Linguistics* (Routledge, 2010) and has worked as a consultant and expert witness in a number of criminal cases where spoken language was at issue. Grebler is an adjunct faculty member in anthropology at Santa Monica College and is currently President of the Southern California Applied Anthropology Network (SCAAN, a subgroup of the American Anthropological Association), which serves practicing anthropologists throughout Southern California.

Joanna Jemielniak Ph.D is an Associate Professor at the Faculty of Law, University of Copenhagen. She was a Fulbright Fellow at Harvard University in 2004/2005, and subsequently held visiting appointments at UNIDROIT (2006), Harvard Law School (2007) and the University of California, Berkeley School of Law (2008). She is a member of the Editorial Board of the *International Journal for the Semiotics of Law* and an international collaborator on the International Commercial Arbitration Practices: A Discourse Analytical Study. She specializes in international business law and arbitration, as well as in theory of legal discourse. Her recent work focuses on legal interpretation and argumentation in international commercial arbitration.

Kim McCaul spent ten years as Senior Research Officer at the Native Title Section of the South Australian Crown Solicitor's Office, and has extensive experience of litigated and mediated land claim processes. He studied Anthropology at the University of Kent and at Adelaide University, and Applied Linguistics at the University of New England, where he also contributed to developing an online unit called "Language and the Law." He is currently an independent consultant based in Adelaide, South Australia. His research interests include cross-cultural relationship-building and dispute resolution, and cross-cultural understandings of altered states of consciousness and their role in personal development.

Richard Powell studied history, politics, law and Japanology in the UK before switching to applied linguistics and taking up a post as professor at Nihon University in Tokyo. His research areas include forensic linguistics, LSP, language planning and cross-cultural pragmatics. His recent books include *Motivations for Code-choice in Malaysian Courtrooms* (University of Malaya Press, 2008) and *English in Asia, Asia in English* (Prounsoop, 2010), and he has also contributed chapters to T. Hoffmann and L. Siebers (eds.), *World Englishes: Problems, Properties and Prospects* (Benjamins, 2007) and J. Gibbons and M.T. Turell (eds.), *Dimensions of Forensic Linguistics* (Benjamins, 2008).

Roxana Rycroft was born in Romania. She settled in the UK in 1991, and has been a practicing freelance interpreter and translator since 1993, specializing mainly in immigration and the Criminal Justice System. In 2001 she obtained a BSc. in Sociology from the University of Surrey Roehampton, and in 2003 completed an MSc. in Human Rights at the London School of Economics. Her research into interpreting within legal settings focuses on the legal model of interpreting and on the sufficiency or otherwise of the mere provision of interpreters to overcome barriers in communication. Her study "Communicative Barriers in the Asylum Account" was published in Prakash Shah (ed.), *The Challenge of Asylum to Legal Systems* (Cavendish, 2005). She lives in London.

Dr Petrina Schiavi holds a Ph.D in Sociology as well as academic and professional qualifications in law. She was admitted as a solicitor of the High Court of Australia in 1999, and practiced law for several years before moving into academia. She currently works as a Research Associate at the Regulatory Institutions Network at the Australian National University, where she conducts research on the role and influence of large corporations in global climate change governance. Petrina has ongoing research interests in critical discourse analysis, the function and effectiveness of regulatory institutions and instruments, and the environmental and social impacts of large corporations.

Anne Wagner Ph.D is an Associate Professor at the Université du Littoral Côte d'Opale (France). She is editor-in-chief of the *International Journal for the Semiotics of Law* (Springer) and co-editor for the book series *Law, Language and*

Communication (Ashgate). She is president of the International Roundtables for the Semiotics of Law. She has extensively published papers and edited volumes in the area of law and semiotics, legal discourse, law and culture, plain language and legal translation.

Foreword
Power of and to Language in Law

Deborah Cao

Whether one admits or not, or whether one knows or not, language entails power. Linguistic power often works in a subtle and invisible way because language is so natural and innate to all of us that it often works its power and influence without us realizing it. This is particularly the case in the courtroom and the legal process, where language sometimes exerts tremendous power as this book and the many chapters in it show us.

Thus, it seems to me that there are two kinds of power at work here: the power of language and the power of the law. The power of the law is much more visible and overt, seen and experienced every day by many and all of us. The power of language or linguistic power, on the other hand, is much more subtle and invisible, and most people are unaware of it even though most use that power every day and exert its power to achieve one's ends in different circumstances and contexts for better or worse. Importantly, language has the power to reveal as well conceal. It has the power to inform and enlighten as well as misinform and mislead.

Increasingly, the importance of language to law and the legal process is being studied and examined by linguists and legal scholars. Law is expressed in language and performs its functions through language. "Law would not exist without language," declares Danet (1980, 448). Similarly, Schauer (1993, xii) writes: "Language plays a central role in the operation of law that is different from, even if not necessarily greater than, the role it plays in facilitating many other forms of human interaction." The discipline of forensic linguistics—that is, the studies of language and law or language used in law and legal process—has now come of age as a discipline (Johnson and Coulthard 2010, 1). Forensic linguists are now involved in many areas related to the legal process, such as the analysis of language for evidentiary purposes in criminal and civil matters, including voice identification, author/speaker identification, legal interpreting/translation, discourse analysis of writing and spoken utterance and linguistic proficiency of the accused as in understanding a Miranda warning or police caution.

Of the many areas of forensic linguistics, it is believed that courtroom language represents the most dramatic of language use. I am pleased to read that this collection of essays specifically examines language in the courtroom in order to understand the law, or rather law's power. As Conley and O'Barr say correctly (1998, 2), for most people, and may I add that this is true for jurisdictions beyond the American borders, "the law's power manifests itself less in the Supreme Court decisions and legislative pronouncements than in the details of legal practice, in the thousands of mini-dramas re-enacted every day in lawyers' offices, police, stations, and courthouses," and the dominant element in almost every one of these mini-dramas is language. As they further point out: "To the extent that power is realized, exercised, abused, or challenged in such events, the means are primarily linguistic" (Conley and O'Barr 1998, 2). Language plays many crucial roles in the establishment and maintenance of relations of the many legal actors, be they lawyers, judges, jurors, criminals or victims. We often reveal who we are and our relations to others through the subtleties of language such as accent, choice of words, grammar, spelling and style, even the forcefulness of our voices as part of our linguistic capital. As Bourdieu (1991) tells us, language is a mechanism of power, and one's relational position in a social space is indicated by the language one uses, and the existing social structures affect or determine who has the right to be listened to, to interrupt, and to pose questions, and to what extent. Similarly, as Habermas (1998) postulates, language is not only the primary means of understanding and consensus, but also the potential instrument of power and inequality in the public sphere, and conversely, communicative action can be distorted by power and inequality, especially in institutional contexts. For our purpose, in the legal context, we need to understand meaning and power of language in relation to the specific parameters and in the light of the connections between the meaning of utterances and social practices and institutions in which communicative activity is embedded. Courtroom discourse, which represents the most institutionalized legal language use, can tell us much about the power of language and of the law, as well as the power of language in law.

Despite the progress in the law's ideals in most democratic countries around the world in the last few decades, there is still unease about the fairness of the law's application, especially today, in the increasingly globalized world where people from different backgrounds and cultures move much more frequently across national boundaries. As we are told, one can sense some of the problems just by listening to how language is used in a courthouse:

> Listen to the way that police officers and judges speak to women seeking domestic violence restraining orders. Listen to the way that mediators interact with husbands and wives in divorce cases. Observe the reasons of judges and jurors to the testimony of different kinds of witnesses. Talk to small claims magistrates about what constitutes a persuasive case … it is hard to escape the feeling that the law's power is more accessible to some people than to others. (Conley and O'Barr 1998, 3)

The courtroom is a stage for the display of linguistic power at work, with various actors performing largely linguistic acts in the discursive choices in (re) presenting and (re)constructing stories or events in real life. As was once described vividly, words can inform our mind, caress our feelings, excite our spirit, and kindle the flame of our hearts. They can also slap our face, punch us in the stomach, rattle our nerves or destroy our confidence.

Despite the importance of language in the judicial process, and despite the fact that language evidence can be as important as physical evidence, as Shuy (2005) points out, the reality is that linguistic evidence or the roles of language do not enjoy the same degree of scrutiny by investigators, lawyers and the courts. Furthermore, many of the legal professionals are unaware of the existence of forensic linguistics or forensic linguists (Gray 2010). This makes works such as the present book all the more important in bridging the communication gaps between lawyers and forensic linguists.

Before the reader embarks on reading this worthy book, perhaps it is fitting to remind ourselves: the pen or the *word* in deed is mightier than the sword!

References

Bourdieu, P. (1991), *Language and Symbolic Power*, ed. John Thompson, Cambridge: Polity Press.

Conley, J.M. and O'Barr, W.M. (1998), *Just Words: Law, Language, and Power*, 2nd edn., Chicago, IL: University of Chicago Press.

Danet, B. (1980), "Language in the Legal Process," *Law and Society*, 14(3): 447–563.

Gray, P.R.A. (2010), "The Future for Forensic Linguists in the Courtroom Cross-cultural Communication," in M. Coulthard and A. Johnson (eds.), *The Routledge Handbook of Forensic Linguistics*, London and New York: Routledge, 591–601.

Habermas, J. (1998), *On the Pragmatics of Communication*, ed. Maeve Cooke, Cambridge, MA: MIT Press.

Johnson, A. and Coulthard, M. (2010), "Introduction: Current debates in Forensic Linguistics," in M. Coulthard and A. Johnson (eds.), *The Routledge Handbook of Forensic Linguistics*, London and New York: Routledge, 1–15.

Schauer, F. (ed.) (1993), *Law and Language*, Aldershot: Dartmouth.

Shuy, R.W. (2005), *Creating Language Crimes: How Law Enforcement Uses (and Misuses) Language*, Oxford: Oxford University Press.

Chapter 1

Language, Power and Control in Courtroom Discourse

Anne Wagner and Le Cheng

Language is a powerful tool for social manipulation and seduction. Linguistic utterances are widely used or abused in court for the benefit of the defense or accusation. Throughout the volume, Goffman's "face-work" (for example, 1959) is the invisible link. In Goffman's (1967) terms, face is a mask that changes depending on the audience and the variety of social interaction and is the image of the self that is presented. Ordinarily, maintenance of face is a condition of interaction, not its objective (Goffman, 1967, 12). Emphasizing the conventionality on the one hand, and the diversification on the other hand, "face-work," according to Goffman (1967, 12), is to:

> designate the actions taken by a person to make whatever he is doing consistent with face. Face-work serves to counteract 'incidents'—that is, events whose effective symbolic implications threaten face. ... Whether or not the full consequences of face-saving actions are known to the person who employs them, they often become habitual and standardized practices .... Each person, subculture, and society seems to have its own characteristic repertoire of face-saving practices.

He stresses the analysis and understanding of role-playing in the social world and focuses his attention to the micro-sociology of daily life with an attempt to trace the meanings behind various ways of acting in different social situations. According to Goffman (1959, 1961), the mundane daily interaction can be approached from a broad social framework:

> The self ... is not an organic thing that has a specific location, whose fundamental fate is to be born, to mature and die; it is a dramatic effect arising diffusely from a scene that is presented .... (1959, 252–3).

> The self ... can be seen as something that resides in the arrangements prevailing in a social system for its members. The self in this sense is not a property of the persons to whom it is attributed, but dwells rather in the pattern of social control that is exerted in connection with the person by himself and those around him.

> This special kind of institutional arrangement does not so much support the self as constituted it. (1961, 168).

Besides the social reflection of the self, there are some face saving techniques that establish distance between a degrading situation and the self. His face theory helps us to shape and control the impression we make on others (audience) in order to influence their reactions and offers an alternative conception of the self as an aspect of social and cultural arrangements. In other words, we shall pay attention to the invisible links between front stage and back stage (Goffman 1959). The inter-semiotic interaction between the two stages enables us to step back from a subjective reality and symbolize instances, and therefore helps us to understand the inter-semiotic operation between the daily and individual activities to larger institutional social structures and processes of power and control in a given discourse community. These issues will be widely discussed in this volume.

Part I: Power and Control in Language

Mapping the contours of power and control in the courtroom equals an interpretation of linguistic utterances and their uses and abuses. This interpretation of law is apt to contribute to the changing needs of institutionally anchored functions, like those of judges, lawyers, legislators or citizens. In Part I, the contributors will highlight that communication (verbal or nonverbal) is a prerequisite of interaction of law and power in the courtroom.

Balkin suggests (1990/91):

> When people speak of the relationship between law and "politics," they mean law's relationship to the many different forms of power—economic, social, cultural, political, military and technological—that law constrains, enables or propagates. They also mean the ideals, ideologies and arguments that people use to justify these forms of power. "Politics" refers to people's contrasting visions and to the values that they want to realize or recognize in public life. But it also refers to the power to realize or recognize those values and visions. So when one considers the relationship between "law and politics" one is also interested in the question of law and power—how people justify and legitimate power directly or indirectly through law. And one must also account for law's own methods of proliferating its own power, whether it be through legal concepts, legal institutions, legal culture, legal education, legal officers, or the legal profession as such. In any case, law is not simply politics; rather it is a surprisingly plastic medium of discourse about power and for the exercise of power.

In Chapter 2, "Understanding Courtroom Communication through Cultural Scripts," Kim McCaul emphasizes the way in which the linguistic power imbalance of the courtroom perpetuates the colonial experience of Indigenous people in Australia today. By treating courtroom communication as a natural result of legal culture, the author explicitly avoids the kind of value judgments that some linguists arrive at when analyzing the seemingly asocial use that barristers often make of language. Instead, McCaul focuses on identifying and exposing the implicit assumptions that underpin the adversarial process, particularly exploring the logic of communication in the courtroom and how it arises naturally from the culture of the law. In this chapter the author pursues two aims: (1) to highlight a number of usually unstated premises that underpin courtroom communication, and (2) to propose a method by which those premises can be explained to lay people entering the courtroom, including L2 speakers of English and non-English speakers. To achieve this, Kim McCaul uses a tool from cross-cultural linguistics called the "cultural script."

In Chapter 3, "Witnesses on Trial: Address and Referring Terms in US Cases," Sarah Dettenwanger begins by discussing legal and linguistic backgrounds relevant to courtroom discourse. She then explains her choices for finding data through ethnography in DC courts, interviews with two US attorneys and a complete transcript from a federal case in Texas. Her findings focus on results from the DC ethnography and the trial transcript, with the interview data reinforcing facts and hypotheses. These findings indicate how witnesses can be treated differently based on their experience and comfort within the courtroom, using address terms and referring expressions as a "way in" to interaction and credibility.

In Chapter 4, "(False) Confessions Become Compelling at Trial," Gillian Grebler looks at several high-profile US cases built on confession evidence to see how attorneys manage these tasks. According to her, the purpose of a police interrogation is to get an admission or confession to a crime. Confessions have been called "the queen of proof," and they come laden with social and moral meaning. Prosecutors repackage confessions strategically and emotively, using a full complement of narrative devices. Their purpose is to provide jurors with a coherent, dramatic and compelling account of the confession. Defense attorneys have to arm jurors with enough knowledge of to evaluate whether or not the confession is reliable and trustworthy, and with knowledge of the ways this confession could be false.

In Chapter 5, "The Role of Metadiscourse in Counsels' Questions," Silvia Cavalieri focuses on the role of metadiscourse in counsels' questions during the witness examination, considering in particular the case of public inquiries in the UK. She discusses the functions of both textual and interpersonal metadiscourse in the realization of lawyers' argumentative strategies to build up effective questions in the two phases of the witness examination, namely the examination-in-chief and the cross-examination. In particular, this chapter aims to describe how counsels exploit the metadiscursive features to control both the form and the ideational content of the exchange through textual metadiscourse, as well as the power relationship with the witness through interpersonal metadiscourse. The results show that metadiscourse completes the argumentative strategy used by lawyers in order to control the witness's narrative, giving precise means to shape both the formal and the relational sides of their questions.

In Chapter 6, "Constructing Legal Narratives: Client-lawyers' Stories," following postmodern trends in the study of law, Flora Di Donato takes into consideration the development of theoretical orientations aimed at merging sociological, psychological and anthropological approaches with the observation of legal practice (that is, the law and literature movement, legal constructivism). Inside this theoretical framework, the qualitative approach of the chapter traces the birth and the evolution of legal narratives. It shows that narrations are determined by violation of the legal and cultural orders typical of a given context, and that they originate from the relationship between two or more actors. The hypothesis is that the trouble triggering the violation of the initial legitimate state stems from the tension existing between two or more interacting actors – that is, within a work or family context.

Part II: Power and Control Behind Language

Language has been identified as the "primary medium of social control and power" (Fairclough, 1989 [2001], 3), most notably in legal settings (Coulthard and Johnson 2007, 37), where the use of language is structured in such a way as to facilitate control through the exercise of power (for example, O'Barr 1982; Conley and O'Barr 1998 [2005]; Cotterill 2003). As exposed in this part, legal discourse is an essential tool in implementing and applying the law, to the point that it might plausibly be argued that legal reasoning is primarily a question of semantics and language interpretation. Courtroom discourse serves as an instrument of institutional empowerment and control. Exploring one of the dominant discursive legal interpretations of the courtroom eventually leads us to reflect upon alternative modes of resolution.

In Chapter 7, "Magical Images in Law," Christine A. Corcos examines the uses of magical images in law and the extent to which we can analogize similarities between law and magic, particularly as they are expressed in terminology, in dress, in venue and in ritual. A number of similarities come readily to mind. Lawyers and magicians perform a script, before an audience, in an effort to present a particular view of a set of circumstances. "Magic words" make up part of legal terminology. Though they may not realize it, lawyers, particularly defense lawyers, may imitate and adopt what are in essence a magician's skills, such as misdirection, to persuade juries of the validity of their arguments. In such ways, attorneys redirect the attention of factfinders, just as magicians redirect the attention of their audiences. Lawyers are interested in telling stories and creating illusions, just as magicians tell stories and create illusions. Both trial lawyers and magicians create a cohesive whole, for an extended period. When that time is over, when the trial is concluded, an attorney's work is over, just as the magician's performance concludes. Indeed, a number of lawyers are themselves amateur or professional magicians. Both magicians and lawyers educate those who would enter their ranks, and use special terminology, oaths and other rites to set themselves apart, for a number of reasons: to separate themselves from the lay public, to guard their special knowledge, to create an air of mystery about their roles, and to preserve their gatekeeper functions. In the courtroom, while the client may wish that her lawyer will provide deception as the return for the fee paid, the lawyer cannot promise deception. Instead, the lawyer can only promise a narrative constructed to persuade the factfinder (the audience) to a certain extent and no more. The lawyer cannot lie to the court. Though some popular culture commentators might have it otherwise, the law does not truly intend to reward deception. The secular magician is a professional deceiver who tells her audience that she intends to deceive for pay, and the audience willingly accepts the bargain. That agreement is the fundamental pact between performer and audience member. Indeed, the deception must be so successful that the customer will feel cheated if he does not feel that impossible feats have been demonstrated. Once he leaves, however, he knows he and all the rest of the audience are returning to reality and leaving the world of illusion. The world of magic exists only (or at least) for the duration of the performance.

In Chapter 8, "The Construction of Admissions of Fault through American Rules of Evidence: Speech, Silence and Significance in the Legal Creation of Liability," Janet Ainsworth examines two American evidentiary rules—the rule governing adoptive admissions and the rule construing apologies as admissible evidence of actionable fault—and reveals that both rules incorporate assumptions about language usage based, not on empirical evidence of linguistic practices, but instead upon the law's presumptions about the speech habits of the "reasonable man." The adoptive admissions rule provides that, when a person confronted with an accusation of wrongdoing fails to deny it, the allegation is deemed to be admitted through the accused person's silence. This legal rule presumes that the "reasonable" reaction to being accused of something would be an immediate and direct denial, such that silence is fairly interpreted as a tacit confession. This rule legally privileges direct, assertive and confrontational modes of speech, and ignores the ways in which factors such as cultural conventions of speech and power asymmetries in interactions impact choices in responding to accusation. Similarly, the evidence rule construing apologetic-sounding language to be an admission of fault rather than an expression of empathy penalizes expressions of emotional solidarity by presuming that "I'm sorry" is best interpreted as meaning "I'm sorry I did something wrong" rather than "I'm sorry that something bad has happened to you." By imposing these legal presumptions on the interpretation of the utterances of socially situated actors, the legal rules of evidence operate to channel and constrain interpretation of the language used by juridical actors, and frequently fail to give effect to their intended meaning.

In Chapter 9, "The Construction of Truth in Legal Decision-making," Petrina Schiavi examines the construction of "truth" by judges in legal decision-making. It investigates how judges operating within an adversarial system of law are able to "find the true facts" from the competing evidence presented to the court by parties to a dispute. In the process, it identifies the techniques used by judges to explain the phenomenon of conflicting accounts of reality in such a way that the belief in a single reality is not threatened. Fundamental to this analysis is the notion that language plays an integral role in the production and reproduction of social facts and social order. The chapter takes as its focus the rulings made by federal judges of the Family Court of Australia between 1976 and 1995 in which allegations of domestic violence were considered as part of the decision-making process. It employs theoretical approaches drawn from the fields of ethnomethodology, the sociological analysis of motivational accounts, and studies of narratives in discourse.

In Chapter 10, "Hidden Penalties Faced by Non-English Speakers in the UK Criminal Justice System: An Interpreting Perspective," Roxana Rycroft addresses some of the specific challenges faced by non-English speakers (NES) when dealt with by police and criminal courts with the assistance of interpreters. It also aims to analyze a number of limitations of the legal model of interpreting also known as "the conduit role," as set out by the National Register of Public Service Interpreters, the national database of public service interpreters in the UK. The methodology used in this chapter includes a mixture of primary and secondary data. The secondary research relates to literature concerned with the role of interpreters working in legal settings, the source of helpful concepts for evaluating the primary data deriving from the researcher's direct experience while working as an interpreter in the UK criminal justice system. She describes a number of interpreter–witness challenges faced by NES that sometimes occur outside the interview room or court hearing, or are difficult to capture unless experienced firsthand. They include statement-taking, use of unqualified interpreters, difficulties faced by NES in talking through interpreters, non-provision of interpreters, and credibility issues in relation to interpreters' use of register. Particular attention is paid to the question "How is the need for an interpreter assessed?" In exploring this topic, Rycroft highlights the lack of procedures in place to determine NES' linguistic ability to participate in and fully understand legal proceedings taken against them without the use of an interpreter, and proposes the introduction of a comprehension test. The author adds voice to the chorus of critics by presenting and evaluating examples from interpreter colleagues' and her own experience. These examples illustrate how, by being informed by the interpreted event taken as an ideal situation rather than a situated and constrained activity, the "conduit role" creates predicaments in instances such as: improper use of "footing," conflicting expectations of court interpreters, interpreter interventions, and coping with dialogue taking place partly in English. The author therefore contends that interpreters resolve such predicaments by use of personal strategies in order to stick to the "conduit role" and fulfill its dictum of "interpreter invisibility." This assumed invisibility serves the legal discourse best in that, as the legal profession's legitimacy resides in its claim to dispensation of justice according to findings of "truth," it simply cannot own up to the interpreter's participatory presence in legal encounters. As the personal strategies used by interpreters to disguise or minimize their presence during legal encounters are not known, they have the potential of introducing distortions in the interpreted event. The instances in the legal procedure described in this study command the attention of the legal profession and policy makers.

In Chapter 11, "Language Alternation in Kenyan and Malaysian Courts," Richard Powell and Maya Khemlani David compare language alternation in the courtrooms of two multilingual societies: Kenya and Malaysia. One starting point for comparison is the way in which languages are alternated, with four distinct patterns apparent in both countries: (1) lexical code-mixing, where words from one language are embedded in utterances with a lexicogrammatical matrix largely drawn from another; (2) code-switching, in which a speaker juxtaposes clauses and whole sentences in different languages; (3) code-shifting, whereby a speaker uses one language with one interlocutor and a different language with another, and (4) non-convergent dialogues, with two speakers conversing in separate languages and understanding each other without the help of an interpreter. Another area inviting comparison is the motivation behind courtroom language alternation. In Malaysia, where code-switching is particularly frequent, courtroom interlocutors appear to switch languages for a number of reasons, including clarification, emphasis, coercion and actual or metaphorical citation. Many of these motivations have been identified in Kenyan courtrooms as well. For example, defense lawyers routinely use English to gain an advantage over police witnesses who are less proficient in it, even after using Kiswahili quite competently in order to accommodate their own witnesses. In many ways, the situation in Kenyan courts today is similar to that which prevailed in Malaysia before the language planning of the 1980s. While there is very little sign that the Kenyan government will bring its national language into the legal domain to anything like the extent that this has been done in Malaysia, its use in combination with English indicates how such a transition might be phased in. Drawing upon courtroom observations and interviews with legal practitioners, this comparative investigation shows how bilingualism in courtroom settings may yield insights into motivations for language alternation in general while shedding light upon the complex nature of legal discourse. Its findings suggest that even though language alternation is often used as a discursive weapon to coerce or isolate courtroom participants, it can also serve to make the workings of the law more transparent without sacrificing the interests of justice.

In Chapter 12, "The Place of Arbitration in Online Proceedings as a Simulacrum," Joanna Jemielniak revisits loci arbitri from a rhetorical perspective. In the last few decades, international commercial arbitration (ICA) has become a significant alternative to state-administered adjudication. Growing popularity of this method of dispute resolution has resulted in introducing new means of communication to the arbitral proceedings. This chapter refers to this phenomenon, discussing consequences of the use of such intermediary tools, available now for the parties and for the arbitrators. The main topic of the chapter is the problem of loci arbitri, which in virtual proceedings has to a large extent become a highly conventional concept. It is discussed in a context of the territoriality principle and the status of arbitration as an arguably a-national method of dispute resolution.

After the explorations of courtroom discourse analyses, we can admit that law is *a discourse of power*, and that formula opens new dimensions. Once citizens become aware of the fact that they are speakers of a specific discourse, they are indeed empowered *to speak differently*—to each other as well as to their respective social institutions. Balkin (1990/91) formulates:

> by choosing to speak in the language of law, powerful people and interests can sometimes be called to account because they try to legitimate what they are doing in those terms. The people they take advantage of can argue that this is a misuse of law, an illegitimate attempt at mystifying rhetoric. They can appeal to the values that law seeks to protect to promote better, more just, and more humane practices and forms of human association.

References

Balkin, J.M. (1990/91), "The Promise of Legal Semiotics," 69 *Texas L. Rev.*

Conley, J.M. and O'Barr, W.M. (1998, 2nd edn. 2005), *Just Words: Law, Language and Power*, Chicago, IL: University of Chicago Press.

Cotterill, J. (2003), *Language and Power in Court: A Linguistic Analysis of the O.J. Simpson Trial*, Basingstoke: Palgrave.

Coulthard, M. and Johnson, A. (2007), *An Introduction to Forensic Linguistics*, London: Routledge.

Fairclough, N. (1989, 2nd rev. edn. 2001), *Language and Power*, London: Longman.

Goffman, E. (1959), *The Presentation of Self in Everyday Life*, Garden City, NY: Doubleday Anchor.

—— (1961), *Encounters*, Indianapolis, IN: Bobbs-Merrill.

—— (1967), *Interaction Ritual*, Chicago, IL: Aldine.

O'Barr, W.M. (1982), *Linguistic Evidence: Language, Power, and Strategy in the Courtroom*, New York: Academic Press.

PART I
Power and Control in Language

Chapter 2
Understanding Courtroom Communication through Cultural Scripts

Kim McCaul[1]

The courtroom offers a rich and fascinating field of linguistic research. It represents a unique space of social engagement and a distinct domain of language usage. Linguists have been particularly interested in the way barristers use language to construct particular narratives and evoke specific images in the minds of the judge or jury (for example, Aldridge and Luchjenbroers 2007; Coulthard and Johnson 2007).

While outsiders might think that confusion, ambiguity and misunderstandings should be avoided during the process of "justice," barristers are not only comfortable with those conditions, but may seek them out to the advantage of their client. To the lawyers, they are seen as a natural part of the adversarial system's competing narrative process. In this chapter I explore courtroom communication and its origin in legal *culture*, explicitly avoiding the kind of value judgments that some linguists arrive at when analyzing the seemingly asocial use that barristers often make of language (for example, Laster 2001). Instead, I intend to show how such language usage arises naturally from the culture of the law, and highlight a number of usually unstated premises that underpin courtroom communication. In particular, I will explore how the relationship between barrister and witness is determined by the culture of advocacy.

I will use a tool from cross-cultural linguistics called the "cultural script," which not only helps to develop succinct synopses of those premises, but could also provide a method by which they can be explained to lay people entering the courtroom, including L2 speakers of English and non-English speakers.

The Natural Semantic Metalanguage and Cultural Scripts

Cultural scripts are an example of the practical application of the Natural Semantic Metalanguage (NSM), first proposed by Wierzbicka (1972) and further developed principally by Wierzbicka and Goddard but increasingly also other researchers (various authors in Goddard 2006b; Goddard and Wierzbicka 2002; Goddard and

---

1 I would like to thank Professor Cliff Goddard and Dr. Nick Reid of the University of New England for their generous assistance, comments and encouragement. Any shortcomings are, of course, my own.

Wierzbicka 2004). The NSM is a mini-language that consists of approximately 60 semantic primes—words, bound morphemes or fixed expressions (see Table 2.1) that can be combined according to specific grammatical principles.

Table 2.1 Semantic primes adapted from Goddard (2009) and Wierzbicka (2006)

Grammatical/semantic category	Primes
Substantives	I, YOU, SOMEONE/PERSON, SOMETHING/THING, PEOPLE, BODY
Relational substantives	KIND, PART
Determiners	THIS, THE SAME, OTHER/ELSE
Quantifiers	ONE, TWO, SOME, ALL, MUCH/MANY
Evaluators	GOOD, BAD
Descriptors	BIG, SMALL
Mental/experiential predicates	THINK, KNOW, WANT, FEEL, SEE, HEAR
Speech	SAY, WORDS, TRUE
Actions, events, movement	DO, HAPPEN, MOVE
Existence and possession	THERE IS/EXIST, HAVE, BE (SOMEONE/ SOMETHING)
Life and death	LIVE, DIE
Time	WHEN/TIME, NOW, BEFORE, AFTER, A LONG TIME, A SHORT TIME, FOR SOME TIME, MOMENT
Space	WHERE/PLACE, BE (SOMEWHERE), HERE, ABOVE, BELOW, FAR, NEAR, SIDE, INSIDE, TOUCHING
Logical concepts	NOT, MAYBE, CAN, BECAUSE, IF
Augmentor, intensifier	VERY, MORE
Similarity	LIKE (AS, HOW)/WAY

These semantic primes share two qualities:

1. their concepts are intuitively clear and almost impossible to define without self-reference;
2. they have equivalents in all human languages (Wierzbicka 2006).

The second point makes the NSM an ideal vehicle to articulate complex cultural concepts in terms that are not ethnocentrically linked to any particular language or culture. It is from these semantic primes of the NSM that cultural scripts are constructed:

> The term "cultural script" refers to a technique for articulating culture-specific norms, values and practices in terms which are clear, precise and accessible to cultural insiders and outsiders alike. … The main goal of the cultural scripts approach is to understand speech practices from the perspective of the speakers themselves. (Goddard 2006a, 1)

Cultural scripts are developed on the basis of linguistic evidence, and often drawn from key lexical items used by a given group of people, but can also shed light on the non-linguistic aspects of culturally based behaviors. Wierzbicka suggests that cultural scripts offer a framework within which an *ethnography of thinking* can be meaningfully and methodically pursued (Wierzbicka 2006, 23). In this approach, "culture" is located in the shared thought processes, some conscious but mostly unconscious, of a given group of people. It is this "culture" that is reflected in the way a group of people uses language.

Two cultural groups are not necessarily distinguished through the lexical level of language. Since English has spread as a world language, it is now spoken by many peoples who are not Anglo-English. But though people may seem to be speaking the same language, the way they use that language differs significantly. According to Wierzbicka, the NSM "provide[s] a paradigm that … could guide future research into 'differences in communication across cultures,' including different cultures associated with different varieties of English" (Wierzbicka 2006, 18). While the language is ostensibly the same—English—the underlying thought-emotional connotations are not. The same can be said of legal English, a specialist language the acquisition of which includes acculturation into legal culture.

Communicative competence of legal professionals, within the domain of their profession, is built on a foundation of their communicative competence as members of Anglo society generally (Engberg and Janich 2007, 216). Specialization is such, however, that once a fair degree of communicative competence in the legal profession has been achieved, specialists can converse in ways that will only be understood with difficulty, if at all, by those with good communicative competence in English, but no specialization (cf. Gibbons 2003, 163–4).

My argument here is that acquiring communicative competence in a specialist area goes hand in hand with acquiring competence in specialized forms of thinking, that is, a specialist culture. Consequently, those lawyers who truly master their art are not only skilled in the specialist communication of their profession; they are essentially bicultural (cf. Laster 2001, 243).

My conclusions are based on extensive courtroom attendance, interviews with barristers, and analysis of legal textbooks and court transcripts to explore the underpinnings of this thinking and provide the basis for the cultural scripts developed here. While one could develop scripts for many aspects of the legal process, due to space limits I here focus on one key dynamic of legal communication: advocacy and what it means for the examination of witnesses.

The Culture of Advocacy

Legal culture strongly reflects a number of values that Wierzbicka identifies as core Anglo values. These include the "imperative of acknowledging the limitations of one's knowledge" (Wierzbicka 2006, 35) and the "emphasis on distinguishing what one knows from what one thinks" (Wierzbicka 2006, 37). Both these values have been encoded in guidelines for expert witnesses before the Australian Federal Court,[2] and arguably underpin the law's evaluation of every witness.

Wierzbicka's study provides clear evidence for the key role of the following words and values in Anglo culture, each of which we could readily associate with legal decision-making: "accuracy," "fact," "truth," "right," "wrong" and "fairness." We speak of "fair" trials, the "facts" of a case and an "accurate" transcript. Legal processes are implicitly designed to sift "right" from "wrong" and establish the "truth," or as one lawyer I interviewed said, "the truth on the basis of the facts of the matter."

Despite this semantic overlap, communication in court is not like everyday communication. It is highly regulated and conducted for a specific purpose, and that is to present information relevant to a particular matter to one or more judges or a jury. To present this information, each party puts evidence before the judge by way of one or more witnesses who have something to say about events or facts relevant to the matter at hand. Even where the evidence is really a "thing," such as CCTV footage or a blood sample, a witness will need to give evidence about its authenticity, origin and so on.

A barrister is a communication specialist whose role it is to present information to the court in such a way that it favors his or her client's case. Barristers place their communicative skills at the service of their clients. Being an *advocate* for their client's cause is their fundamental role in the courtroom. I here explore their role as advocates in the context of the so-called *Pinkenba* case, analyzed by Eades in a number of publications (Eades 2004b; Eades 2006; Eades 2007; see also Alter 2004).

Very briefly, in the *Pinkenba* matter, three Aboriginal teenagers (aged 12, 13 and 14) had brought charges against six police officers for unlawful deprivation of liberty. The six officers had picked the three boys up in a Brisbane shopping center. The boys had not committed any offense and were just hanging around. However, they had committed offenses in the past, and apparently the officers wanted them to think about their misdemeanors. For some reason they thought that this could be achieved by taking the three boys in three separate cars to an industrial estate 14 kilometers out of town and leaving them to walk back.

During the trial, the police officers were represented by two of the most senior barristers in Queensland, while the boys' case was brought by a junior lawyer from the Office of the Director of Public Prosecution. Most of the trial

2 See Practice Notes for Expert Witnesses in Proceedings in the Federal Court of Australia, <http://www.fedcourt.gov.au/how/practice_notes_cm7.html>.

was taken up by the defense barristers cross-examining the three boys in an extremely intimidating and harassing manner, as in the following sample:

> **Barrister**: And you knew when you spoke to these six police in the Valley that you didn't have to go anywhere with them if you didn't want to, didn't you?
>
> **Witness**: No.
>
> **Barrister**: You knew that, Mr Coley I'd suggest to you, PLEASE DO NOT LIE. YOU KNEW THAT YOU DIDN'T HAVE TO GO ANYWHERE if you didn't want to, didn't you. DIDN'T YOU? DIDN'T YOU MR COLEY?
>
> **Witness**: Yeh.
>
> **Barrister**: WHY DID YOU JUST LIE TO ME? WHY DID YOU SAY "NO" MR COLEY? YOU WANT ME TO SUGGEST A REASON TO YOU MR COLEY? THE REASON WAS THIS, THAT YOU WANTED THIS COURT TO BELIEVE THAT YOU THOUGHT YOU HAD TO GO WITH POLICE, ISN'T THAT SO?
>
> **Witness**: Yeh.
>
> **Barrister**: AND YOU LIED TO THE COURT, TRYING TO, TO … YOU LIED TO THE COURT TRYING TO PUT ONE OVER THE COURT, DIDN'T YOU?
>
> **Witness**: No.
>
> **Barrister**: THAT WAS YOUR REASON, MR COLEY WASN'T IT? WASN'T IT? WASN'T IT, MR COLEY?
>
> **Witness**: Yeh.
>
> **Barrister**: YES. BECAUSE YOU WANTED THE COURT TO THINK THAT YOU DIDN'T KNOW THAT YOU COULD TELL THESE POLICE YOU WEREN'T GOING ANYWHERE WITH THEM. THAT WAS THE REASON, WASN'T IT? WASN'T IT?
>
> **Witness**: Yes.
>
> **Barrister**: Yes. (quoted in Eades 2004a, 171; capitals indicate raised volume)

While the blatant harassment of minors in this and other transcript excerpts Eades provides is disturbing, on the basis of the fundamental value of advocacy on which the barrister's practice is based, this kind of cross-examination is entirely logical. One could say it is culturally logical, and this logic is reflected in a number of legal textbooks.

One striking aspect of legal texts is the frequent analogy between courtroom work and war. For example, Napley suggests that "the conduct of a trial at law is, in many respects, comparable with the conduct of a military operation. Going to law is a great deal like going to war" (Napley 1991, 74; see also Phillips 1985, 64). Similarly, Gibbons suggests that "adversarial proceedings … take the form of a ritualized battle between the prosecution and the defence" (Gibbons 2003, 6). Building on this analogy, the barrister is both a general, carefully planning a strategy, and the frontline soldier executing the plan. Obviously, there are certain rules of engagement regarding a barrister's relationship with other legal representatives, witnesses and the judge. But within those rules the barrister is duty bound "to use every means fairly open on behalf of your client" (Phillips 1985, 4). Tronc and Dearden provide more detail on how barristers should represent their clients:

> Ultimately you are there in the interests of the client and you are paid … to represent that client's interests *unashamedly, firmly, vigorously, persuasively and relentlessly*. (Tronc and Dearden 1993, 23; my emphasis)

This role of the barrister is considered fundamental to the English legal system. A historic trial in England in the late eighteenth century provides a logical and often-cited foundation for the role of the barrister (for example, Napley 1991; Phillips 1985). In that matter, a barrister by the name of Erskine defended the author Thomas Paine, who had written a book that included negative depictions of the royal family for which he was being sued. Erskine accepted the brief, despite much personal insult and direct threats from senior government figures. In court he gave a rousing speech setting out the role of the advocate that included the following passage:

> From the moment that any advocate can be permitted to say that he will or will not stand between the crown and the subject arraigned in the court where he sits daily to practice, from that moment the liberties of England are at an end. If the advocate refuses to defend from what he may think of the charge or the defence, he assumes the character of the judge; nay, he assumes it before the hour of judgment, and in proportion to his rank and reputation puts the heavy influence of perhaps a mistaken opinion into the scale against the accused, in whose favour the benevolent principle of the English law makes all presumptions and which commands the very judge to be his counsel. (quoted in Napley 1991, 60)

Napley comments on this quote:

> This is a passage which all advocates should read and read again …. (Napley 1991, 60)

Similarly, Phillips suggests that:

> At the core of the modern democratic state are the ideals of freedom from arbitrary arrest and freedom from conviction and punishment without fair trial. … But such ideals will wither unless there exist men and women who are prepared to strive to see that they are given practical application and effect—regardless of personal considerations. Hence, the necessity in every civilised community for a body of skilled and honourable advocates. (Phillips 1985, 18)

It is this fundamental logic within which the barristers defending the police officers in the *Pinkenba* matter would have been operating. From an outsider's perspective they may look like manipulating bullies. On the basis of their own cultural logic, their actions were upholding fundamental social principles. In fact, they may have been negligent in their professional duty had they acted otherwise. Here is another statement, this time from a judge, that really brings the point home:

> Every counsel has a duty to his client fearlessly to raise every issue, advance every argument, and ask every question, *however distasteful*, which he thinks will help his client's case. (Lord Reid in *Randel* v. *Worsely*, cited in Dal Pont 2001, 445; my emphasis)

It may seem obvious to the outsider that three young Aboriginal boys are not in a position to assert themselves when confronted by six police officers. The law on the particular charge leveled against the police officers, however, required definite evidence that they had forced the boys, and this is what the barristers successfully undermined. As seen above, the judge has to presume the police officers innocent and maintain their innocence as long as he has any doubt as to whether they forced the three boys into the cars against their will. The officers' barristers succeeded in creating such doubt.

As recently as 1998, the full bench of the High Court confirmed that "confrontation and the opportunity for cross-examination is of central significance to the common law adversarial system of trial" (*Lee* v. *The Queen*, cited in Ross 2007, 340). A fundamental principle of that system is that the two (or more) sides are both competently represented to bring their best case. The *Pinkenba* case highlights a crucial problem with the adversarial system. While it may support "the ideals of freedom from arbitrary arrest and freedom from conviction and punishment without fair trial," as suggested by Philips (1985, 18), it does so only when the advocates on either side are evenly matched.

The extent to which the barristers for the police were permitted to use their linguistic and social dominance in their favor reflects badly on the prosecution counsel and on the judge, who should not have permitted the harassment and intimidation of minors. As a result, the barristers for the police were able to push their clients' case much further than they may have been able if the boys had also had senior counsel representing them. To that extent, the *Pinkenba* case is an example of the adversarial system failing its own principles.

None the less, it is easily seen how such a situation can arise from the very logic on which the adversarial system is premised. The logic from which barristers are operating could be captured in the following script that describes their relationship to the client.

Cultural script for advocacy 1

You are "my client". When I do something for you, it is good to think like this:

(a) You say some things happened/are like this.

(b) Other people say the same things did not happen (are not) like this.

(c) I will say many times that the things happened/are like you say. I will say it well.

(d) Other people may think something bad of me because of this. I will not think about that.

Commentary

(a) and **(b)** set out the adversarial nature of the legal process. The client has one story about a particular set of circumstances, while the other party has another story. The "things" that "happened like this" in this context can be something as specific as a string of events leading up to a fight in a pub, or more abstract like someone's state of mind or intention.

(c) is the core of the advocates' role: to represent his or her client's case, continuously and well within the given legal framework in which the action is taking place.

(d) sums up the possible by-product of this action, namely that people on the other side might think something bad about the barrister. This could be even wider, so that, for example, barristers defending people who are publicly branded as evil (a rapist or pedophile for example) can become associated with those people in the media and the public mind. However, the committed barrister will not let this interfere with his or her advocacy.

Their role as "questioner" clearly defines the barrister as the dominant character in the courtroom:

> The art of effective questioning lies in the relentless building up, step by step, of an inescapable conclusion. In the questioning which takes place both in examination-in-chief, and also in cross-examination, the advocate is constructing a wall of evidence. Each question is a brick in that wall. (Tronc and Dearden 1993, 12)

The manner in which barristers ask questions is a salient cultural feature of legal English. In standard English, people may ask direct questions, but usually only about "safe" topics, such as "What did you do on the weekend?" Béal (1992) has shown that in standard English, such questions are frequently mere routines for the sake of being polite. The answer may or may not be of actual interest, and it is uncommon to follow up the original question with further direct questions. When people do ask a series of direct questions, they frequently accompany this with an apology. It is usually considered rude, to openly doubt the veracity of an answer during commonplace conversations. Not so, however, in the court of law.

Barristers communicate information to the judge by way of questions to witnesses. Essentially, the barrister is not asking questions for the sake of the information, but to provide a particular picture of events or facts to the judge. This may include wanting to paint a particular picture of the witness being questioned, and during cross-examination direct attacks against the witness's honesty and integrity are perfectly permissible.

The two domains of legal questioning, examination-in-chief and cross-examination, are a consequence of the adversarial system, where (usually) witnesses are called by one or the other of the parties because their evidence in some way supports that party's case. The party calling the witness will lead them through their "evidence-in-chief" and is not allowed to ask either leading or probing questions. Commonly, the barrister will have gone through the questions with the witness in advance (known as "proofing the witness"). When it comes to asking the questions before the judge, the witness will expect the questions, and the barrister the answers that are likely to be given. Depending on the confidence the barrister has in the witness, questions can be either closed or open.

During cross-examination, the barrister for the other side "tests" the narrative provided by the witness during evidence-in-chief. This barrister has not had the benefit of proofing the witness, but is permitted to ask leading questions and to explore issues probingly. Essentially, the barrister calling the witness will seek to portray the witness as credible and use the evidence favorably to his or her case. The barrister for the other side will seek to discredit the witness and minimize the reliance that can be placed on the evidence, or ideally show it to be in fact favorable to *his or her* case. The barrister does what he or she does for one purpose only: to convince the judge of the merits of his or her client's case. The following script seeks to describe this underlying motivation.

Cultural script for advocacy 2

You are "the judge." When I say things to you I think like this:

(a) There are many things people can say to you.

(b) I want you to hear some things. When you hear those things it is good if you think:

"Those things are true. That is what happened."

(c) Someone else wants you to hear some other things. When you hear those things it is good if you think:

"Those things are not true. That is not what happened."

(d) I will say many things to you because of this.

Commentary

(a) makes the point that there are many possible accounts that could be given to the judge of any given issue.

(b) points out that the barrister wants only particular accounts to be given to the judge and wants those accounts to be compelling.
(c) points out that others will have other accounts to give the judge. What the barrister wants to achieve is that those accounts are not as compelling as his or her own.
(d) clarifies what the barrister does to achieve this—he or she speaks to the judge at length, either indirectly through witnesses or directly in making submissions.

Having considered the advocacy role of the barrister, I will now turn to the position of witnesses and what is expected of them.

Witnesses

> The witnesses to be called in your trial are simply the means of conveying to the tribunal of fact events that happened at other times and other places. They are the medium by which the story will unfold. (Phillips 1985, 25–6)

This story is told for the benefit of the judge, and it is only witnesses who can provide the judge with information, not barristers. This is one reason why there is a lot of pressure on witnesses to answer questions cogently.

According to Wierzbicka, "one of the central values of Anglo culture is … the value of personal autonomy" (Wierzbicka 2006, 50). She develops the following cultural script for that value, which she refers to as the "autonomy script":

> [People think like this:] when I do something it is good if I do it because I want to do it, not because someone else wants me to do it. (Wierzbicka 2006, 52)

Witnesses in legal proceedings leave this script behind, and are obliged to respond to questions put to them by the barristers and judge. From the witness's perspective, the two rounds of questioning can be quite distinct experiences. Evidence-in-chief often takes a more narrative form, while cross-examination has quite a different emphasis. Usually, the witness will be asked very specific questions and the barrister may seek to confine the witness to very specific and brief answers.

One of the reasons for this is that the two barristers are either looking for totally different narratives of an event or a set of circumstances, or at least trying to emphasize different aspects to the same narrative. The multiple-narrative approach may go beyond merely the information conveyed by the witnesses, and also extend onto the witnesses themselves. Usually, a barrister calling a witness will want to portray the witness as honest and willing to assist the court to the best of his or her ability. A cross-examining barrister, on the other hand, may raise doubts about the witness's honesty, memory, character in general or ability to make any meaningful contribution to the matter at hand. The transcript from *Pinkenba* quoted above provides a vivid illustration of a barrister seeking to portray the witness as a deliberate liar.

Navigating these competing demands from the different lawyers can be daunting and challenging, especially when the lawyers enjoy natural linguistic dominance. From the witness's point of view, what is important is to answer questions carefully and precisely, but without agreeing with propositions one does not actually agree with. Nor should a witness try to outsmart or "play games" with the cross-examiner, as that can easily make a bad impression before the judge. Working with witnesses can be very challenging for barristers, as even the most competent seeming witnesses can stray from their proofing session once in the witness box.

The following script summarizes key characteristics of what would be considered a good witness: clarity, credibility, and making an honest attempt at saying everything one knows without being motivated by anything other than a desire to tell the truth.

Cultural script for impression in court

When I say things in court, it is good if people can think about me like this:

(a) "When this person says something about a thing, all the people at this place can hear him/her and know something about the thing because of this."

(b) "When this person says something happened/is like this they know it well. They won't say something happened/is like this when they don't know it well."

(c) "When this person says something about a thing he/she says all he/she knows about the thing."

(d) "When this person says something about a thing many times, he/she says the same thing many times. He/she does not say one thing one time and some other thing some other time."

(e) "When this person says something, he/she says it because he/she thinks it is true, not because he/she wants other people to think something good about him/her because of it."

Commentary

(a) refers to clarity of answers, so that if a person says something about a topic, people actually know what is being said about that topic.

(b) emphasizes the witness sticking to "facts," that is, things they know about from their own knowledge not something they have been told, and that the person knows this thing well, not just a little bit.

(c) makes the point that it is good to say as much as one can.

(d) emphasizes the need for consistency, especially between that which is said during evidence-in-chief and during cross-examination.

Finally, **(e)** makes the very important point about the motivation of the witness. Even though this script emphasizes that people will think good things about a witness if he or she behaves in a certain way, it is important that the judge does not think the witness is motivated by anything other than a desire to tell the truth.

As indicated earlier, a cross-examiner is entirely permitted to "test" the honesty and integrity of a witness, even to the extent of introducing extraneous material, as long as the overall point, for example that the witness is not credible, can be argued to be relevant to the proceedings. The following script could serve as a primer to give witnesses an understanding of the possible intentions of the cross-examiner.

Cultural script for intention of the cross-examiner

You are "the other lawyer." When you say something to me, it is good to know this about you:
(a) You want other people to think something.
(b) You may want other people to think something bad about me. You may say things like this to me because of this:
"The thing you say is not true. The thing you say is not what happened."
"What you say happened, you can not know happened."
"What you say now is not what you said before."
(c) You may want other people to think something else about the things I say. You may say things like this to me because of this:
"When you say one thing, it is like this other thing that I say."
(d) You may say things like this to me many times.

Commentary
(a) outlines the driving intention of the cross-examiner, namely to create an impression in the minds of other people in the court, most importantly the judge.
(b) implies that it may be in the lawyer's overall scheme to create a bad impression about the witness being cross-examined. The three examples of what might be said to the witness all go towards doubting the credibility, or at the least the coherence or relevance, of the witness.
(c) sums up the relabeling of a witness's statement in a way favorable to the lawyer's case (this is explored in more detail below).
(d) makes the point that cross-examiners can relentlessly cover the same topic.

Having explored both barristers and witnesses, I will end by looking at a key dynamic in their communication: the battle over the meaning of key words.

Relabeling

Part of the competing narrative approach of the adversarial system is that two barristers may seek to label the same events in different ways:

> Lawyers choose their language carefully. Words create images which colour our perceptions of events and people. In an Israeli rape trial, for example, the prosecutor characterised the sexual act as "sexual torture" whereas the defence referred to it as "romance". In a United States manslaughter case, the alleged victim was referred to variously as a "baby", "child", "premature human being" and "foetus". (Laster 2001, 268)

The purpose, of course, is to persuade judge or jury to accept whichever version of events the barristers are arguing for.

As a result, witnesses under cross-examination may have to navigate the barrister trying to impose his or her interpretation, his or her label, on the evidence that is being given (cf. Aldridge and Luchjenbroers 2007; Eades 2006). We saw above how in the *Pinkenba* cross-examination, the barrister was demanding that the witness agree with his description of the witness's motivations. In that case, the witness's age and background meant he was not in a position to resist the barrister's linguistic dominance. In the following example, taken from a South Australian Royal Commission known as the *Hindmarsh Island Bridge* case, the Aboriginal witness is articulate and confident, but the barrister still insists on imposing his own label:

> **Barrister**: How did you know that connecting the island to the mainland by a bridge, that is, the linking of the island to the mainland by a bridge, was somehow offensive to its significance as being a place of women's business?
>
> **Witness**: I think it is just common sense.
>
> **Barrister**: But you didn't know anything about the content of the women's business?
>
> **Witness**: No, I still don't know any of the content.
>
> **Barrister**: It may be that a bridge to the island from the mainland would have no effect on—
>
> **Witness**: It is still going through our waters.
>
> **Barrister**: I beg your pardon?
>
> **Witness:** It is still going through the waters.
>
> **Barrister**: You don't say the waters is the women's business, do you?
>
> **Witness**: I am saying the importance of the waters.
>
> **Barrister**: The importance of the waters is something to do with women's business, is it?
>
> **Witness**: It very well could be, but it is important to the Ngarrindjeri culture because of the meeting of the waters. I didn't want to say this, but the place of the waters relates to what we call—the Ngarrindjeri people call Ngatji, which is each clan group's symbolic totem, so to speak. Those places like that is where these things breed, where they live, where they feed, all those things. You upset

the totem area, you are upsetting everybody. But I don't expect you would understand that, the Ngarrindjeri Ngatji.

Barrister: Let me put a suggestion to you: what you are talking about is a disturbance to the environment. Is that right?

Witness: No, more than that. To what those Ngatji are to the people. They are not just animals and fish and snakes and things to us. They are real. They are more like people. Spiritual.

Barrister: So it is really nothing to do with women's business, is it?

Witness: It is combined with all those things.

Barrister: But—

Witness: You can't get it.

Barrister: You make an attempt to convey it to us please.

Witness: I have no—

Barrister: You were saying that the island is significant because it is a place of women's business, and that a bridge linking the mainland to this place of women's business would be a desecration. That's what you are saying, is it?

Witness: Yes, there is no way—

Barrister: And you don't know, do you, by necessity, a jot about what the women's business is, do you?

Witness: (Witness shakes head)

Barrister: So you cannot tell us, can you, in what way a bridge would affect the spirituality of the island, which is women's business, can you?

Witness: No, I have no way in the world of trying to explain that to you. I never come here to talk about the women's business on that site.

Barrister: You are in no position to talk to us about it, are you?

Witness: Because I can't, I am a man.

Barrister: That's right. So your objection to the bridge really comes down to an environmental objection, isn't it?

Witness: No, a spiritual.

Barrister: A bridge is going to—

Witness: Spiritual.

Barrister: Pardon?

Witness: A spiritual.

Barrister: Is there some other spiritual aspect to the island which would be affected by a bridge, is there, not women's business?

Witness: I just finished talking to you about it, Ngatji related.

> **Barrister**: I want to put a label on it so we can understand it. Is it the case that what you are talking about—that is, that a bridge cannot go to the island—is to do with some other spirituality of the island, not women's business?
>
> **Witness**: I am talking about my business.
>
> **Barrister**: Can you tell us as much as you can about that?
>
> **Witness**: I said it just now, N-G-A-T-J-I.
>
> **Barrister**: Which is what you are talking about, is a question of protecting the environment from a lot of people coming to the island and ruining it? That's what it is, isn't it?
>
> **Witness**: You can interpret it as environment, I don't. We have different interpretations it seems. We cannot, as Aboriginal people, separate environment and culture. They go hand in hand.
>
> …
>
> **Barrister**: I am suggesting to you that your objection to the bridge, in the end, boils down to really protecting the island from too many people coming onto it and the degradations that would lead to in terms of wildlife, plants, and that sort of thing. That's what it is about, isn't it.
>
> **Witness**: Well, that's what you are calling it.
>
> **Barrister**: You say it is more than that, do you?
>
> **Witness**: *Yes*. (transcript quoted in Hemming 1996, 27–9)

Immediately after first mentioning Ngatjis, the witness sought to explain their significance:

> **Barrister**: Let me put a suggestion to you: what you are talking about is a disturbance to the environment. Is that right?
>
> **Witness**: No, more than that. To what those Ngatji are to the people. They are not just animals and fish and snakes and things to us. They are real. They are more like people. Spiritual.

The barrister does not engage with this information, but turns to another topic, and then proceeds to simply ignore the witness's repeated assertion that he is talking about something spiritual. The barrister instead insists on using the label "environment" as a way of re-framing the witness's statement in a way beneficial to his client's case.

In doing so, he was acting in full coherence with his culturally ascribed role to "create a particular perception of reality and a set of convincing impressions that highlight your client's case" (Tronc and Dearden 1993, 5).

The following script summarizes the obligation on a witness to answer, and the pressure that a cross-examiner may exert in seeking to relabel a witness's evidence.

Cultural script for cross-examination from the witness's perspective

You are "the other lawyer." When I say things to you it is good to think like this:
(a) Many times you will say something like this to me:
"I want to know something. I want you to say something in one way about it because of this."
(b) When you want me to say something, I cannot not say something.
(c) When I say something, it is good if I say something because I think it is true, not because you say it is true.

Commentary
(a) highlights that the cross-examiner is likely to put a predetermined set of events and get the witness to agree or disagree, that is, "say something in one way."
(b) sums up the obligation on the witness to answer the question.
(c) expresses the tension that can arise when the cross-examiner tries to put words into the witness's mouth. So even though the witness has to answer the lawyer's questions, and often answer them in a very particular way, for example "yes" or "no," it is important that the witness does not agree with things put by the barrister that are not true as far as the witness is concerned.

Conclusion

According to Laster, "techniques and strategies used by lawyers have caused linguists to describe courtroom dialogue as 'dysfunctional' or even 'absurd' or 'pathological' communication" (Laster 2001, 268). In this chapter I have sought to demonstrate that despite such evaluations, courtroom communication arises from an internally consistent logic, in which "truth" or "justice" is pursued by pitching two parties against each other before an impartial judge. That this way of pursuing a "good" outcome is deeply embedded in our culture can be seen by the similar logic that underpins the partisan discourse of politics. In both law and politics, the aim of communication is not to foster a "meeting of minds," but to prove one version of events and debunk another. In neither forum does communication so based necessarily lead to the best outcome. That this has been recognized in the legal context is indicated by the increased use of mediation to settle disputes in the English-speaking world.

Linguistics offers valuable tools to distinguish some of the potential risks that legal communication poses for the process of justice. It can also assist in legal education of lay persons involved in court matters. The benefit of cultural scripts is that they can provide an easily translatable framework that could be used for education or briefing of witnesses from diverse cultural backgrounds to help them participate more effectively in the process. More substantially, cultural scripts can highlight the foundation on which courtroom interaction is built, and thereby raise the serious question whether such a foundation really is the best place from which to start a pursuit of justice.

As long as we depend on the adversarial system, however, I think it is beneficial to describe it clearly and make such description available to the non-legally trained actors in legal proceedings. Ideally, I would like to see whether these scripts could actually be put to practical use in the process of briefing witnesses. Because they are composed in NSM, the texts I have developed should be translatable into other languages, for example indigenous Australian languages. It would be a great test of the practical applicability of the NSM process to see whether producing such translations and having lawyers use the scripts to brief witnesses provides any benefit to those witnesses when appearing in court.

References

Aldridge, Michelle and Luchjenbroers, June (2007), "Linguistic manipulations in legal discourse: Framing questions and 'smuggling' information," *International Journal of Speech, Language and the Law* 14(1), 85–107.

Alter, Adam (2004), *Aborigines and Courtroom Communication: Problems and Solutions*, Australian Human Rights Centre, Working Paper 2.

Béal, Christine (1992), "Did you have a good weekend? Or why there is no such thing as a simple question in cross-cultural encounters," *Australian Review of Applied Linguistics*, 15(1), 23–52.

Coulthard, Malcolm and Johnson, Alison (2007), *An Introduction to Forensic Linguistics: Language in Evidence*, Abingdon: Routledge.

Dal Pont, G.E. (2001), *Lawyers' Professional Responsibility in Australia and New Zealand*, 2nd edn., Sydney: LBC Information Services.

Eades, Diana (1992), *Aboriginal English and the Law*, Brisbane: Queensland Law Society.

—— (2003), "'I don't think the lawyers were communicating with me': Misunderstanding cultural differences in communicative style," *Emory Law Journal*, 52, 1,109–34.

—— (2004a), "'Evidence given in unequivocal terms': Gaining consent of Aboriginal young people in court," in Janet Cotterill (ed.), *Language in the Legal Process*, Basingstoke and New York: Palgrave Macmillan, 162–79.

—— (2004b), "Understanding Aboriginal English in the legal system: A critical sociolinguistics approach," *Applied Linguistics*, 25(4), 491–512.

—— (2006), "Lexical struggle in court: Aboriginal Australians versus the State," *Journal of Sociolinguistics*, 10(2), 153–81.

—— (2007), "Aboriginal English in the criminal justice system," in Gerhard Leitner and Ian G. Malcolm (eds.), *The Habitat of Australia's Aboriginal Languages: Past, Present, Future*, Berlin and New York: Mouton de Gruyter, 299–326.

Engberg, Jan and Janich, Nina (2007), "Über die Komplexität fachkommunikativer Sprachkompetenz und ihrer Beschreibung," in Dorothee Heller and Konrad Ehlich (eds.), *Studien zur Rechtskommunikation*, Linguistic Insights: Studies in Language and Communication No. 56, Bern: Peter Lang, 209–34.
Gibbons, John (2003), *Forensic Linguistics*, Oxford: Blackwell.
Goddard, Cliff (2006a), "Cultural Scripts," in Jan-Ola Östman and Jef Verschueren (eds.), *Handbook of Pragmatics 2006*, Amsterdam and Philadelphia, PA: John Benjamin, 1–16.
—— (ed.) (2006b), *Ethnopragmatics: Understanding Discourse in Cultural Context*, Berlin: Mouton de Gruyter.
—— (2009), "The 'communication concept' and the 'language concept' in everyday English," *Australian Journal of Linguistics*, 29(1), 11–25.
—— and Wierzbicka, Anna (eds.) (2002), *Meaning and Universal Grammar: Theory and Empirical Findings*, Amsterdam: John Benjamins.
—— (eds.) (2004), *Cultural Scripts: Special Issue of Intercultural Pragmatics*, 1(2).
Hemming, Steve (1996), "Inventing Ethnography," *Journal of Australian Studies*, 48, 24–39.
Laster, Kathy (2001), *Law as Culture*, 2nd edn., Sydney: The Federation Press.
Napley, David (1991), *The Technique of Persuasion*, 4th edn., London: Sweet and Maxwell.
Phillips, John (1985), *Advocacy with Honour*, Sydney: The Law Book Company.
Ross, David (2007), "Criminal Law Practice: Defending Aboriginal People," *Criminal Law Journal*, 31, 332–44.
Tronc, Keith and Dearden, Ian (1993), *Advocacy Basics for Solicitors*, Sydney: The Law Book Company.
Wierzbicka, Anna (1972), *Semantic Primitives*, Frankfurt: Athenäum.
—— (2006), *English: Meaning and Culture*, Oxford: Oxford University Press.

Chapter 3

Witnesses on Trial: Address and Referring Terms in US Cases

Sarah Dettenwanger[1]

In an idealistic sense, trials are supposed to prove how the examination of facts through rules of evidence ensures personal freedom under the state. Whatever one's views are about how successfully the adversarial system accomplishes this, the strict rules of evidence supposedly limit the facts presented to peers in jury trials. Once an individual's testimony is deemed admissible, however, lawyers and judges have greater freedom in how they interact with the witness. Through these interactions, it is possible that non-evidential language and behavior will affect the judgments of jury members and, ultimately, the verdicts they reach.

Language biases can occur at many levels, from conscious efforts to control a witness through question forms to unconscious prejudice towards a particular dialect. The degree of intentionality when affecting social position and credibility means little when someone's freedom, life or appropriate punishment is at stake. This is particularly worrisome when considering the substantial forethought that lawyers devote to their courtroom preparation and performance, and how juries respond to such efforts.

Legal Background

In order to understand the described behavior and events I will be analyzing, some legal background information is necessary.[2] My own academic knowledge has been built up through reading research articles about language and the law, courses dealing with forensic linguistics and language and the law, and prior research on direct and cross-examination in US courts.

The following is a basic overview of what occurs in a United States criminal trial. During the life of a case, there are hearings and other events that take place in

1 The author would like to thank Professor Heidi Hamilton and Dr. Anna Trester for their immeasurable help with this research and document through its many stages.

2 This researcher is not a lawyer, nor an expert in legal procedure. Discrepancies between this chapter and actual law could be the result of variation between federal and state policies, or mistaken understanding of observed behavior. This chapter focuses on criminal, not civil, law.

the courtroom regarding the development of evidence and possible plea bargains, but do not involve a jury. Before a defendant in a federal felony case goes to trial, he or she must be indicted by a grand jury. The prosecution presents its evidence to the grand jury and compels witness testimonies. If a witness who testified at the grand jury also testifies in the trial, then a transcript of the previous testimony is provided to the defense.

The trial itself begins with the judge explaining basic legal information and outlining events to jurors, followed by opening statements from both the government (assistant US attorney, hereafter AUSA) and the defense (hereafter DEF). The government presents its case to the jury first. The AUSA will examine his or her own witnesses, and there are certain requirements regarding the types of questions a lawyer can ask on direct examination—for example, one cannot lead the witness to certain answers. For each witness, the defense has the option of cross-examination. Cross-examination is essentially a re-examination of the testimony by the opposing attorney, generally in order to discredit the witness and testimony, or to emphasize additional information the direct examination did not focus on. The scope of the cross-examination often focuses on information brought out on direct examination, the witness's reliability as an expert or eyewitness, and in some circumstances, previous convictions. The government generally calls the most witnesses, since it carries the "burden of proof," and must convince the jury that the defendant committed the crime(s). The defense only needs to establish a reasonable doubt[3] of the government's account of events for the accused to be acquitted. After the government rests, the defense presents its case. The defense calls its own witnesses, and the same process of direct examination, cross-examination and re-direct examination goes on, though now DEF handles direct and re-direct testimony, while the AUSA cross-examines.

After the defense rests, the government begins closing arguments by summarizing its position and highlighting the "deciding proof" of what occurred. Then the defense summarizes its case and seeks to at least reach a point of "reasonable doubt" regarding the defendant's involvement in the crime. The government is allowed to speak to the jury once more in response to the defense's closing arguments, and then there are jury instructions.

Jury instructions are frequently studied in linguistics,[4] and contribute to this research. Jury instructions are established through a combination of written guidelines, local and federal laws, lawyer agreements and the judge's supervision. Jury instructions direct the jury on what evidence to consider, the relevant law and what they are to deliberate on. The judge from the Texas case reminded jurors: "as I told you at the beginning and throughout the trial, and in final instructions,

3 Reasonable doubt, as defined for a Superior Court case, is "doubt that would cause a reasonable person, after careful and thoughtful reflection, to hesitate to act in the graver or more important matters in life. However, it is not … a doubt based on speculation or guesswork …."

4 See Gibbons (2003) for an overview of several studies.

that what the attorneys say to you is not the evidence. The evidence is what you heard from this witness stand and the exhibits" (US v. Ramos et al.). In one trial in Superior Court (SC), jurors were reminded to consider just the sworn testimony, facts, stipulations and exhibits. Yet jurors were also instructed to weigh the testimony of witnesses, assessing their credibility. When considering the weight to give a witness's testimony, jurors could factor in the individual's demeanor, behavior, manner of testifying, memory and so on. None of these factors were defined or elaborated upon. The ambiguity of this credibility evaluation gives jurors significant liberty for personal judgments about the capabilities of a testifying witness. Such judgments will be created through interaction, and are therefore affected by the lawyers' and judges' own communicative choices.

In SC, after receiving these instructions, the jurors are sent to deliberate. The deliberations themselves are private, outside of the presence of the lawyers, judge and defendant(s). The time for jury deliberations varies, but many take anywhere from a few hours to a few days to return with a unanimous guilty or a not guilty verdict for any number of charges of which the defendant may be accused. Judges handle sentencing of the defendant, which normally takes place some time after the jury's decision, so the judge is able to gather information pertinent to his or her decision.

Literature Review: Language and Law

Legal institutions worldwide provide constrained and formulated interactions that need to accommodate a variety of situations involving diverse populations. These interactions provide an abundance of entry points for research. A number of ethnographic studies and other linguistic analyses have focused on multilingual concerns for reference and politeness (Angermeyer 2006), bias in mediation (Marinova 2007), and question forms and poetic devices in cross-examination (Matoesian 2001). Though opinion questionnaires, re-enactments and perception studies are popular for measuring jury bias, gender bias and other research interests (Kaplan and Miller 1987), ethnography is also well situated to incorporate linguistic particulars within the fabric of courtroom interaction. Lawyers and judges have years of schooling and practice in order to fully engage in the courtroom, so there must be significant contrasts to other "everyday" social environments (Heritage 1997).

Trials are, in many ways, performative presentations of fact to an audience with the power to determine guilt or innocence, with potentially serious ramifications. This has led to studies of factors that can affect jury perception, or ignite social biases. As Hahn and Clayton (1996) detail:

> the attorney's presentation style operates within a system: Not only the attorney is being evaluated, but also the attorney's relationships with witnesses and defendants, and the defendant in light of those relationships. … [M]ore

> important in the courtroom is how an attorney's interactions with witnesses and defendants affect the evaluation of those individuals and of their testimony. (Hahn and Clayton 1996, 536)

In their test of attorney styles, they found that aggressive lawyers were more successful than passive lawyers, and male lawyers more successful than female lawyers. Hahn and Clayton's (1996) study also looked at juror gender, and found that male jurors are more affected by presentation style than their female counterparts. An earlier study (Conley et al. 1979) focused on the linguistic behavior of witnesses, and also found that gender plays a distinctive role in juror perception. One of a number of features[5] of a powerless speaking style was the inclusion of polite forms (including "sir" and "please"), which significantly lowered the perceived competence, professional judgment and believability of witnesses (Conley et al. 1979). This style was especially more likely to be used by witnesses of "low social status," meaning poor and uneducated individuals, and more often by women than men (Conley et al. 1979, 1,380). Address terms or referring expressions were explicitly cited as part of the research in the previous study, as well as in Riger et al. (1995). The latter was a survey for attorneys and judges to examine factors that might contribute to either real or perceived bias towards female attorneys. In the section of the survey aimed at observable examples of bias, both male and female attorneys were asked if a judge used informal forms of address with female counsel. While the general results are not significant for this study, address terms were acknowledged as contributing to perception and bias within the courtroom among participants who feel more at ease and aligned with the legal system (compared to witnesses, defendants and others unfamiliar with the experience).

Discomfort and unease among certain populations in trials is not unique to US courts. Eades (2000; 2005) investigated Aboriginal populations in Australian courts and published a lawyers' handbook about the linguistic, cultural and discourse systems available to Aboriginal speakers. Eades utilized the cultural difference approach (Gumperz 1982; Tannen 1994) in the information provided to the legal community, an approach she later criticizes (Eades 2005) since it does not address power inequalities of the Aboriginal population in many social and legal spheres. Acknowledging the social realities that can feign, reinforce or destroy credibility is an important factor in moving forward language and law studies.

Linguistic Research: Reference and Address Terms

In addition to research about legal institutions with their own linguistic concerns, there is pertinent linguistic research regarding address terms and referring

5 Some of the other features included hedges, hesitation forms and intonation; Conley et al. (1979).

expressions. Schiffrin (2006) examines reference, and constructs frameworks for considering the role and realization of referring expressions, and when such efforts go awry. As Schiffrin (2006) defines:

> Referrals are communicative attempts by a speaker to evoke a referent (the idea a speaker has of something in the world) through a referring expression (a linguistics expression that can represent and evoke an entity) …. As first-mentions, we can think of the speaker as "accessing" the referent; as next-mentions, as "maintaining" the referent. (Schiffrin 2006, 36)

She goes on to discuss how successful communication is a negotiation between speaker intention and hearer interpretation that mediates their shared world of knowledge. This presents problems in "ordinary" conversation, though confusion can be conveyed through questions or misunderstandings brought to light in dialogic conversation. In the courtroom, however, jurors do not normally participate in discussions or voice confusion over terms or references. Jurors are generally allowed to ask questions of the court during and after trial, but they do not do so frequently (never in the observed SC trials). Whether allowed or not, jurors are more constrained in opportunities for resolving confusion as compared to everyday small group interactions. Since many courts do not have recurrent, structured openings for jurors to talk, it is difficult to break through the structure and flow of institutional talk with respected, powerful and possibly more institutionally fluent lawyers, judges and witnesses.[6] Witnesses are likewise limited in their capacity to speak beyond answering questions, and while generally encouraged to seek clarification, may feel they do not have the conversational right to voice uncertainty, or that doing so will adversely affect their credibility. At least as far as jury comprehension goes, attorneys desire a clear and persuasive argument, so they will likely do their best, in order to fulfill their own ends, to keep referrals straightforward and simple. But as Schiffrin (2006) points out, manifest "disfluencies do not always indicate problematic referrals … [and] problematic referrals are not always overtly displayed by disfluencies" (Schiffrin 2006, 41).

Not only can there be problematic referrals, but also troublesome address relationships. Dickey (1997) begins with a discussion about the meaning of references and address terms and their similarity in that both are defined by social usage and not determined solely by indicating a referent. She states that there are myriad choices for referring or addressing someone (for example, Jane, Jane Smith, Mrs. Smith), but that the choice among these options is based on social meanings. In her study of family interactions and academia, Dickey (1997) found different schemas for hierarchical divisions and resultant distinctions in reference and address (age and generation for the former, academic or departmental standing for the latter). Incorporating this into the courtroom could be quite

6 There are asymmetries in everyday conversation, and assuming equal participation is always dangerous; Heritage (1997).

complicated, as witnesses are brought in as authorities (either through personal or expert knowledge), yet attorneys hold much of the interactional power. Juries have the power of deciding guilt or innocence, but do not often talk, while judges have institutional authority. This institutional authority comes from their role in resolving points of law, their experience within the courtroom, and their ultimate ability to control courtroom conduct. Deciding which is most salient at any given point is a challenge, and the formal nature of the courtroom that often deals with personal situations (death, rape, violence, addiction and so on) further complicates the available options and behavior.

It is also necessary to acknowledge the complicated nature of the "listener." For everyday discourse, Goffman (1981) delineates this category as follows:

> broadly speaking, there are three kinds of listeners to talk: those who *over*hear …; those … who are ratified participants but are not specifically addressed by the speaker; and those ratified participants who *are* addressed, that is, oriented to by the speaker in a manner to suggest that his words are particularly for them, and that some answer is therefore anticipated from them …. (Goffman 1981, 9–10)

This description applies to the courtroom, with examples of unratified listeners (the public), ratified but not addressed by the speaker (during most of the examination, the judge and jurors) and the ratified and addressed individual (the witness, the attorney, or the judge if a ruling is necessary). The speaker and addressee can take any or all of these individuals into consideration when choosing address or referential expressions. All of this potential complication and variation highlights the difficulty of explaining with certainty why X chose Y expression in a specific situation.

Methodology

This study was an effort to supplement discourse analysis with another qualitative research method, ethnography, to give a richer picture of address and reference in a courtroom. Given the low frequency of address and reference tokens, great variation among personal styles and the importance of discourse sections (opening statement, closing argument, direct examination and so on), a nuanced, qualitative investigation allows for a more definitive conclusion than numerical data alone would suggest. Some quantitative data will be included from the transcript below, but is not the focus of this investigation.

Ethnographic and Interview Data

In order to better understand courtroom behavior and practices, I observed felony trials in SC for over 50 hours. The observation covered a variety of cases, but generally included multiple lay and court witness testimonies, and for two trials, the closing arguments. I also conducted two interviews with practicing US attorneys. The ethnographic observations and interview data will be used to augment and situate some of the data from the Texas trial transcript, and was considered in the above introduction to US criminal procedure.

Transcript Data

Court transcripts provide an opportunity to study many of factors that contribute to address terms, reference and witness credibility. With such information, it is possible to follow the role of a witness in each case's theory of events and track references across multiple witnesses, as well as in opening statements and closing arguments.

The following provides some information about this particular case, which received media attention in 2006 and 2009. The case is US v. Ignacio Ramos et al. (2006), from a Texas district court. Defendants, Ignacio Ramos and Jose Compean, were working for the Department of Homeland Security as Border Patrol agents on the US–Mexican border. The incident took place on February 17, 2005 near San Elizario. A Mexican citizen, Jose Aldrete-Davila, was shot in the back after fleeing from the agents. Defendants were charged on 11 counts, including assault with intent to commit murder, aiding and abetting, assault with a dangerous weapon and multiple instances of tampering with an official proceeding. Some of the charges relate to Mr. Aldrete-Davila's injuries, but others address the lack of reporting for discharging firearms. Agents Ramos and Compean were found guilty of all charges except the first counts of assault with intent to commit murder and aiding and abetting. The case was back in the news when former President George W. Bush commuted their sentences before leaving office.

This criminal case was notable in a number of respects. To begin, in comparison to observed SC cases, this is the only instance of law enforcement officials as defendants. There could be a number of differences in criminal law and procedure between SC cases and this case in Texas, but they did not appear to alter the flow of questioning, statements or other courtroom behavior. It is also possible that besides personal style differences, regional style differences could affect features of courtroom interaction, including address terms and referring expressions.

Having two defendants who were charged with some separate crimes yet tried together also complicated this trial. Thus, for the government, there were two assistant US attorneys and four lawyers for the defense, two for each agent. While it was not necessary for each lawyer individually to examine and cross-examine witnesses, it did occur. There were also the options of re-cross and re-direct examination for government and defense attorneys. Both AUSAs also provided closing arguments, as did both of Agent Ramos's attorneys. That brings the relevant transcript sections for analysis to a total of three opening statements, five closing arguments, five direct/re-direct examinations and seven cross/re-cross-examinations spanning three witnesses.

In selecting witnesses to focus on the lay/court distinction, I chose the victim and two doctors. The victim, a Mexican citizen shot in US territory, was an outsider in many ways and not familiar with US courtroom practices. Other than the victim, almost all of the witnesses were Border Patrol agents, and while I was unsure of each individual's courtroom experience, law enforcement officers often have to testify for their work. Instead of dealing with the uncertainty of these individuals, I chose two doctors who provided medical testimony in the trial, since both verbally acknowledged their previous experience of testifying and aligned in role and function more closely with expert testimony observed in SC. These three witnesses testified about their personal experience. The two doctors also testified about their opinions and judgments as medical professionals. For this case, there were no solely "expert" testimonies; possible witnesses were listed, but then specific facts were entered in as stipulations.

The transcript was prepared by an official court reporter and totaled 2,606 pages in 18 volumes. Searching this document, I highlighted addresses to witnesses on direct examination, on cross-examination and any from the judge. I also identified address terms the witness used for the judge and lawyers on direct and cross-examination (see Table 3.1).

Table 3.1 Address options

	Address direction	
Direct and re-direct examination	Prosecution/Defense → Witness	Witness → Prosecution/Defense
Cross- and re-cross-examination	Defense/Prosecution → Witness	Witness → Defense/Prosecution
Judge	Judge → Witness	Witness → Judge

After delineating these six possibilities for address terms, I examined the entire trial for references made to each witness. Using one copy per witness, each document became a view into the way a single individual was not only addressed while on the stand, but how that person (in terms of credibility, testimony and so on) was involved and reference in other testimonies or remarks.

Results

These results hinge on differences between these familiar or "court" witnesses, who were at ease or had knowledge of courtroom conduct, and lay witnesses, who were new to the courtroom and were unable (or unwilling) to adjust to proper trial deportment. Court witnesses, for the purpose of this research and SC observations, included social workers, expert witnesses and law enforcement. Lay witnesses included those not testifying in a formal (legal) capacity, generally defendants, eyewitnesses and victims.

Clearly, the issue is not straightforward enough to boil down to simply "who uses what" terms. Identity production is an interactive and dynamic construction, and different aspects can be highlighted at different stages (Bogoch 1999). In the same vein, the different actors' relationships to the testimony, audience, and specific witness can change with different facts and narrative elements as they arise. All of these variables necessitate an awareness of co-reference between interlocutors, as does more information about the discursive moves and information going on simultaneously.

The comparison for this point of the analysis is how attorneys will refer to and characterize the witnesses once they are no longer physically present—that is, in closing arguments. While these statements are not evidence, they can be very influential. Without the need to attend to face-work with any of the witnesses or worry about how the jury will view the interactions, attorneys are free to play around with referrals to access the referent and maintain it as they see necessary and helpful for characterization. Closing arguments are essentially "insider talk," since the attorneys, judge and jurors are the only people who have heard the entire story and are responsible for putting the facts together. This insider status emphasizes the solidarity between the speaking attorney and jurors, and highlighting this solidarity is critical to the attorney who wants his or her view to succeed.

Court Witnesses: The Doctors

The doctors' testimonies in *US* v. *Ramos et al.* (2006) had similar subjects, namely the victim's injury and treatment when they saw him, and their opinion on other facets of the injury or its causes. And as skilled experts who had previously testified in court, they were familiar with expected behaviors and needed little guidance on answering questions. Generally speaking, both doctors were treated similarly and were grouped together referentially, and will be for this analysis.

Though the doctors are grouped together, it is worth noting that there are differences between them that could affect address term usage, mainly that one doctor was in the military. This doctor's military experience, style or norms might have affected his use of polite address terms, though the other doctor could also have unknown motivations for his choices in address terms. Table 3.2 shows the rate of address terms used by the attorneys, judge and the military doctor, and shows how difficult it can be to measure the use and impact of address terms. The doctor was called by the prosecution to testify, which could possibly suggest alignment with its case, though the doctor's testimony was not really a point of contention between the prosecution and defense. To measure the frequency of address terms used by the attorneys (Colonel, Dr. X, Doctor) and the witness's responses ("sir," "ma'am"), I counted the individual tokens of these addresses and

Table 3.2 Rate of address usage

	Institutional actor		Witness	
Direct/re-direct examination (prosecution)	8/144	5.56%	9/109	8.26%
Cross/re-cross-examination (Defense)	4/69	5.6%	0/51	0%
Further explanation (judge)	0/7	0%	0/7	0%

Note: The ratios are address terms per sentence-unit, with percentages to the right.

compared them to the sentence-units for each section (direct examination, cross-examination and so on). The "sentence-unit" was an attempt to control for the length of speech, without being able to measure the time each person had. Each completed statement and question counted towards total sentence-units, but not interrupted/overlapping statements or questions unless they were eventually completed. The "further explanation" section took place after re-direct and re-cross-examinations, and was an attempt by the judge to clarify the victim's body position.

It is interesting that though the prosecution used twice as many address terms as the defense, the rates of usage were extremely close because of the large difference in sentence-units overall. This could mean that attorneys have similar rates for addressing expert witnesses (though this contradicts SC observations where address terms were often non-existent on cross-examination), but it could also mean that the sheer volume of information the attorney needed to work through on direct examinations masked attempts to bolster witness credibility. There could also be unknown reasons for the defense attorney to use address terms with such frequency.

It is also worth noticing the witness's responses and his rate with different individuals—namely, that he did not use any responses ("ma'am" and "sir") for the defense attorney or judge. Since the attorney rates are essentially the same, it is likely that the witness had his own differing interactional rules on cross-examination. The interaction with the judge was comparatively short, so it is hard to tell if they disregarded politeness opportunities or there were simply not enough occasions.

Regarding possible and likely occurrences of address terms for court witnesses, they were found at the beginning of an examination block (whether direct or cross-examination), when refocusing on testimony (after an objection or bench conference) or when a lawyer moved onto a new line of questioning. The following occurred after an attorney was re-starting questioning on direct examination about a particular exhibit:

> "Okay. With regard to the actual x-ray, then, Doctor, instead of the diagram …."
> (*US* v. *Ramos et al.* 2006, 218)

This example contrasts with lay witnesses in SC, who often have their names repeated when things go awry and the lawyer is trying to focus the witness or highlight the lack of cooperation to jurors. SC witnesses rarely got into such disruptive situations or needed help to refocus.

Analogously, the judge in this case only used one address term for either of the doctors, though she did have to talk with one for specific clarification (see Table 3.2, above). For the non-military doctor, the judge merely said at the end of his testimony, "Thank you, Doctor. You're free to go" (US v. Ramos et al. 2006, 614). Since the role of the judge is often to ensure the courtroom is running smoothly and decide on the admissibility of evidence, a well-behaved witness creates little need to talk continually or to do so formally at all. This contrasts with lay witnesses who interact less frequently with the court and may introduce an incentive for judicial guidance and politeness in a recognizably foreign environment.

Another fascinating difference among court and lay witnesses was the reference to individuals before they testified, throughout the rest of the trial and in closing arguments. These references can prepare (or predispose) jurors for certain testimony, and can continue affecting perception as reference is linked throughout multiple witnesses and closing arguments. The two doctors, for instance, were referenced by their job (for example, urologist or surgeon), as "medical testimony," and even by the institution where they worked. The following is from the government's opening statement:

> "[The victim] went to Beaumont [Hospital] and Beaumont removed the bullet." (*US* v. *Ramos et al.* 2006, 188)

This association of individuals with respected professions and institutions could reinforce their testimony as definitive fact and bias the jury in favor of such individuals before they even take the stand. These characterizations and associations were not being disputed by opposing counsels since their testimonies largely provided background information (the case was not about whether the victim sustained injuries), and were probably reinforced by the address terms and interaction during examination.

Lay Witness: The Victim

For this particular case, there were significant differences between court witnesses and lay witness. The victim was not only unfamiliar with courtroom behavior, he was a foreigner to the US, and his native language was Spanish. An interpreter was provided who translated contemporaneously, which has its own concerns, which are not considered in this study (see Berk-Seligson 2002). Some issues that I am unable to account for are different markers between Spanish and English to show interactional deference, and whether the interpreter translated these accurately or at all. For instance, in English it is simple to tack on "sir" or "ma'am" to a question, but Spanish can require conjugating a verb differently (*usted* versus *tú*) to convey a similar deference. I am limited to what is included in the court transcript, which only had one example of "sir" attributed to the victim. Regarding the translation more generally, there were two minor issues of clarifying which question the witness was answering, as well as the meaning of a Spanish word and the interpreter's choice for the English translation (some of the lawyers knew Spanish and questioned the translation). By and large, however, the parties seemed satisfied in the interpretation for the witness.

Another issue, related to the witness's Mexican heritage, was his three-part name. Most American English names have a first/personal name, an optional middle name and a last/family name. The witness's name was Osvaldo Aldrete-Davila, and attorneys varied in how they addressed him. On direct examination, the lawyer addressed him as "Mr. Aldrete-Davila," in one cross-examination he was "Mr. Davila," and in another he was "Mr. Aldrete." This confusion for defense attorneys was not resolved until a re-cross-examination, when the lawyer asked:[7]

> **Q**: Mr. Aldrete—or should I—I'm sorry. Should I call you—I was calling you Mr. Aldrete, and Ms. Ramirez is calling you Mr. Davila. How should I address you?
>
> **A**: I am Aldrete-Davila. What you wish. Whatever you wish.
>
> **Q**: Well, how—what do you go by?
>
> **A**: Aldrete-Davila.
>
> **Q**: Mr. Aldrete-Davila. Okay. (*US* v. *Ramos et al.* 2006, 623)

Not only is this a concern for the witness's right to be properly identified (even if the problem is eventually resolved), it can be confusing for jury members to not have a clear, coherent line of reference throughout a trial, which is full of random and unresolved information. And it can negatively impact the credibility of a witness if lawyers cannot seem to get his name correct, or the lawyer may appear unwilling to learn the customs of a large segment of the population in the region. This is an excellent example of a problematic referral (Schiffrin 2006), which was necessarily resolved, though late in the course of the trial and in the witness's time on the stand.

The judge, for this lay witness, stepped in to help more often. As the victim in this case, a large amount of this witness's testimony was at issue in the case. For example, depending on the victim's behavior, the gunshots and injury could be considered "justified" and thus not a criminal act for the two defendants. This witness's reason for being in the United States was also problematic (he was drug-running across the border), and though given immunity to testify, the judge had to be careful that he understood his right to not testify in a way that would

---

7 "Q" stands for question and indicates the lawyer for a particular section, in this instance a defense attorney. "A" stands for answer and is the witness's response.

further harm himself. So she did more work clarifying questions, asserting which questions had to be answered and when the witness had to answer without help from the prosecution. All of this necessitated that the judge talked more to the lay witness, and in order to be polite or even assertive (depending on situation and prosody), she employed address terms for him more often than she did with the court witnesses. Most jurors should recognize circumstances that necessitate guidance, but it is still possible to question the witness's credibility based on the labor-intensiveness of his testimony.

Unsurprisingly, on direct examination, the government lawyers addressed the witness as "Mr. Aldrete-Davila" and "sir," likely to bolster credibility. Likewise, the defense lawyers used some "Mr. Aldrete" and other names to address the witness, but less frequently. The defense lawyers did not want to be (or perceived to be) rude, which was arguably why they didn't use "Osvaldo" as they did in opening statements. At the same time, it did not necessarily help them to repeat the respectful address expression over and over. Through repetition of these respectful references, it could be possible to elevate the victim's perceived credibility, which would go against the defense's objective of discrediting his testimony and person. Repetition can also have other effects, as in this excerpt from the victim's cross-examination:

> **Q**: Did you get the description, possibly, from Rene Sanchez?
>
> **A**: I don't understand the question. The description of Rene Sanchez or of the agent?
>
> **Q**: Okay. Let me go back. On March 11th you had a conversation with Christopher Sanchez. Is that correct, **Mr. Davila**?
>
> **A**: Yes.
>
> **Q**: And you had previously told … the jury that you did not talk to him about specifics about the incident on February 17, 2005. Is that correct, **Mr. Davila**?
>
> **A**: I don't understand very well this thing between 11 and 17. Was it on the 11th that I talked with Chris?
>
> **Q**: Well, I don't know. You tell me. When did you talk to Agent Christopher Sanchez, **Mr. Davila**? (*US* v. *Ramos et al.* 2006, 589; emphasis added)

This cluster of "Mr. Davila" appeared when the witness began claiming confusion about what a few questions meant, but it is hard to tell without audio or visual data if the increased use of an address term was meant to be authoritative (emphasizing the witness's uncooperativeness) or if it was an attempt to focus the witness in order to have the question answered. The 11 pages of cross-examination before this only had three other instances of "Mr. Davila," which were used in the initial greeting or after breaks in the testimony.

Not only is it important to consider address terms and referring expressions in their own manifestation, but also comparing them to nearby references can reveal much about social positioning and relative credibility. For instance, in one of the defense's opening statements there is a juxtaposition of the victim and one of the defendants in a sentence, which boiled down to "Osvaldo Aldrete-Davila and Mr. Ramos." Clearly one could argue that a certain professionalism is due to one's own client, but the relative prestige of the defendant over the victim can have effects for positioning their relative credibility. Another defense attorney had a similar juxtaposition and inequality, but this time the pair was "Mr. Aldrete-Davila" and "Agent Juarez." The attorney actually self-corrected when the two were identically referenced:

> **Q**: … Do you have any idea of the distance apart that Mr. Aldrete-Davila and Mr.—Agent Compean were at the time that that—the shooting happens? (*US* v. *Ramos et al.* 2006, 1,673)

"Agent" is arguably more appropriate for someone who is a Border Patrol agent, but this correction could also be a (sub)conscious attempt to differentiate the credibility and respect afforded to different individuals in the trial.

Such strategies vary not only according to trial unit (examination versus opening statements), but depending on who is utilizing the names. Though witnesses are supposed to just be relating the truth as they remember it, it is impossible to deny that some are more or less affiliated with either the government or defense. Different sides have at least varying stakes in the credibility of particular witnesses. For example, each side can call their own witnesses, who they question with more open-ended forms than the other side will, which is one difference between direct and cross-examination. And it can be argued that each witness may be aligned with the interests of one party more than the other (Luchjenbroers 1997). Obviously, the defense lawyers would like to see the defendants acquitted, and could achieve this end by discrediting the victim's testimony. The government, on the other hand, does not represent the victim in this case, but believes him enough to initiate action and have him testify.

Just as the court witnesses were referenced throughout, there was competition for which characterization of the lay witness the jury would latch onto. As seen in Figure 3.1, there were diverse options available for attorneys to employ for the witness's construction during closing statements. While not controlled for the statements' lengths, the prosecution referenced the witness 67 times, while the defense referenced the witness 53 times. References that strictly filled syntactic roles ("he," "him" and so on) were not counted, since it would be difficult to argue any strategy in the use of these terms without hearing the tone or emphasis used with them. The numbers in Figure 3.1 represent the combined efforts of attorneys for each side.

Clearly, for the prosecution, there was a strong preference for using the witness's first name or full name, without the use of "Mr." or rarely the more distant "Aldrete-Davila." It was surprising to see the prosecution refer to one of its most important witnesses as a "drug dealer," but context adds some clarity:

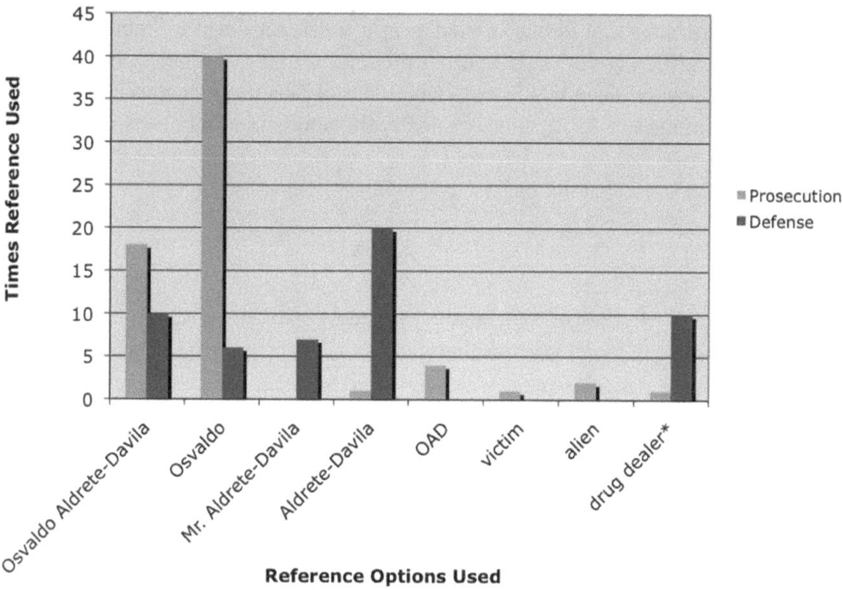

Note: * This category also includes instances of "drug smuggler" and "drug trafficker."

Figure 3.1 Victim references in closing statements

> And then they come before you with this concocted story that **Osvaldo Aldrete-Davila** had a gun. It's—it was shameful. The person who had some of the most credible testimony is **the drug dealer**. The agents' stories do not hold up. (*US* v. *Ramos et al.* 2006, 2,237; emphasis added)

This potentially biasing fact about the witness becomes a way to make the dishonesty of the Border Patrol agents even more shocking. The defense's reasons for continuingly associating the witness with drug-trafficking are probably not as generous, and are explicitly justified by one defense attorney:

> I'm calling him a drug trafficker, and I want to make it quite clear. Our theory … is not that he's a drug trafficker and he deserves to be shot. … That's not our defense, he's a drug trafficker and he deserves to be shot. Or, he's a drug trafficker, therefore you can't believe anything he says. That's not our theory, either. I'm calling him a drug trafficker because that's what he was that day. He was a drug trafficker. And you know what? He's not just a little mule.[8] (*U.S.* v. *Ramos et al.* 2006, 2,261)

8 "Mules" are defined as "the very low-level participants who bring the marijuana across the river"; *US* v. *Ramos et al.* (2006), 2,262.

And though she says that being labeled a drug trafficker does not mean all these negative things, the lawyer is still taking this opportunity to repeatedly associate the lay witness with "drug trafficker," which could bias the jury that he deserved to be shot or should not be trusted—basically the opposite of what she is claiming to deny.

Conclusion

> Language is a reflection of context, roles, attitudes ... and an element in creation and negotiation of social structure, institutions and relationships. (Bogoch 1999)

While address terms and referrals are just two features among the gamut of linguistic and paralinguistic communicative cues, the accumulation of these performances and their effects can still be very compelling for jury members. As Miller and Burgoon (1982) established in their study, people (that is, jurors) are not very good at judging deceptive practices of strangers. Though people may believe they are adept at evaluating others, they rely a great deal on observing witnesses' interactions with attorneys and judges to assess credibility. So a lawyer could alter a witness's identity with the varied, available means of creating negative opinions. An attorney could suggest, for instance, that a witness was being "difficult" through intonation, pacing, body language, showing concerted efforts at politeness, provoking the witness through question content or many other alternatives. While people acknowledge the performative aspect of trial, it is hard to remove all of these elements from consideration when deliberating.

Beyond this, there are other important considerations for names and referrals in trial. There is, for instance, the practice of identifying an individual to a witness by saying "the man you know as Youngin" and having to repeat this phrase over and over. It appeared that substituting the nickname for an actual name was not allowed because that would be introducing information the witness did not know. This involves rules of evidence and making witnesses appear more comfortable or authoritative. This could also potentially confuse witnesses or jurors if lists of nicknames and given names get too long and would, in more natural conversation, be easily addressed by explanation.

It would also be worthwhile to take a look further back into the history of cases to see how victims, suspects and potential witnesses interact with institutional actors such as the same judges and attorneys they will eventually see in trial. Trinch and Berk-Seligson (2002), for instance, studied how paralegals shaped the "facts" of protective order interviews. Not only could credibility be affected at an earlier stage in the judicial process, but participants' satisfaction in sharing their story and seeing justice done begins long before entering the courtroom.

This study addresses a gap of investigation into address terms and referring expressions in the courtroom, but there are of course a number of directions that could develop this area of research further. Through accumulating shared knowledge and understanding of modest linguistic building blocks, we can properly inform larger studies of courtroom behavior incorporating all of this information. Overall, my research has been an exercise in discourse analysis in the courtroom, a field-test for linguistic theories in an institutional setting, and a contribution to an awareness of all the small things which are necessary considerations for relationships, testimonies and credibility within a trial.

References

Angermeyer, P.S. (2006), *Speak English or What?: Codeswitching and interpreter use in New York Small Claims Court*, doctoral dissertation, New York: New York University, <http://homepages.nyu.edu/%7Epsa208/Dissertation.pdf>.

Berk-Seligson, S. (2002), *The Bilingual Courtroom: Court Interpreters in the Judicial Process*, Chicago, IL: University of Chicago Press.

Bogoch, B. (1999), "Courtroom discourse and the gendered construction of professional Identity," *Law and Social Inquiry*, 24(2), 329–75.

Conley, J.M., O'Barr, W.M. and Lind, E.A. (1979), "The Power of language: Presentational style in the courtroom," *Duke Law Journal*, 6 (1978), 1,375–99.

Dickey, E. (1997), "Forms of address and terms of reference," *Journal of Linguistics*, 33, 255–74.

Eades, D. (2000), "I don't think it's an answer to the question: Silencing Aboriginal witnesses in court," *Language in Society*, 29(2), 161–95.

—— (2005), "Beyond difference and domination? Intercultural communication in legal contexts," in S.F. Kiesling and C.B. Paulston (eds.), *Intercultural Discourse and Communication: The Essential Readings*, Malden, MA: Blackwell Publishing, 304–16.

Gibbons, J. (2003), *Forensic Linguistics: An Introduction to Language in the Justice System*, Malden, MA: Wiley-Blackwell.

Goffman, E. (1981), *Forms of Talk*, Philadelphia, PA: University of Pennsylvania Press.

Gumperz, J. (1982), *Discourse Strategies*, Cambridge: Cambridge University Press.

Hahn, P.W. and Clayton, S.D. (1996), "The effects of attorney presentation style, attorney gender, and juror gender on juror decisions," *Law and Human Behavior*, 20(5), 533–54.

Heritage, J. (1997), "Conversation analysis and institutional talk: Analysing data," in D. Silverman (ed), *Qualitative Research: Theory, Method and Practice*, London: Sage Publications, 161–82.

Kaplan, M.F. and Miller, L.E. (1987), "Reducing the effects of juror bias," in L.S. Wrightsman, S.M. Kassin and C.E. Willis (eds.), *In the Jury Box*, Newbury Park, CA: Sage Publications, 114–37.

Luchjenbroers, J. (1997), "In your own words ...: Questions and answers in a Supreme Court trial," *Journal of Pragmatics*, 27, 477–503.

Marinova, D.S. (2007), *Neutrality in Mediation Hearings: Managing the Mediation Process without Bias*, doctoral dissertation, Washington, DC: Georgetown University.

Matoesian, G.M. (2001), *Law and the Language of Identity: Discourse in the William Kennedy Smith Rape Trial*, New York: Oxford University Press.

Miller, G.R. and Burgoon, J.K. (1982), "Factors affecting assessments of witness credibility," in N.L. Kerr and R.M. Bray (eds.), *The Psychology of the Courtroom* (New York: Academic Press), 169–94.

Riger, S., Foster-Fishman, P., Nelson-Kuna, J. and Curran, B. (1995), "Gender bias in courtroom dynamics," *Law and Human Behavior*, 19(5), 465–80.

Schiffrin, D. (2006), *In Other Words: Variation in Reference and Narrative*, Cambridge: Cambridge University Press.

Tannen, D. (1994), *Gender and Discourse*, Oxford: Oxford University Press.

Trinch, S.L. and Berk-Seligson, S. (2002), "Narrating in protective order interviews: A source of interactional trouble," *Language in Society*, 31(3), 383–418.

US v. *Ignacio Ramos et al.*, No. 05-CR-856-KC (5th Cir. Mar. 8, 2006), <http://www.usdoj.gov/usao/txw/press_releases/Compean-Ramos/index.html>.

Chapter 4
(False) Confessions Become Compelling at Trial

Gillian Grebler

> Storytelling has a pragmatic efficacy. In pretending to recount the real, it manufactures it. It renders believable what it says, and it generates appropriate action. … The voices of narration transform, reorient and regulate the space of social interaction. (de Certeau 1986, 200)

False Confessions as Evidence

Confessions are given inordinate weight at every stage of a criminal case. Interrogators are trained to pursue them, but interrogation can induce innocent people to confess falsely. And false confessions are counterintuitive: most jurors cannot imagine that they would ever confess to a crime they did not commit (Kassin 2002). In two large studies of proven false confessions in the United States, false confessors who pled not guilty and took their cases to trial were convicted by juries 73–81 percent of the time (Leo and Drizin 2004).

Academic studies of wrongful conviction cases show that 15–20 percent contained confessions in evidence (Leo and Drizin 2004; Gross et al. 2005). Of over 250 people exonerated by DNA testing, more than 40 confessed falsely to rapes and murders (Garrett 2009).

Studies with mock jurors have shown that confessions are powerful even when they are known to have been elicited under pressure, are not consistent in their chronology or compatible with forensic or witness evidence, and are retracted soon after they are given. These studies have consistently shown that "confession evidence boosts conviction rates even among jurors who believe the confession was coerced" (Kassin et al. 2009).

Neither police nor prosecutors nor judges expect the post-interrogation confession to be complete, coherent or completely true. Police interrogators expect suspects to withhold and distort information. They expect "lying and gauging" (cf. the Hayat rebuttal page 63 of this chapter). Prosecutors tell the story that way: defendants' admissions are incomplete or inconsistent because defendants are wily, lying, hiding key information, protecting themselves.

How do suspects come to admit after initially denying involvement in the crime? What makes them stop telling what we know in retrospect to be the truth, and be willing instead to take the officers' cues, imagine, hypothesize or simply play along and "lie"?

There is now a large and growing literature by psychologists and linguists which attempts to explain this phenomenon. They have studied the way false confessions arise from the use of tactics and ploys used by interrogators (see, for example, Ofshe and Leo 1997a; Shuy 1998), the effects of different kinds of interrogation questions (Tully and Cahill 1984; Oxburgh et al. 2010) and the psychological vulnerabilities of the suspects who make them (Gudjonsson 1992; Kassin and Gudjonsson 2004). They have determined that children and juveniles are especially vulnerable to interrogation, especially when it is accusatory (Redlich and Goodman 2003; Drizin and Colgan 2004; Redlich et al. 2004), as are mentally retarded and mentally ill suspects (Cahill et al. 1988).[1] Non-native or non-English speakers interrogated without effective interpreters are also particularly vulnerable to interrogation (Berk-Seligson 2002; Berk-Seligson 2009).

Proven false confessions show that police officers can alight on the wrong suspect, sometimes in ways that reveal racial or cultural bias. At times they misinterpret behaviors and demeanor. Interrogating officers may assume a suspect is guilty, or be under pressure to solve a crime, and in an accusatory, guilt-presumptive interrogation drive for an admission, and whether intentionally or inadvertently, supply critical details of the narrative (Hill 2003; Garrett 2009).

Police-induced False Confessions

Research has shown that invoking a suspect's rights as prescribed in *Miranda* v. *Arizona*[2] does little to protect against "unknowing" rights waivers (Leo 2008; Ainsworth 2010), uphold the right to an attorney (Ainsworth 1998; Ainsworth 2010; Solan and Tiersma 2005), prevent self-incrimination or protect against false confessions.

According to Miranda, a suspect should be able to control the interaction during police interrogation. The suspect should be able choose whether or not to speak, how much to say, which questions to answer, when he or she needs a break, and when to end the interrogation.

Interrogators, however, are trained to dominate the interaction (see Inbau et al. 1986; the John Reid website;[3] Walkley 1987) and they do this by various verbal and non-verbal means, including bombarding the suspect with large quantities of talk, interrupting continually, controlling the topic, questioning accusatorily, shouting and ignoring the suspect's denials.

1 In a recent study of 42 DNA exoneration cases, Brandon Garrett (2009) found that 13 were juveniles at the time they gave false confessions and 14 were mentally retarded or borderline retarded. Three were diagnosed as mentally ill.

2 384 US 436 (1966).

3 <www.reid.com>.

Some innocent suspects cannot maintain their innocence in the face of this coercive interaction. They reach an emotional breaking point and begin to admit. After this breakdown (or, according to the prosecution, "breakthrough"), the false confessor finds relief, a semblance of synchrony (Gumperz 1982) and a degree of interactional harmony by agreeing to tell the story, to cooperate, to work with the officer to construct an account of a crime.

The final push by the officers and the breakdown by the suspect are almost never recorded. And even when the entire interrogation has been recorded, we can never hear those crucial comments made in the car, in the hallway, in the restroom or when the tape is being changed, though we can sometimes see what Richard Ofshe calls their "footprints" (Ofshe and Leo 1997a; Ofshe and Leo 1997b).

When the line is crossed from denial to admission, real world consequences flow: from false confession to charge to custody to trial to conviction. There is no more pivotal moment in the entire criminal justice process. And yet interrogators, like jurors, believe that innocent people do not stop denying. As the Reid interrogation training says:

> It is very rare for an innocent suspect to move past this denial state. He remains steadfast in the assertion of his innocence. The sincerity with which he presents his case is a clear indication of his truthfulness.

Research has also shown that "actual innocence" does not protect suspects, but may put them at risk (Kassin 2005). Suspects waive their rights, "naively believing in the transparency of their innocence", and once armed with a confession, police investigators often proceed with "tunnel vision," excluding alternative lines of investigation and other possible suspects (Findley and Scott 2006; see also Solan 2010).

Once the suspect has "admitted" and the videotape is on, the interrogator struggles to elicit the kind of details that confirm and corroborate the "admission" or confession. It is this post-admission interrogation that needs more study (Leo 2008).

The purpose of the post-admission phase of interrogation is to confirm, corroborate and fill in the details of the admission. In Reid interrogation training, this is Step Eight, and here "the investigator's objective is to obtain a brief oral review of the basic sequence of events involved in the commission of the crime, while obtaining sufficient detail to corroborate the suspect's guilt."

Haworth (2010) writes of the "interview as evidence." She cites Baldwin (1993), saying that "instead of a search for truth it is much more realistic to see interviews as mechanisms directed towards the 'construction of proof.' At trial it is de and recontextualized" (Briggs 1996). As Cotterill (2002) puts it: "each part of the (re)constructive process of the crime narrative is potentially the site of influence from previous interviews and hearings and, equally significantly, has an eye on potential future appeal proceedings."

Mysteriously, false confessors tell about people and places, actions and events they never actually observed. They describe conversations they never heard and feelings they could not have felt. They seem to draw on memories we know they do not have. And yet these details, co-produced during the post-admission portion of interrogation and all unfounded, are transformed by the prosecution at trial into a compelling story. Impugned by the defense, the confession is revived and re-legitimized by the prosecution as emotive and highly probative evidence.

Leo and Davis (2009) point out an important gap in knowledge: too little is known, they say, about what leads inexorably from a police-induced confession to a conviction. To fill this gap, the "post-admission" stage of interrogation needs more study (Leo 2008). Beyond this, we have to understand the way the confession and interrogation are repackaged as evidence and used strategically at trial. It is at trial that both the pre- and post-admission interrogation become the grist for "adversarial storytelling" (Amsterdam and Bruner 2002), and the defendant is characterized through them and other evidence, as well as by his or her demeanor in court (Levenson 2007), as the kind of person who is capable of committing the crime in question.

We look at the confession's repackaging at trial because that is where the jury meets it. Jurors may have been exposed to the confession by the media when it was repackaged into an affidavit or charge long before they became jurors. But the only real "confession" the jurors take to the deliberation room is the one that has been presented to them during the examination and arguments of a trial.

At trial, jurors may be influenced by the believability, verisimilitude and compellingness of the prosecution story, persuaded by what clinical psychologist Donald Spence (in Ochs and Capps 2001) calls narrative truth. Narrative truth depends on "continuity and closure and the extent to which the fit of the pieces takes on aesthetic finality" (Spence, in Ochs and Capps 2001, 285). Historical truth, on the other hand, aims to come as close as possible to what "really" happened. Is the confession reliable? Does it "fit" what else is known about the alleged crime (Ofshe and Leo 1997b)? Are there inconsistencies in it (Shuy 1998)?

Discovering the answers to these questions should be the goal of jurors considering confession evidence that has been retracted, is weakly or not at all corroborated, and according to information presented by the defense, likely to be false. As Heffer (2002; 2010) points out, a jury trial is a complex genre whose opening address and closing arguments are in story mode. Jurors make decisions to a large extent through story-making, transforming narratives which emerge in testimony to "reconstruct reality in the courtroom" (Bennett and Feldman 1981; Pennington and Hastie 1994; Amsterdam and Bruner 2002).

Laurence Rosen (2006) describes the process of collective decision-making that juries undertake as they strive for a verdict. Individual jurors "put together a narrative as they individually listen to the trial, matching each new piece of information to the story they've been telling themselves along the way." When they adjourn to discuss the evidence they work towards a "collective narrative, one that necessarily depends on the ways in which narratives are generally created in their culture" (Rosen 2006, 148).

The "confession" the jurors take to the deliberation room, then, is the one that has been shaped for them during the trial, and that they then shape again together during deliberation. The prosecution rebuttal argument is the final filter through which they hear about the confession, and it can pack an "emotional punch" (Read 2007). This final narrative doesn't "simply describe ready-made events," but provides "central means by which we create notions as to what took place and how the action unfolded" (Briggs 1996, citing Bauman 1986).

Jurors adjourn for deliberation after the prosecution rebuttal argument and after receiving instructions from the judge about how much weight to give the confession. These instructions may also play an important role in the jurors' decision-making.

Human memory does not distinguish among various sources of information; it doesn't distinguish who said something, but only the fact that it was said, (the fundamental attribution fallacy); it doesn't consider the conditions under which something was said. The rebuttal plays on these weaknesses. The jury will remember the confession through this filter.

False Confessions at Trial

> Although we have constructed an elaborate system of evidentiary rules and courtroom procedures, an American criminal trial is much more than a mere sum of its evidentiary parts. Rather, it is a theater in which the various courtroom actors play out the guilt or innocence of the defendant for the trier of fact to assess. (Levenson 2007)

The fabrication of legal evidence out of a false confession is effective even though it is based on fiction. It is constructed with the same attention and intentionality as any piece of (acknowledged) fiction, striving for verisimilitude. However, because the confession on which it is based is not identified as fictional but rather as sincere, serious and true, it is not critically analyzed.

Political scientist Kristin Bumiller, writing as "an observer of spectacles of interracial gang rape," describes the way the prosecutor in the 1991 Central Park Jogger trial builds a narrative out of what we know now to be false confessions. According to Bumiller, the prosecutor is author of a story about the crime that "has the explicit purpose of making the case for the guilt of the defendants."

In this important case, one black and two Hispanic teenage boys were charged with the sexual and physical assault of a young professional woman in Central Park. The prosecution case was based on forensic photography of the woman's body and the written and videotaped confessions of the defendants. Bumiller says that in this trial, the prosecutor's primary role was as a "scenographer" who created "narrative structure" by arranging and placing objects, persons and events within a "landscaped vision." In closing argument, "the prosecutor tells the story in a way which suggests that the jogger is 'picked' as the victim; as she runs North on East Drive, she becomes 'illuminated for the defendants and others ….' The boys took 'positions' behind trees and ambushed her: she fell to the ground and then was dragged into the woods and darkness off the roadway."

Bumiller's interpretation focuses on how prosecutors produce stories that do more than satisfy "love of justice."

In a recent Stanford Law Review, Brandon Garrett (2009) looked at 42 cases of proven false confessions amongst 252 DNA exonerations. Rather than join scholars who look at "the psychological techniques that can cause people to falsely confess and document instances of known false confessions," he takes a different approach. Garrett examines the substance, or content, of false confessions, including what was said during interrogations, and then, importantly, how the confession statements were litigated at trial and afterwards.

In this chapter I take a similar approach, although I look at the life of only one problematic confession: its "production" at FBI headquarters, and the ways it was strategically repackaged and commented on at trial. We see how the defendant's own original story was rejected by his interrogators and replaced by the government story, how that story went to trial as a probatively powerful confession, and the strategic repackaging of the confession in closing argument. This retelling used a number of narrative devices to create a compelling narrative.

The Hayat case, like other anti-terrorism cases in the United States after September 11, 2001, is one which the prosecution characterized as pre-emptive: its purpose is to prevent a crime. No crime had actually been committed. In fact, it may have been wholly fabricated, a case built on entrapment and self-incrimination, where actual truth may have been trumped by narrative truth. And yet the repercussions for the defendant, his family and the Moslem community in Lodi are pervasive.

There are instances of true stories suppressed and supplanted (under duress) by false stories which are then so compellingly told (by the state) that they convince decision-makers of their reliability. This is what happens when a person is convicted on the basis of a false confession, and Hayat's trial may be an example. In the closing arguments, the original interaction on which the evidence was co-produced (both between the cooperating witness Khan and the defendant, Hamid Hayat, and between the police officers and Hayat) is erased while other, imagined relationships are created and new interpretations made. By using as evidence words that were spoken by the defendant, these closing arguments gain a superficial air of authenticity (Komter 2002) especially with regard to the so-called confession – a speech act which always seems to generate an expectation of sincerity and seriousness (Brooks 2000).

The Case

Surveillance and Arrest

After September 11, 2001, the United States government began to identify and investigate Pakistani American youths who had been to Pakistan to study at religious schools (madrasas) affiliated with banned militant groups. Twenty-two-year-old Hamid Hayat, born in Stockton, California in 1983, was the first to be arrested.

Hayat is part of a small, largely working-class Pakistani community whose families began to arrive in Lodi during the early 1900s to work on the railroads and in the fields. The FBI's Joint Terrorism Task Force, set up in Sacramento after September 11, had been investigating the Lodi Moslem community since 2003. Cooperating witness Nassim Khan had infiltrated the community in 2002, and begun secretly tape-recording his conversations with Hamid Hayat in March 2003. In February 2006 the Director of National Intelligence, John Negroponte, told the Senate Intelligence Committee that federal authorities had uncovered a network of Islamic extremists in this San Joaquin County farming town.

Hamid Hayat was first interviewed on May 30, 2005, when his flight from Pakistan was rerouted to Japan. He was interviewed by an FBI agent and deemed safe to return to the United States.

When Hayat was eventually charged with three counts of lying to the FBI, the interview in Japan was the basis of the first count. The second count was based on an interview on June 3, 2005 at his home. At this time FBI agents took various publications, Hamid's scrapbook and a tawiz (traveler's prayer) from his wallet.[4] Hamid and his father, Umer Hayat, were asked to come to FBI headquarters the next day to help with the investigation. When they arrived, Hamid was taken into an interview room to be questioned by Agent Harry Sweeney. Sweeney read Hayat his rights at 12.30 p.m. The third count was based on the first three and a half hours of a four-hour interrogation during which Hamid again answered questions about his time in Pakistan, telling the agents that he played cricket, helped his mom, and spent time with his cousins.

Interrogation and Admissions

A false confession raises a challenging question: what does it take to get an innocent suspect to put his or her own reality on hold, to move into the frame of guilt insisted upon by the interrogator, and then to produce a fictional account in apparent cooperation with this powerful "co-teller" (Ochs and Capps 2001, 259e)?

4 This prayer was translated by the government expert as "Oh Allah, we place you at their throats, and we seek refuge in you from their evil," and played a significant role in Hayat's trial.

At 4 p.m. Hamid Hayat stopped denying his presence at a training camp and made what Agent Sweeney considered his first "admission," saying that he had been to a training camp in 2000. Forty-five minutes later he made his second admission: that he had been to a training camp in 2003.

Hayat's confession has all the risk factors that are by now well known from the analysis of proven false confessions: the defendant was young, not exceptionally bright, with a compliant personality. His language abilities in English were weak, and at the time of interrogation he was exhausted because of the time difference between Pakistan and California, and from working the night shift. We do not know whether he understood his rights, and he certainly did not understand the implications of waiving them. Although he was interrogated for over thirteen hours, he never seemed to grasp the fact that he was a suspect; he thought, and was allowed to think, that he was helping the agents with their investigation.

This crucial first three and a half hours of the thirteen-hour interrogation of June 4 and 5 were not videotaped, so our only way to evaluate the voluntariness of the confession is through Agent Sweeney's notes and the things he said during cross-examination. Hayat's initial admission came after repeated denials and the use of several well-known interrogation tactics.

Before what Sweeney calls Hayat's first admission, Sweeney used a "minimization" tactic (Inbau et al. 1986), suggesting to Hayat that perhaps he had been to a religious rather than a military training camp, mitigating the serious of the accusation. This tactic of Sweeney's also framed the admission as hypothetical, another familiar interrogation tactic. It took repeated questioning, but when Hayat finally answered that yes, it was possible, perhaps all his subsequent answers also referred to the possible and not the real.

To secure Hayat's second admission, Sweeney used two other familiar tactics: he told Hayat, falsely, that there were satellite photos of him at a training camp, and later, that he had failed his polygraph test.

The Post-admission Interrogation

Once FBI Agent Sweeney considered that Hayat had made admissions, he made ready to videotape and handed Hayat on to Agent Schaaf, whose job (with the occasional help of Agent Leticia Lucero) it was to seek details to corroborate, verify and bring to life the sparse admissions. Two further interrogations were conducted that same evening, and both were videotaped. During these nine hours, agents and suspect worked together until the early hours of the morning to shape "the unfolding tale" (Ochs and Capps 2001), the joint production of an admission narrative. What began as two opposing stories was transformed into one—the FBI version—and became the key evidence in the trial.

At the beginning of the first tape-recorded interrogation, Special Agent Gary Schaaf encourages Hamid Hayat to take off where he'd left off (GS is Agent Schaaf, HH is Hayat, and LL is Agent Leticia Lucero, another FBI interrogator):

> **GS**: Now my understanding uh Hamid is that you uh you attended some camps.
> **HH**: OK.
> **GS**: Um and that's that's true right? (HH nodding)

In a coerced-compliant false confession, the interrogator sometimes leads a suspect to his first admission by asking him for a hypothetical description. This seems to have happened during the first interrogation. During the second interrogation, the agent invites Hayat to imagine a scene and tell what he sees:

> **GS**: So, all right. And uh, so tell me, what put, put me in the front seat of the bus. What am I seeing as you're coming into the camp? Uh here I am, I mean through your eyes tell me what you're seeing as you come out.
> **HH**: Um just go inside and you're not gonna go try to take bus inside.

When the agent tries the same approach again a little later, Hayat does not seem to understand and fails to come up with anything:

> **GS**: So that's, do you go up the main route into the camp?
> **HH**: I mean, on walk we go?
> **GS**: Yes.
> **HH**: Yeah, we walk.
> **GS**: OK.
> **HH**: We walk.
> **GS**: OK. And so tell me, alright, take me on the walk. What happens on the walk?
> **HH**: Nothing happens.

When the agent tries to get a description of the camp setting, this is the exchange:

> **GS**: You said this was almost in the jungle.
> **HH**: (unclear)
> **GS**: What, well, like jungle ah to me means like ah, you mean like pine trees?
> **HH**: (unclear)
> **GS**: Like, like the mountains?
> **HH**: Regular trees, yeah like that ….
> **GS**: Ah, so you like, like just lots of tall, very tall trees.
> **LL**: Like a forest.
> **HH**: Yeah.
> **LL**: Or just trees.
> **HH**: Trees.

When dominant co-tellers such as police interrogators insist that the truth is a lie and "contend that certain unremembered events transpired" (Ochs and Capps 2001), the story that emerges often has signs of what linguists call the language of uncertainty—it is full of vagueness, hedging, pauses and self-repair. It may contain the subjunctive and conditional formulations indicative of what Ofshe and Leo (1997b) call the "grammar of confabulation."

Throughout Hayat's interrogation, we hear the interrogating officer, who is trying to ask questions about something he knows little or nothing about, and the defendant, who is trying to cooperate by answering his questions, both using this language of uncertainty. Agent Schaaf is trying to help Hayat describe a place where Hayat may never have been and which in fact may not even exist. Here he suggests that there are usually hundreds of people at a training camp:

> **GS**: So, um during the course of the time that you're there um how many people did you ob— I mean, usually these camps have, you know hundreds of people coming and going so that I assume that this is, the way you're describing it, would sound similar in that regard. Is that, is that right?
> **HH**: Like hundreds of people.
> **GS**: Yeah, yeah, you know.
> **HH**: I didn't see that much like uh over 50 people I'll say. I didn't see over 50 people there, sir.

Schaaf persists. Perhaps Hayat means he saw 50 people at a time but there could be more, and Hayat complies. The number rises:

> **GS**: At any one time?
> **HH**: One time you know I see, I see like you know all together all the time I like you know, about like 70.

In the early hours of the morning, when Hayat was asked again about possible targets of terrorist action, he was still vague:

> **HH**: Like buildings and I'll say buildings.
> **TH**: What kind of buildings?
> **HH**: Bigger building, you know, buildings.
> **TH**: Buildings? Commercial buildings?
> **HH**: You know commercial, projects and like those kind of buildings. I'll say.

And a little later, asked yet again,

> **TH**: But I need you to tell me details about targets, what they said you know. And, this is where I need your memory to come back.
> **HH**: Like I said sir, you know, big buildings and you know hospitalities and you know, finance buildings, banks and what's it called ah, hmmm maybe like you know uh stores, stores.
> **TH**: What kind of stores?
> **HH**: Stores, like food stores, anything like that.

This exchange was cited in the first affidavit for Hayat's arrest, which read: "Hamid advised that he specifically requested to come to the United States to carry out his jihadi mission. Potential targets for attack would include hospitals and large food stores" (affidavit, June 2005). Agent Timothy Harrison offers to help Hayat in exchange for his cooperation. One example of several is in this excerpt from his interrogation. It's 2 a.m.:

TH: OK I'll meet you, I'll meet you halfway, alright.
HH: What's that mean, halfway? You want me to cooperate.
TH: Cooperate.
HH: Cooperate, yeah I get that, sir.
TH: Yeah, you gotta give me something, in order for me to go help you.
HH: OK.
TH: You know, to tell my bosses that you're cooperating, that you're working with us. You know, you're in a bad situation, you know, but it could be a lot worse, and there's a lot we can do to help you. But you got to help us, you gotta work with us. (HH nodding) All right.

Like people who have made what we know to be false confessions, Hayat did not seem to understand the implications of his admissions. Like others, he may have been aiming simply for a short-term result, an end to the interrogation. Hamid repeatedly asked to see his father, he offered to return another day, he offered to take the agents' numbers and report anything suspicious to them. At about 6 p.m., after two hours of interrogation by Agent Gary Schaaf, Hayat seems to think the interview is over. He asks Schaaf:

HH: Do you have a card, sir?
GS: I will. I don't have one on me.
HH: I contact you (unintelligible).
GS: Yeah.
HH: How 'bout beeper to (unintelligible) remember anything to contact you.

Later, after nearly thirteen hours of interrogation, Hamid still did not seem to understand that he was a suspect. He offered to return the next day. He was surprised that he was about to be arrested and that he was going to jail. He had stopped asking for his father. Now all he wanted was sleep:

HH: So I come back here tomorrow? Again.
TH: No, no. You're not leaving here tonight, no.
HH: No, I mean ah, tomorrow. I'm going to be here tonight. Staying here? In the building?
TH: No, no, you're going to go, you're going to go to jail.
PA: Hamid, you're going to jail.
HH: Yeah, so am I going to get a place to sleep over there like that?

PA: It's jail, Hamid, you understand that?
HH: Yeah, I know, I know it's a jail, but can I lay down because my head (HH points to his head) is hurting, I want to sleep.

The Confession at Trial: Adversarial Storytelling

At the trial we hear about three aspects of the confession: the interrogation itself (Was it given voluntarily, is it reliable?), the crime (Did Hamid Hayat go to a training camp and get trained there?) and the character and intent of the defendant based on "his own words" and actions.

First, we will look at the confession's evidential value. If the apparently remembered experience of being at a training camp is not reliable, then there is no evidence with which to charge Hamid Hayat. As the defense attorney said at trial:

> And so that's what you have, Ladies and Gentlemen, you have a meaningless confession. You have Hamid Hayat being intimidated into saying things that the FBI wanted him to say .... The entire interview was meaningless, and it does not prove that Hayat went to a camp. And because [Hayat's] statements come from a meaningless confession and they are completely unreliable, the government ladies and gentlemen, is left with nothing.[5]

But the prosecution case depends on a jury beginning its deliberations with the confession intact. Because the government has the burden of proof, the prosecution gets the last word with a "rebuttal" argument. David Deitch uses this "extremely powerful tool for the plaintiff" (Read 2007, 279–80) to great effect.

In rebuttal, Deitch discredits the defense closing argument. He "re-legitimizes" (Rosulek 2008, 2010) the confession which the defense attorney had carefully presented as "meaningless" and "unreliable." He retells the story of the interrogation, erases apparent gaps, uncertainties and contradictions in the confession, and characterizes the defendant as a youth capable of committing great violence for ideological reasons. He plays on the fears and uncertainty jurors may feel in a post-9/11 United States, and leaves them with a sense that it is their responsibility to protect the public by upholding the government case.

Interrogation: Did Admissions Follow Breakthrough or Breakdown?

The first weakness that Deitch set out to re-legitimize is the point where Hamid Hayat stopped denying and began to admit, a pivotal moment upon which the voluntariness of the admission and the reliability of the narrative details hinges.

5 Transcript of defense closing argument, Reporter's Transcript, Jury Trial, February 16–April 12, 2006, 4,319–20.

The defense attorney had brought this crucial moment into question during the trial in her careful cross-examination of Agent Sweeney.

> **Q**: And your recollection is during that first three and a half hour period in all of his responses he denied any connection to jihadi training?
> **A**: That is correct
> **Q**: Okay. Now let's move into that second portion, when he makes his initial – did you call it an admission.
> **A**: Admission. Confession. Yes.
> **Q**: Do you recall the question that you asked when he ultimately said that at about 3:30? …
> **A**: My question to him was, Is it possible, Hamid, that you didn't know that you were going to a jihadi training camp? Is it possible that you may have thought it was something else, like a religious education camp?
> **Q**: Okay. Did he give you any inclination that that may have been a possibility?
> **A**: No, he did not.
> **Q**: And when you asked that question, what was his response?
> **A**: His response was that, yes, that, in fact, was the case.
> **Q**: What were the words he uttered; do you recall?
> **A**: I don't recall the exact words.

She wonders whether Hayat offered details of the camp after his supposed decision to admit:

> **Q**: Do you recall, was it a yes, or was it a yes with detail?
> **A**: I recall that it was a yes with detail.

"Yes with detail"—but she does not leave it at that. What did it take to get Hayat to offer details? Were they freely given?

> **Q**: The first time you asked?
> **A**: No. Actually, the first time I brought up that topic and asked that direct question or that direct issue, it wasn't necessarily an automatic yes, that's it. There may have been several times that I raised that particular issue.

The police officer asked "several times." We are left thinking that he may have badgered and put pressure on Hayat.

Deitch tells the story of the interrogation differently. Here is his description of the first interrogation, the one with Harry Sweeney, during which Hayat begins to admit. In the rebuttal, Deitch characterized that crucial turning point as a "breakthrough," to overcome jurors' concerns about its elicitation:

> Hamid Hayat told Harry Sweeney, in response to questions, that he had gone to Pakistan to help out his mom, that he had gone to get married, that he played

> cricket, that he hung out with friends, and that he'd sometime go and travel to eat in American style restaurants. Hamid Hayat specifically denied to Special Agent Sweeney that he had ever received any weapons training at a jihadist training camp, and that he had ever received any training at a jihadist camp to fight against the United States. He denied that more than once. After doing that though, there was a moment in which there was a breakthrough. Harry Sweeney asked Hamid Hayat, Is it possible that you didn't know that you were going to a jihadi training camp? Is it possible that you may have thought it was something else, like a religious education camp?

After Harry Sweeney posed that question, Hamid Hayat confessed for the first time. Examining Sweeney, Hayat's defense attorney carefully demonstrates that Hayat's second admission came after he was offered false evidence, another common police tactic when driving for a confession:

> **Q**: And when he made the second admission, was there a different question that was posed to him?
> **A**: Yes.
> **Q**: And what was that question?
> **A**: My answer to him—the issue that I raised was that I knew that he attended a camp in 2003. … I … asked him the question, in essence, why would we have a picture of you on satellite image in 2003 in your most recent trip to Pakistan. And it was at that time, in response to that issue being raised, that he said he was, in fact, at a camp in 2003 for a much longer period.
> **Q**: Do you, in fact, have a satellite image picture of him at a camp—
> **A**: We do not.
> **Q**: In 2003—Okay.

Deitch tells his own story about the second admission:

> He later changed his tune, and you know the moment he did so. The defining moment was with Agent Sweeney, when Agent Sweeney, among other things, asked him if there was any reason why Hamid Hayat's image would be on a satellite photo during Hayat's most recent visit to Pakistan. It was from this point forward, ladies and gentlemen, that Hamid Hayat honestly believed that the FBI had at least some evidence to prove that he went to a camp, but Hamid Hayat didn't know how much.

He uses this to characterize Hayat as highly skilled at deception, a jihadi trained to keep inside and outside information separate:

> This evidence suggests that at point, ladies and gentlemen, Hamid Hayat felt profoundly conflicted. On the one hand he knew that he had been caught but on the other hand he didn't want to reveal the full and true nature of what he did.

> Like his uncle, inside, outside, keep as much as you can. That's what a jihadi is trained to do, knows to do, when confronted.
>
> So what did he do? He admitted what he thought the FBI knew, but otherwise he tried, when he could, to minimize, and he even tried to hide the true extent of his conduct.

Developing the characterization of Hayat in the rebuttal argument, David Deitch develops a theme of inner and outer behaviors. He describes Hayat as garrulous and open during the Khan recordings, and secretive in the FBI interrogation.

Characterizing the Defendant: Jihadi Heart and Mind

In closing argument, government prosecutor Tice-Raskin repackaged this problematic and possibly false confession to paint a picture of a young man with a jihadi heart and mind, who admitted "in his own words" to having attended a military training camp. To do this, he draws on the surreptitiously recorded conversations between Hayat and cooperating witness Khan:

> These recorded conversations, ladies and gentlemen, allow you, the jury, to be live and to hear the actual words, the actual words that that man spoke in 2003. What did these recordings reveal? On March 11, 2003, Hamid Hayat himself indicated that jihad is the duty of all Muslims. He stated "Jihad is the duty of every Muslim. It is our duty to go and help other Muslims anywhere in the world where Muslims or Muslim countries are attacked.

The prosecutor quotes in full a disturbing conversation in which Hayat speaks approvingly about the murder of Daniel Pearl. Although the defense successfully attacked Khan's credibility at trial, Hayat's jury was not given the benefit of a linguistic analysis of the tapes (Shuy 1993; Shuy 2005; Shuy 2010). This kind of analysis would have revealed to the jury the "stock" conversational strategies Khan used to elicit and encourage Hayat's anti-American talk, and the "troublesome, seductive and ultimately unfair" kind of evidence it is (Shuy 2005). Khan played on his "friendship" with Hamid to try to persuade him to go to a training camp. Hayat's jury hears his apparently damning words doubly removed from their interactional context because they are translated from the Pashto (and occasional Urdu).

The Training Camp

The government had to prove that Hayat was at a militant training camp, and according to the prosecutor in his closing argument, they had done just that.

The defense attorney, on the other hand, was certain that the prosecution had failed to prove that Hayat had been to a training camp. In discussing Hayat's confession during her closing argument, she reminded the jury that the police had intimidated Hamid, used questionable tactics, he was exhausted, and he was asked many leading questions. He didn't "know what was happening to him."

> He didn't realize that by telling the FBI what they wanted to hear, that he attended a camp in Pakistan, that he had just gotten himself into a whole lot of trouble. It's really quite sad to watch that video and watch [Hayat] say things that make no sense. They don't even make sense to the agents who are listening to them. And you really see him trying to cooperate and provide the answers the best that he can.

The agents tried to establish the location of a training camp, but got vague and contradictory information from Hayat. The rebuttal repackages this to produce what prosecutor David Deitch calls the "consistent thread" of Balakot, making it sound as if Hayat told Agent Sweeney three times that he was there. Deitch's phrasing gives the impression that Hayat himself repeated the name out loud six times in a row:

> So when Hamid Hayat goes on video, he's already given away a lot of information. And perhaps the most important piece of information he's given away, I'll say it in one word, Balakot. Balakot. He told Harry Sweeney the camp was in the area of Balakot. … And he repeated … at least six times during the videotaped interview, Balakot, Balakot, Balakot, Balakot, Balakot. Balakot.

In the rebuttal argument details that emerged at length and which were often later contradicted in the interrogation are presented as if they are undisputed facts. Vague images invariably suggested first by the interrogator and then integrated into the account become vivid in rebuttal.

> (An exchange about Kalashnikovs)
> **GS**: OK. And then what about Kalishnikov training?
> **HH**: No, I never did that.
> **GS**: Ah, I mean they have there, I assume?
> **HH**: They do have it over there.
> **GS**: You can hear it, it sounds dit, dit, dit, dit, dit.
> **HH**: Yeah.
> **GS**: Yeah.
> **HH**: I can hear that but I never did that.
> **GS**: So you saw they have Kalishnikov training and then they have ah I mean they they have explosives training.

Deitch transformed that exchange into "He also stated that he was aware that they had kalashnikovs and indicated that he, in fact, had seen one." Information about possible explosive training proposed by Schaaf became amplified in rebuttal: "Hamid Hayat also admitted that he consistently heard a lot of explosions while he was at camp."

Deitch uses subjective verbs which cannot be contradicted: Hayat, he says, "admitted," "indicated," "remembered" and "recalled" details of the training camp. This way of casting narrative events as what they or another "remember" (Ochs and Capps 2001, 284) is strategic and provides an "authenticating power" by presupposing "that the events truly occurred".

In her closing argument, the defense attorney demonstrated that every detail about the training camp was introduced by the agents. This is a serious indictment. But research has shown that human memory does not always distinguish among sources of information (Shuy 1993; Schachter 2001), and the rebuttal argument plays on this weakness:

> Hamid Hayat didn't just make up these details about this camp. Why was he able to describe a camp in the outskirts of Balakot, with this trail through the woods, over the mountains, opening into a field and so forth?
>
> He may have gotten a lot of the details wrong either because of lack of recollection or because of the kind of lying and gauging that I've talked about, but he sure got a lot of the details right. Someone who had not been to that camp, it would be an awful coincidence to get all of those right and for it to match.

In the rebuttal argument, events are "materialized" and arranged in a temporal and causal order to achieve an appearance of reality. Disparate physical details that came into the narrative through a series of alternative, either/or, questions are pulled together to portray a journey with a beginning and an arrival: Hayat's movement from home to camp entails a bus journey and then a trail that goes through woods, over mountains, into a field:

> **GS**: Um and uh and then you're uh what time do you, do you leave at night or in the daytime or—
> **HH**: From where to the camp?
> **GS**: From from Pindi yeah.
> **HH**: Uh daytime, sir.
> **GS**: So you left in daytime. Did you arrive in dark or was it—
> **HH**: Yeah it was dark when we arrived, yes, sir.

In Deitch's version (and here we see the trees so painstakingly garnered by the interrogator):

> He recounted to the agents that he arrived by bus at nighttime, that he followed an unidentified male who had a flashlight, and then they went up a zigzag road up a mountain. And you will recall, when you see him on videotape, the way Hamid Hayat would describe with his hands how he would go up the various zigzag portions of that road. Hamid Hayat indicated that at the end of that hike he reached a field, and that there were trees all around him.

To make the description even more concrete, Deitch reminds jurors that they saw Hayat gesturing on videotape when "describing" the road. He creates a sense of heightened reality by highlighting Hayat's "live" appearance on videotape, calling upon jurors' sense of televisual reality to give them confidence in the existence of the road Hayat described. Richard Sherwin (in an interview in Scelfo 2001) warns us that "visual persuasion" can be used to "short-circuit the ideal of rational deliberation and supplant it by a more emotional form of judgment." In the next excerpt, Deitch compounds the emotional impact by repeating the word "repeatedly":

> During the course of the videotaped interviews, again, where you had chance, folks, to see Hamid Hayat live, he gave a fairly detailed confession in which he repeatedly, repeatedly confirmed that he had attended a jihadi camp both in 2003–4 as well as earlier in 2000.

In fact, Hayat's interrogators never heard him "repeatedly, repeatedly confirm" that he had attended a jihadi camp. On the contrary, they struggled with him to produce a coherent, convincing and legally sound confession narrative, and although Hamid Hayat wanted very much to cooperate, they did not succeed. Toward the end of the third interrogation, after 3 a.m., Agent Aguilar, sitting in with Agent Harrison, says:

> **PA**: Hamid, we keep asking you these questions and, and you're giving us the answers you are taking I mean why, why aren't you being truthful here?
> **HH**: I don't get that, like the questions you guys are asking again, you know. What question, you ask me again, I try my best you know.

Dangerousness

In a pre-emptive trial such as this one, intended to prevent a violent crime, the jury has to believe that the defendant is capable of committing that crime. Deitch ends his argument by describing a highly emotive, imagined scene in which he discredits the defense portrayal of Hayat as harmless and projects him instead as the possible future agent of horrific violence. Toward the end of the rebuttal argument, Deitch says this:

> But there is a more important point here. Let's say that Hamid Hayat came back, how thin or not thin do you think you need to be to spray a crowd with an AK-47? How thin or not thin do you think you have to be to wear a backpack full of explosives into a crowded shopping mall? How thin or not thin do you think you need to be to drive a Ryder truck full of explosives into a public building?

Then, in a bold rhetorical move he "animates" Hamid Hayat, by creating a fictionalized confession as if actually spoken by him in an uninterrupted monologue. The attributed words imply clear intention on Hayat's part to carry out the charged actions:

> There is lots of evidence here, ladies and gentlemen. Lots of evidence to show that a man, Hamid Hayat, said, I'm going for training, I'm going to be trained to commit jihad, and that he returned and said, Yes, I did go, and I was trained to commit jihad, and I came back here with the intent to do just that, consistent with his conversations and consistent with the physical evidence that you've seen in this trial.

Hayat is made to tell a very simple story with a clear chronology, and Deitch's "breakthrough into performance" (Hymes 1981), his use of direct discourse, carries inordinate power: "By giving voice to characters, dialogue makes story into drama and listeners into an interpreting audience to the drama…Thus understanding [of this type of] discourse is in part emotional" (Tannen 1989, 133).

Briggs (1996) points out how "reported speech provides narrators with the ability to embed their assessment of a character's affective and/or moral state in the way his or her words are replayed on the narrative stage." Kandel (2002) points to the persuasive force of reported speech in legal settings, where it can give a strong appearance of veracity, specificity and accuracy of memory, involve the hearer emotionally, and make what is narrated in this form especially salient, memorable and significant to the hearer.[6]

6 Diez (2005) looks at reported speech in asylum interviews, and Holt and Johnson (2010) in police interviews. Galatolo and Mizzau (2005) describe yet another specific function of direct reported speech that they say has emerged from the analysis of their testimony data from an Italian court: "in the context of lay witness' testimony, direct reported speech can be a tool for covertly expressing one's point of view about events, bypassing the rule that prevents one from expressing individual opinions and evaluations while testifying." Shonna Trinch (2010), in her study of direct reported speech in Latina domestic abuse affidavits, suggests that the role of direct reported speech varies by setting, but is always contextual, always meaningful.

The Verdict

In a pre-emptive prosecution like that against Hamid Hayat, the defendant is charged with having undertaken an action such as military training considered preparation for terrorism, or having shown sympathy and support for terrorism. Jury foreman, Joseph Cote (Waldman 2006) called the issue of intent the most perplexing question in the entire indictment, but maybe the most morally significant. The jury's biggest challenge, said Cote, was whether Hayat was capable of engaging in terrorism (Waldman 2006): "We're not being asked 'Did the defendant commit the crime? …' but is the defendant capable of doing a crime? And I don't think that that is in the level of understanding of the jurors."

According to United States Attorney, MacGregor Scott, the significance of the notebooks and the prayer seized from Hayat's home was to show his mindset, his beliefs and his intent. According to Cote, the Arabic prayer (translated by the government expert as "Oh Allah, we place you at their throats and we seek refuge in you from their evil") was especially influential: "It carried a lot of weight. Even though he's an American citizen, his love and his home are in Pakistan."

In the end, says Waldman, Cote decided they couldn't take a chance. There are, he said,

> He looked at Hayat and saw what he called a nice young man. But in his mind was the specter of other nice young men, three of them also of Pakistani origin, who had carried out the London subway bombings.

After nine days of deliberation, the jury found Hayat guilty on four counts: one count of providing material support or resources to terrorism, and three counts of lying about it to the police.

In October 2006, Hayat's attorneys submitted a motion for retrial.[7] The motion was denied by Judge Burrell. While the jury seems to have struggled with the evidence, according to Cote reaching its decision "with a heavy heart," Burrell showed no sign of such struggle. On September 10, 2007, at the Federal District Court in Sacramento, he sentenced Hayat to 24 years in prison. According to

---

7 In its motion for a retrial, Hayat's defense contended that there was not enough evidence to legally corroborate Hayat's confession. Judge Garland E. Burrell, Jr. of the Federal District Court in Sacramento rejected the motion in May 2007: "The government contends that Hayat's confession was corroborated by: his possession of a jihadi supplication; his multiple recorded conversations with Khan related to his belief in jihad and desire to attend a jihadi camp; testimony regarding the existence of camps in Pakistan (including in the Balakot area) by Eric Benn and Hassan Abbas; Hayat's self-made jihadi scrapbook; and Hayat's possession of numerous well-known jihadi publications. The government is correct that sufficient independent corroborating evidence is in the record on Hayat's actus reus. Therefore, Hayat is not entitled to a new trial on this ground."

an article in the New York Times (September 11, 2007), Hayat was solemn and attentive as the words of Judge Burrell were translated into Urdu:

> Hamid Hayat attended a terrorist training camp and returned to the United States, ready and willing to wage violent jihad when directed to do so, regardless of the havoc such acts could wreak on persons and property in the United States, and then lied to the FBI on three separate occasions.

Burrell added that the evidence suggested a likelihood of recidivism and an unlikelihood of rehabilitation. An appeal has been made and its outcome is awaited. Meanwhile, Hamid Hayat has been transferred to a prison in Indiana, far from his family and community in Lodi.

Conclusion

We do not know whether Hayat was ever at a military training camp or whether he admitted only to the *possibility* of having been at one. He may have cooperated with the interrogators to describe a camp he had never been to and which may never have existed. The jury should have been told that Hayat was similar to suspects known to have confessed falsely, and that he was questioned in a manner known to have generated false confessions. They should have learned about the psychological process of "influence" (as in Leo 2010), how it is enacted and embodied verbally and non-verbally during interrogation and can generate false confessions

The jurors should also have learned about how the post-admission interrogation process may have contaminated Hayat's statements (Garrett, 2010). They could have been helped to understand that the familiar constraints of sociality, cooperativeness, politeness and "preference for agreement" play on confession-makers even more than they do on ordinary conversationalists. They could have been guided to understand "linguistic coercion" and to see how the "interlocutory relationship" between suspect and interrogator is a relationship which, as Peter Brooks (2000, 6) says, "urges towards speech."

The jurors and the judge should have been guided to see that legal evidence is gathered and presented strategically, with intentionality (Shuy 2005), so that they could understand their "subtle strong persuasive effect" (Kandel 2002). They could have learned that narrative strategies make a story compelling, seem to give it an anchor in reality, generate emotion and enhance audience involvement, and that they can also be used to manipulate listeners and obscure reality. As Jerome Bruner (2004 [1987], 15) says: "We seem to have no other way of describing 'lived time' save in the form of narrative' and that makes us very susceptible to the persuasive power of stories."

In an ideal world, jurors and judges would hear about the vagaries of human memory (Schachter 2001) and the common mistakes of language use (Shuy

1993). And in an ideal world they would be aware of what Matoesian (2009) calls "the most complex tension in the study of discourse: that there were aspects of talk that were not only or even primarily in the talk, and these aspects constitute socially structured and historically inherited forms of domination that permeate the microcosmic fabric of situated forms of conduct."

Videotaping Interrogations

Overwhelmingly, academics, lawyers and advocates call for mandatory videotaping of police interrogations. In order for these recordings to be useful, however, we need to understand what can go wrong when they are used at trial, and to develop ways to explicate them for judges and jurors.

During the Central Park Jogger trial, the videotaped "confessions"—now known to be false—were used to the detriment of the defendants. Prosecutor Elizabeth Lederer replayed two of the videos numerous times during the month-long trial, According to political scientist Kristin Bumiller, who attended the trial:

> In the videotaped confessions we see the boys cornered in a small room, answering a series of questions about their own and others' participation in the rape. We are told that the first boy gripped her shirt and started to feel her. Steven Lopez covered her mouth when she started screaming, "smashed her," and said, "shut up you bitch," yet she keep on screaming and he "just kept smashing her and hitting her with a brick." The defendant explained: "She was like shocked, she just stood there and didn't do anything."

In Hayat's trial Cote said just after the trial (Waldman 2006) that the outcome was uncertain when they began deliberations, and it was reviewing the videotaped interrogation for a second time that made the difference. The first time the jurors saw the videotape, he says, they were bothered by the leading questions and "pressure tactics" used by the FBI interrogators. But they had received an instruction from US District Judge Garland E. Burrell stating that "the government may utilize a broad range of schemes and ploys to ferret out criminal activity." Also crucial, according to Cote, by the time they viewed the videotape for the second time, the jurors had absorbed all the other evidence, and by this time they had heard the closing arguments.

The prosecution's closing arguments portray a young man with a jihadi heart and mind. And they accomplish this portrayal, they claim, through his own words captured forever on tape. By focusing on his own words, they gain the authenticating power that reported speech can bring. However, the jury isn't reminded that these "own words" emerged from the constraining and coercive context of interrogation.

It is essential to evaluate videotaped evidence multimodally, considering prosody, gaze, gesture and other nonverbal aspects of the interrogation (Goodwin

1994; Goodwin 2000; Goodwin 2007; Matoesian 2010), attending to the effect of camera angle (Lassiter 2004; Lassiter et al. 2006), intentional "audience manipulation" by interrogators doing the recording (Coulthard 2002), the ways gesture, gaze and postural orientation "are interwoven into the stream of verbal activity" in legal proceedings (Matoesian 2010), and remembering (Sherwin 2002) that visual evidence has persuasive power of its own.

Implications for Justice

There's a new kind of law in America, and the Moslem community in the small city of Lodi, like Moslems across the country, is susceptible to it. United States Attorney McGregor Scott speaks of the "mission" law enforcement has been given by the president and attorney general "in the post-9/11 context," which is to "to prevent deadly acts before they occur. That is the new paradigm for law enforcement." We read in Amy Waldman's analysis of Hamid Hayat's case that Hayat's jury had difficulty deciding to convict. But, said Cote:

> Can we, on the basis of what we know, put this kid on the street? … On the basis of what we know of how people of his background have acted in the past? The answer is no." There are he says, "So-called new rules of engagement and I don't want to see the government lose its case."

Anthropologist Sunaina Maira, who visited Lodi after the trial, was told that some Pakistani families had come to the United States as early as 1908, to work on the railroads. Maira contrasts the Lodi community to the more recent, more upwardly mobile South Asian population in the Bay Area. She points out that since the Lodi community is geographically and politically isolated from their compatriots in the major urban and suburban South Asian enclaves and most do not speak English (Grudin 2005), they are an easier target for surveillance and intimidation. There are no South Asian political organizations in Lodi, and the Pakistani community had not been exposed to workshops on civil and immigrant rights. Hamid Hayat, like other men in Lodi, had opened his door to the FBI when they arrived at his home three days after he returned from Pakistan. Without consulting a lawyer, he had agreed to be questioned and offered to drive to Sacramento to take a polygraph test.

As Umer, Hamid Hayat's father, said in a Frontline interview, they had no reason to be nervous, because they were innocent. They didn't know their rights. They didn't know they shouldn't have spoken to the FBI without an attorney present.

The Hayat case may be an example of the "collateral damage" that can result from the so-called war on terror. Kent Roach and Gary Trotter (2005) warn that the "temptation of departing from normal legal standards and engaging in prejudgment, prejudice, and stereotyping may be particularly high in emotive and devastating cases involving allegations of terrorism and fears of continued acts of terrorism

…." They remind us that "the risk of wrongful convictions in terrorism cases, both before and after 9/11, are likely to fall disproportionately on particular groups, such as racial and religious minorities, or those with radical political views":

"Prosecutors have only had to show that the accused expressed interest in helping—as the government puts it—the 'global jihad movement' …. Under our system you have to show a defendant has done something specific," says national security scholar Peter Margulies. "These charges are really a departure from the usual way of our doing justice."

There are often larger social and political issues at work in false confession-based wrongful conviction cases, and broad social voices and discourses "which shape courtroom interaction" (Cotterill 2002). As in the Hayat case, anti-Moslem sentiments and more general issues of class, racism and cultural and religious stereotyping come into play.

At the Central Park Jogger trial, another high-profile case built on police-induced false confessions, gathered from vulnerable youths after egregious interrogation. Columbia University law professor Patricia Williams attended the trial. She describes the uproar—"Lines extended around the block for admission, as though it were a Broadway show"—and the racialized perception of the defendants: "for all other attendees, the bailiffs would determine at the door whether one was with the prosecution or the defense. When Kristin [Bumiller] and I said neither, they seated us on the right, with the prosecution. Some called it the white side. The other side of the courtroom was usually entirely black" (Williams 2002). Bumiller (1997) says that the "spectacle inscribed fears of racial violence and sexual violation in the modern urban scene" and is about the "brutalities of existence for woman and racial "others."

In 2002, DNA evidence confirmed the confession of Matias Reyes to the 1989 rape of Paula Harris, the Central Park jogger. The convictions of the five African-American and Latino young men wrongly convicted in 1991 were vacated. At a press conference, their mothers and sisters spoke about the case.

Yusuf Salaam's mother, Sharonne, was asked whether civil rights attorney William Kunstler could have made a difference. "Jesus couldn't a won it," she said, "the fix was in …. They had the media, the public, the judge, all they needed was the hangman's noose."

Salaam continues: "We also feel that we have all been victimized just as the Central Park Jogger … we have all been denied justice. … In their rush to judgment innocent lives have been pushed aside … other people who were victims in the park that night never received justice … everyone was eager to point a finger at these children …."

Poignantly, powerfully, speaking as a mother, she says: "We wanted our children to be professionals. We wanted our children to be lawyers and doctors and school teachers. We wanted for our children what all people want for their children."

Angela Cuffee, Kevin Richardson's sister, told the press and the country: "Everybody should be outraged …. Change the laws …. Never let this happen again."

The reliability and trustworthiness of every confession should be considered before it is entered into evidence. Leo and Ofshe (1998) recommend a mandatory "reliability hearing" before a confession is allowed into evidence. Garrett (2009) agrees: "Unless criminal procedure is reoriented towards the reliability of the substance of confessions, contamination of facts may continue to go undetected, resulting in miscarriages of justice." Largely as a result of the growing number of DNA exonerations, "a spotlight of scrutiny has been cast on the processes of police interviewing and interrogation" (Kassin et al. 2009).

Jurors and judges need reminding that even a videotape is simply a partial record of a complex interaction between a suspect and police officers anxious to solve a crime. They should be guided to understand the innocent suspect's experience of domination and deception, frustration and futility, the process by which he or she has been "influenced" (Leo 2008), and how 'influence' was enacted through verbal and nonverbal language.

Linguistic anthropologists interested in the role of narrative in creating and maintaining collective memory and in the functioning of social memory in specific institutions (Mendoza-Denton 2008) can help to explain how the human proclivity to story-making and particular narrative devices such as reported speech influence individual and collective decision-making.

We are reminded by Hayat and similar cases that a confession statement becomes powerful and dangerous evidence at trial. Existing legal safeguards do not protect a suspect from the elusive, emotive and subjective factors which come into play when a confession is the sole evidence. Confessions, and especially uncorroborated confessions, should never play more than a very limited role in any criminal case. If, as in the Hayat case, a judge does allow a problematic confession into evidence, the jurors should be fully informed about the dangers of false confessions.

In all cases, the lives of communities, families and individuals are severely disrupted by these miscarriages of justice. It is easy to miss the quiet comment Hamid Hayat made toward the end of his interrogation about his mother's illness and how her condition has worsened with worry and sorrow about his and his father's situation. We hear a whisper of despair, and it is one that bears attending to.

Further Reading

Gudjonsson, G. (2003), *The Psychology of Interrogations and Confessions: A Handbook*, London: Wiley.

Hepworth, M. and Turner, B.S. (1982), *Confession: Studies in Deviance and Religion*, London: Routledge and Kegan Paul.

Leo, R. (2008), *Police Interrogation and American Justice*, Cambridge, MA: Harvard University Press.

Shuy, R.W. (1993), *Language Crimes*, Oxford: Blackwell.

—— and Thomas, G.C. III (eds.) (1998), *The Miranda Debate: Law, Justice and Policing*, Chicago, IL: Northeastern University Press.

Case Documents

See <www.milnet.com> for many of the case documents and articles regarding the *Hayat* case.

Affidavit, June 6, 2005 Eastern District of California, <http://www.washingtoninstitute.org/documents/42b18c1d93623.pdf>.

USA Plaintiff v. *Hamid Hayat and Umer Hayat*, No. CR.S-05-240.

Reporter's Transcript, Jury Trial, February 16–April 12, 2006.

FBI Interrogations with Hamid Hayat—transcript and video.

Translated transcriptions of Khan tapes (Pashto to English, some Urdu).

Miranda v. *Arizona*, 384 US 436 (1966).

References

Aldridge, M. and Luchjenbroers, J. (2007), "Linguistic manipulation in legal discourse: Framing questions and 'smuggling' information,'" *International Journal of Speech, Language, and the Law*, 14(1).

Ainsworth, J. (1998), "In a different register: The pragmatics of powerlessness in police interrogation," in R.A. Leo and G.C. Thomas III (eds.), *The Miranda Debate: Law, Justice and Policing*, Chicago, IL: Northeastern University Press.

—— (2010), "Miranda rights: Curtailing coercion in the police interview—the failed promise of *Miranda* v. *Arizona*," in M. Coulthard and A. Johnson (eds.), *The Routledge Handbook of Forensic Linguistics*, Abingdon and New York: Routledge.

Amsterdam, A.G. and Bruner, J. (2002), *Minding the Law*, Cambridge, MA: Harvard University Press.

Baldwin, J. (1993) "Police interviewing technique: Establishing truth or proof," *British Journal of Criminology*, 33(3), 325–52.

Bauman, R. (1986), *Story, Performance, and Event: Contextual Studies of Oral Narrative*, Cambridge: Cambridge University Press.

Bennett, W.L. and Feldman, M.S. (1981), *Reconstructing Reality in the Courtroom*, London: Tavistock Publications.

Berk-Seligson, S. (2002), "The Miranda warnings and linguistic coercion: The role of footing in the interrogation of a limited-English-speaking murder suspect," in J. Cotterill (ed), *Language in the Legal Process*, New York: Palgrave Macmillan.

—— (2009), *Coerced Confessions: The Discourse of Bilingual Police Interrogations*, Berlin: Mouton de Gruyter.

Briggs, C.L. (ed.) (1996), *Disorderly Discourse: Narrative, Conflict and Inequality*, New York: Oxford University Press.

Brooks, P. (2000), *Troubling Confessions: Speaking Guilt in Law and Literature*, Chicago, IL: Chicago University Press.

Bruner, J. (2004 [1987]), "Life as narrative," *Social Research* 71(3), 691–710; originally published in *Social Research*, 54(1) (Spring 1987).

Bumiller, K. (1997), "Spectacles of the strange: Envisioning violence in the Central Park jogger trial," in M.A. Fineman, and M.T. McCluskey (eds.), *Feminism, Media and the Law*, Oxford: Oxford University Press.

Cahill, D., Grebler G., Baker, A. and Tully, B. (1988), *Vulnerable Testimony: Police Interviewing of Mentally Handicapped and Mentally Disordered People in Connection with Serious Crime*, London: Royal Society for Mentally Handicapped Children and Adults.

Cotterill, J. (1998), "Metaphor in closing arguments," *International Journal of Speech, Language and the Law*, 15(2).

—— (2002), "Intertextuality in the trials of O.J. Simpson," in J. Cotterill (ed.), *Language in the Legal Process*, New York: Palgrave Macmillan.

Coulthard, M. (2002), "Whose voice is it? Invented and concealed dialogue in written records of verbal evidence produced by the police," in J. Cotterill (ed.), *Language in the Legal Process*, New York: Palgrave Macmillan.

Davis, D. and Leo, R.A. (2010), "Commentary: Overcoming Judicial Preferences for Person- Versus Situation-based Analyses of Interrogation-induced Confessions," *Journal of the American Academy of Psychiatry Law*, 38 (June), 187–94.

de Certeau, M. (1986), *Heterologies: Discourse on the Other*, trans. B. Massumi, Minneapolis, MN: University of Minnesota Press.

Diez, I.G. (2005), "The Transformation of Asylum Seekers' Narratives through the Asylum Procedure," paper presented at the International Association of Forensic Linguists 7th Biennial Conference on Forensic Linguistics/Language and Law, Cardiff University, UK, July 2005.

Drizin, S.A. and Colgan, B.A. (2004), "Tales from the juvenile confession front: A guide to how standard police interrogation tactics can produce coerced and false confessions from juvenile suspects," in G.D. Lassiter (ed.), *Interrogations, Confessions and Entrapment*, New York: Kluwer/Plenum.

Findley, K.A. and Scott, M.S. (2006), "The multiple dimensions of tunnel vision in criminal cases," *Wisconsin Law Review*, 291.

Galatolo, R and Mizzau, M. (2005), "Quoting dialogues and the construction of the narrative point of view in legal testimony: The role of prosody and gesture," *Studies in Communication Science*, special issue.

Garrett, Brandon L. (2009), "The substance of false confessions," *Stanford Law Review*, 62(4), Virginia Public Law and Legal Theory Research Paper No. 2010-11, <http://ssrn.com/abstract=1280254>.

Goodwin, C. (1994), "Professional vision," *American Anthropologist*, 96(3), 606–33.

—— (2000), "Practices of seeing: visual analysis—an ethnomethodological approach," in T. van Leeuwen and C. Jewitt (eds.), *Handbook of Visual Analysis*, London: Sage Publications.

—— (2007), 'Participation, stance, and affect in the organization of activities," *Discourse and Society*, 18(1), 53–73.

Grebler, G. (2005), "Language Issues in (False) Confession Evidence," paper presented at International Linguistic Association, 50th Anniversary Conference on Language and Law, New York City, April 2005.

—— (2010), "A jihadi heart and mind? Strategic repackaging of a possibly false confession in an anti-terrorism trial in California," in M. Coulthard and A. Johnson (eds.), *The Routledge Handbook of Forensic Linguistics*, London: Routledge.

Gross, S.R., Jacoby, K., Matheson, D. J., Montgomery, N. and Patil, S. (2005), "Exonerations in the United States, 1989 through 2003," *Journal of Criminal Law and Criminology*, 95(2), <http://ssrn.com/abstract=753084>.

Gudjonsson, G. (1992), *The Psychology of Interrogations, Confessions and Testimony*, Chichester: John Wiley and Sons.

Gumperz, J. (1982), *Discourse Strategies*, Studies in Interactional Sociolinguistics, Cambridge: Cambridge University Press.

Haworth, K. (2010), "Police Interviews in the Judicial Process: Police Interviews as Evidence," in M. Coulthard and A. Johnson (eds.), *The Routledge Handbook of Forensic Linguistics*, London: Routledge.

Heffer, C. (2002), "If You Were Standing in Marks and Spencers': Narrativisation and Comprehension in English Summing-up," in J. Cotterill (ed.), *Language in the Legal Process*, Palgrave Macmillan.

—— (2010), "Constructing crime stories in court," in M. Coulthard and A. Johnson (eds.), *The Routledge Handbook of Forensic Linguistics*, London: Routledge.

Hill, M.D. (2003), "Identifying the source of critical details in confessions," *Forensic Linguistics*, 10(1), 23–61.

Holt, E. and Johnson, A. (2010), "Formulating facts: Questions and reported speech in police interviews with suspects," in M. Coulthard and A. Johnson (eds.), *The Routledge Handbook of Forensic Linguistics*, London: Routledge.

Hymes, D. (1981), *"In Vain I Tried to Tell You": Essays in Native American Ethnopoetics*, Philadelphia, PA: University of Pennsylvania Press.

Inbau, F.E., Reid, J.E. and Buckley, J.P. (1986), *Criminal Interrogation and Confessions*, Baltimore, MD: Williams and Wilkins.

Johnson, A.J. (2008), "From Interview to Courtroom: The Evidential Narrative as Courtroom Object," paper presented *at Georgetown University Roundtable*, Georgetown University, Washington, DC, 2008.

Kandel, R.F. (2002), "Why evidence scholars should study conversation," *International Commentary on Evidence*, 1(2), art. 7, <http://www.bepress.com/ice/vol1/iss2/art7>.

Kassin, S. (2002), "False confessions and the jogger case" (op ed), *The New York Times*, November 1, p. A31.

—— (2005), "On the psychology of confessions: Does innocence put innocents at risk?", *American Psychologist*, 60, 215–28.

—— and Gudjonsson, G.H. (2004), "The psychology of confession evidence: A review of the literature and issues," *Psychological Science in the Public Interest*, <http://www.williams.edu/Psychology/Faculty/Kassin/research/confessions.htm>.

Kassin, S., Drizin, S., Grisso, T., Gudjonsson, G., Leo, R.A. and Redlich, A.D. (2009), "Police-induced confessions: Risk factors and recommendations," *Law and Human Behavior 2009*, University of San Francisco Law Research Paper No. 2010-13, <http://ssrn.com/abstract=1483878>.

Komter, M. (2002), "The suspect's own words: The treatment of written statements in Dutch courts', *International Journal of Speech, Language and the Law*, 9(2).

Lassiter, G.D. (ed.) (2004), *Interrogations, Confessions and Entrapment*, New York: Kluwer/Plenum.

—— and Geers, A.L. (2004), "Bias and accuracy in the evaluation of confession evidence," in G.D. Lassiter (ed.), *Interrogations, Confessions and Entrapment*, New York: Kluwer/Plenum.

Lassiter, G.D., Ratcliff, J., Ware, J., Lezlee, J. and Irvin, C.R. (2006), "Videotaped confessions: Panacea or Pandora's Box?", *Law and Policy*, 28(2), 192–210.

Leo, R.A. (2009), "False confessions: Causes, consequences and implications," *Journal of the American Academy of Psychiatry and the Law*, University of San Francisco Law Research Paper No. 2009-11, <http://ssrn.com/abstract=1328623>.

—— and Davis, D. (2009), "From false confession to wrongful conviction: Seven psychological processes," *Journal of Psychiatry and Law*, <http://ssrn.com/abstract=1328622>.

Leo, R.A. and Drizin, S.A. (2004), "The problem of false confessions in the post-DNA world," *North Carolina Law Review*, 82, <http://ssrn.com/abstract=1134094>.

Leo, R.A. and Liu, B.L. (2009), "What do potential jurors know about police interrogation techniques and false confessions?", *Behavioral Sciences and the Law*, <http://ssrn.com/abstract=1404078>.

Leo, R.A. and Ofshe, R.J. (1998), "The consequences of false confessions: Deprivations of liberty and miscarriages of justice in the age of psychological interrogation," *Journal of Criminal Law and Criminology*, 88.

Leo, R.A., Drizin, S.A., Neufeld, P.J., Hall, B.R. and Vatner, A. (2006), "Bringing reliability back in: false confessions and legal safeguards in the twenty-first century," *Wisconsin Law Review*, University of San Francisco Law Research Paper No. 2009-04, <http://ssrn.com/abstract=1134948>.

Levenson, L. (2007), "Courtroom demeanor: The theater of the courtroom," *Legal Studies Paper* No. 2007-30, <http://ssrn.com/abstract=999471>.

Maira, S. (2007), "Deporting radicals, deporting La Migra: The Hayat case in Lodi," *Cultural Dynamics*, 19:1.

Matoesian, G.M. (2001), *Law and the Language of Identity: Discourse in the William Kennedy Smith Rape Trial*, New York: Oxford University Press.
—— (2009), "Review of Eades, D. (2008) *Courtroom Talk and Neocolonial Control*," *International Journal of Speech, Language and the Law*, 16(1).
—— (2010), "Multimodal aspects of trial discourse," in M. Coulthard and A. Johnson (eds.), *The Routledge Handbook of Forensic Linguistics*, London: Routledge.
Mendoza-Denton, N. (2008), *Homegirls: Language and Cultural Practice among Latina Youth Gangs*, New York: Blackwell.
Meyer, P.N. (1996), "'Desperate for Love II': Further reflections on the interpenetration of legal and popular storytelling in closing arguments to a jury in a complex criminal case," 30 *USFL Rev.* 931 (1995–96), <http://heinonline.org/HOL/LandingPage?collection=journals&handle=hein.journals/usflr30&div=39&id=&page=n>.
Ochs, E. and Capps, L. (2001), *Living Narrative: Creating Lives in Everyday Storytelling*, Cambridge, MA: Harvard University Press.
Ofshe, R. and Leo, R. (1997a), "The decision to confess falsely," *Denver Law Review*, 74.
—— (1997b), "The social psychology of police interrogation: The theory and classification of true and false confessions," *Studies in Law, Politics and Society*, 16, 189–251.
Oxburgh, G.E., Myklebust, T. and Grant, T. (2010), "The question of question type in police interviews: A review of the literature from a psychological and linguistic perspective," *International Journal of Speech, Language and the Law*, 17(1).
Pennington, N. and Hastie, R. ([1993] 1994), "The story model for juror decision making," in R. Hastie (ed.), *Inside the Juror: The Psychology of Juror Decision Making*, Cambridge and New York: Cambridge University Press, 1993; Thousand Oaks, CA: Sage Publications, 1994.
Radelet, M., Bedau, H.A. and Putnam, C.E. (1992), *In Spite of Innocence*, Boston, MA: Northeastern Press.
Read, D.S. (2007), *Winning at Trial*, Louisville, CO: National Institute for Trial Advocacy.
Redlich, A.D and Goodman, G.S. (2003), "Taking responsibility for an act not committed: The influence of age and suggestibility," *Law and Human Behavior*, 27, 141–56.
Redlich, A.D., Silverman, M., Chen, J. and Steiner, H. (2004), "The Police Interrogation of Children and Adolescents," in G.D. Lassiter (ed.), *Interrogations, Confessions and Entrapment*, New York: Kluwer/Plenum.
Roach, K. and Trotter, G. (2005), "Miscarriages of justice in the war against terrorism," *Pennsylvania State Law Review*, 109(4), <http://ssrn.com/abstract=742628>.
Rosen, L. (2006), *Law As Culture: An Invitation*, Princeton, NJ: Princeton University Press.

Rosulek, L.F. (2008), "Legitimation and the heteroglossic nature of closing argument in criminal trials," paper presented at Georgetown University Roundtable 2008, Georgetown University, Washington, DC.

—— (2009), "The sociolinguistic creation of opposing representations of defendants and victims," *International Journal of Speech, Language and the Law*, 16(1).

Scelfo, J. (2001), "When Law Goes Pop: Interview with Richard Sherwin," *Stayfree Magazine*, 18, <www.stayfreemagazine.org/archives/18/sherwin.html>.

Schachter, D. (2001), *The Seven Sins of Memory: How the Mind Forgets and Remembers*, Boston, MA and New York: Houghton Mifflin.

Scheck, B., Neufeld, P. and Dwyer, J. (2000), *Actual Innocence*, New York: Doubleday.

Sherwin, R.K. (2002), *When Law Goes Pop*, Chicago, IL: University Of Chicago Press).

Shuy, R.W. (1998), *The Language of Confession, Interrogation and Deception*, New York: Oxford University Press.

—— (2005), *Creating Language Crimes*, New York: Oxford University Press.

—— (2010), "Methods in forensic linguistic casework: Linguistics and terrorism," in M. Coulthard and A. Johnson (eds.), *The Routledge Handbook of Forensic Linguistics*, London: Routledge.

Solan, L (2010), "The forensic linguist: The expert linguist meets the adversarial system," in M. Coulthard and A. Johnson (eds.), *The Routledge Handbook of Forensic Linguistics*, London: Routledge.

—— and Tiersma, P. (2005), Speaking of Crime: The Language of Criminal Justice, Chicago Series in Law and Society, Chicago, IL: University of Chicago.

Tannen, D. (1989), *Talking Voice*, New York: Cambridge University Press.

—— (1993), *Framing in Discourse*, New York: Oxford University Press.

Trinch, S. (2010), "Disappearing discourse: Performative texts and identity in legal contexts," *Critical Inquiry in Language Studies*, 7(2).

Tully, B. and Cahill, D. (1984), *Police Interviewing of the Mentally Handicapped: An Experimental Study*, London: The Police Foundation.

Walkley, J. (1987), *Police Interrogation: A Handbook for Investigators*, London: Police Review Publications.

Wrightsman, L.S. and Kassin, S.M. (1993), *Confessions in the Courtroom*, Newbury Park, CA: Sage.

Newspapers, Magazine Articles and Websites

Frontline (2006), "The Enemy Within," Public Broadcasting Service (PBS), July 24.

Grudin, Nicholas (2005), "Pakistani Men Adjust to Life in Lodi," *Wisconsin News-Sentinel* (n.d.).

Kearns, Jeff (2006), "Lodi Muslims: Under the 'Eye of Suspicion,'" *Frontline*, Public Broadcasting Service (PBS), July 24.

Marshall, C. (2007), "24-year term for Californian in terrorism training case," *New York Times*, September 11.

Mojaddidi, W. (2006), "How Politics Influenced the Case of US v. Hamid Hayat," Chance Lecture, Boalt Law School, UC Berkeley, September 5.

See <www.reid.com> for a frequently updated compendium of trial and appeal court decisions regarding Miranda, police interrogation and confession evidence.

Press conference (2002), Mothers and sisters of "Central Park Five" <http://www.democracynow.org/2002/12/6/we_wanted_our_children_to_be>, December 6.

Waldman, A. (2006), "Prophetic justice," *The Atlantic*, October.

Williams, P.J. (2002), "Reasons for Doubt," *The Nation*, <http://www.thenation.com/article/reasons-doubt>.

Chapter 5

The Role of Metadiscourse in Counsels' Questions

Silvia Cavalieri[1]

This chapter focuses on the role of metadiscourse in counsels' questions during the witness examination, considering in particular the case of public inquiries in Great Britain.

The study discusses the functions of both textual and interpersonal metadiscourse (Hyland 1998; Hyland 2005) in the realization of lawyers' argumentative strategies to build up effective questions in the two phases of the witness examination, namely the examination-in-chief and the cross-examination. In particular, this study aims to describe how counsels exploit the metadiscursive features to control both the form and the ideational content of the exchange (Halliday 1994) through textual metadiscourse, as well as the power relationship with the witness through interpersonal metadiscourse.

The analysis is carried out on a corpus of 15 days of witness examination transcripts (507,346 words) collected from three different public inquiries, namely the Bloody Sunday Inquiry (Northern Ireland), the Shipman Inquiry (England) and the Cullen Inquiry (Scotland), to achieve a wider perspective on common law administrative justice. It principally involves a quantitative observation of the data by means of corpus linguistics tools, and in particular by means of WordSmith Tools, which is a suite of programs for text analysis and manipulation. Moreover, the corpus is also tagged in order to create two sub-corpora: one concerning the Examination-in-Chief questions and the other concerning the Cross-Examination questions. This tagging enables us to verify any significant difference in the use of the metadiscursive elements in the two phases of the witness examination.

As regards the choice of the metadiscursive elements to be searched in the corpus, the present work has integrated Hyland's 1998 metadiscourse classifying model to Hyland's 2005 one, modifying them in order to meet the needs expressed by data.

The results will show that metadiscourse completes the argumentative strategy used by lawyers in order to control the witness's narrative, giving precise means to shape both the formal and the relational sides of their questions.

---

1 The author would like to thank Professor Marina Bondi (University of Modena and Reggio Emilia) for her invaluable advice and comments.

Introduction

Legal discourse has been thoroughly investigated from a variety of angles over the last thirty years or so. Investigations of courtroom interaction have involved linguistic analysis of legal style and rhetoric (see Mellinkoff 1963; Goodrich 1987; Tiersma 1999), studies of specific legal genres (see Levi 1990; Bhatia 1993; Maley 1994; Gibbons 1994), as well as ethnomethodological and sociological approaches (see O'Barr 1982; Drew 1985). The analysis of courtroom discourse has recently extended to issues of language power relations and on the legal argumentative strategies employed by counsels during the examination of witnesses (see Walton 2002; Walton 2003).

From this perspective, this chapter analyzes how metadiscourse is used in counsels' questions while examining witnesses during public inquiries in Great Britain. The chapter takes into account the role of textual and interpersonal metadiscourse (Hyland 1998; Hyland 2005) in the construction of lawyers' argumentation in order to ask efficacious questions both in the examination-in-chief and the cross-examination. By textual metadiscourse, we mean all the linguistic devices used by the counsels to create a coherent pattern in their examination by establishing preferred interpretations of the propositional meaning produced in their questions. Indeed, textual metadiscursive features help the lawyers to form an articulate line of questioning relating individual propositions to each other as well as to other evidential resources such as written statements, documents, photographs and so on that are fundamental in the development of the testimony. On the other hand, by interpersonal metadiscourse we indicate all those elements that contribute to creating and maintaining the relationship between the legal professional and the witness, also giving the counsel's perspective on the information brought in the examination. This category involves interactional and evaluative aspects of metadiscourse, and expresses both the lawyer's attitude and commitment to the propositional content and to the witness. In particular, the aim of this study is to show how counsels choose certain items of metadiscourse in order to shape both the form and the ideational content of the exchange (Halliday 1994) through textual metadiscourse, as well to demonstrate their powerful position in respect to the witness through interpersonal metadiscourse.

Metadiscourse: Theoretical Background

The term *metadiscourse* was created and used for the first time by Zellig Harris in 1959, and indicated the ways in which the writer or the speaker conduces the receiver's perception of a text through the use of language. Thus, metadiscourse can be seen as an "umbrella term" used to include both cohesive and interpersonal features that help to relate a particular text to its context. After this first definition, the notion has been further developed in the 1980s by Vande Kopple (1985) and Crismore (1989), who have included in their descriptions discoursal features such as hedges, connectives and various forms of text commentary to demonstrate how a writer or speaker uses their text to influence their interlocutor's reception of it. Influencing the receiver's perspective of a text or of an utterance is a central aspect of metadiscourse, in fact Hyland (2005) argues that metadiscourse includes all those linguistic features of the text which explicitly refer to the organization of the discourse or the writer's stance towards either the content or the reader. As it is possible to notice, metadiscourse is a relatively new concept that has become increasingly important in the research about language.

Metadiscourse is commonly defined as "discourse about discourse or communication about communication" (Vande Kopple 1985, 83); however, as Dahl (2004) explains, it is a concept which is difficult to label because it may be realized by various linguistic forms and may realize numerous pragmatics functions in the text. For this reason, there is also a lack of clarity in the literature concerning what can be defined as metadiscourse, and there are no simple linguistic criteria for identifying it. Thus, metadiscourse can be seen as an open category (Hyland 2005, 27) to which writers/speakers are able to add new items according to the needs of the context.

Many metadiscourse studies have focused on written discourses (see, for example, Vande Kopple 1985; Crismore and Farnsworth 1990; Crismore et al. 1993; Markkanen et al. 1993; Hyland 1998; Hyland 2005; Infantidou 2005; Aedel 2005) and start from a functional perspective on language by making reference to Hallidayan Systemic Functional Linguistics, and in particular to Halliday's distinction into three "metafunctions" or purposes of language: textual, ideational and interpersonal functions of a text (Halliday 1973). Since metadiscourse analysis involves a functional approach to texts, numerous researchers have drawn on Halliday's "metafunctions" to build up their taxonomies of metadiscourse (for example, Crismore and Farnsworth 1990; Hyland 1998; Hyland 2005; Vande Kopple 1985). Indeed, they have distinguished metadiscourse items, categorizing them according to the functions they perform in a text, and they have individuated mainly two wider purposes of metadiscourse: (1) organizing a coherent discourse, defined as textual function; (2) creating a relationship with the audience and conveying the writer's attitude to the text, defined as interpersonal function. The interpersonal–textual duality represents a matter of debate among researchers into metadiscourse. Mauranen (1993) has identified two strands of study into metadiscourse: (1) the integrative approach, which considers both interpersonal and textual metadiscourse; (2) the non-integrative approach, which distinguishes between metadiscourse and evaluation, considering only textual metadiscourse, which is labeled as metatext (Mauranen 1993, 1). The non-integrative model restricts metadiscourse to refer to linguistic elements "whose functions in the first place is to describe the text in which they are located" (Crismore et al. 1993, 142), while interpersonal elements are largely excluded. Since the present work draws on the integrative approach, taxonomies produced by this strand of researchers into metadiscourse will be described in the following passage of the theoretical overview.

Most studies about metadiscourse follow the integrative approach and take Vande Kopple's (1985) classification system as their point of departure, offering their own modifications to it.

Vande Kopple divides metadiscourse into two broader categories, always following the Hallidayan functional framework:

> *Textual metadiscourse*: the devices that principally play the role of organising the text for the reader. ("[It] shows how we link and relate individual propositions so that they form a cohesive and coherent text and how individual elements of those propositions make sense in conjunction with other elements of the text. ...)"
>
> *Interpersonal metadiscourse*: the items of a text that are mainly used to interact with the reader about the propositional content. ("[It] helps to express our personalities and our reactions to the propositional content of our texts and characterizes the interaction we would like to have with our readers about that content. ..." (Vande Kopple 1985, 87)

Successively, Hyland (1998) follows Vande Kopple in distinguishing textual and interpersonal categories, and furthers their taxonomy of metadiscursive elements by classifying more specific functions within this macro-division. Textual metadiscourse is described by Hyland as all the devices which allow the recovery of the writer's intention by creating a coherent and convincing text. On the other hand, interpersonal metadiscourse is defined as the linguistic means that give the author's perspective towards both the propositional content and the readers, contributing to creating a writer–reader relationship. The taxonomy proposed by Hyland is quoted in Table 5.1 (Hyland 1998, 442).

In more recent times, Hyland (2005) furthers his analysis and proposes another model of metadiscourse always based on a functional approach, but that focuses on its contextual specificity rather than on Vande Kopple's distinction between textual and interpersonal functions, by using Thompson and Thetela's (1995) distinction between interactive and interactional resources to acknowledge both the organizational and the evaluative features of interaction.

The interactive dimension concerns the writer's awareness of a participating audience. The writer's purpose is to shape and constrain the text to meet the needs of a particular reader and at the same time to guide him or her through the text. Thus, the metadiscursive resources used in this category addresses ways of organizing discourse.

The interactional dimension concerns, on the other hand, the ways in which writers conduct the interaction by intruding and commenting on their message. The writer's aim is to express his or her perspective and to involve readers. Metadiscourse used in this category is essentially evaluative and engaging, building up an imagined dialog with the reader.

Table 5.1 Synthesis of Hyland's 1998 taxonomy of metadiscourse

CATEGORY	FUNCTION	EXAMPLES
TEXTUAL METADISCOURSE		
LOGICAL CONNECTIVES	Express semantic relation between the main clauses	*In addition; but; therefore; thus; and*
FRAME MARKERS	Explicitly refer to the discourse acts, or text stages	*Finally; to repeat; our aim here; we try*
ENDOPHORIC MARKERS	Refer to information in other parts of the text	*Noted above; see Fig. 1; Table 2; below*
EVIDENTIALS	Refer to source information from other texts	*According to X; Y; 1990; Z states*
CODE GLOSSES	Help readers grasp meaning of ideational material	*Namely; for example; such as; in other words*
INTERPERSONAL METADISCOURSE		
HEDGES	Withhold writer's full commitment to statements	*Might; perhaps; it is possible; about*
EMPHATICS	Emphasize force or writer's certainty in message	*In fact; definitely; it is clear; obvious*
ATTITUDE MARKERS	Express writer's attitude to propositional content	*Surprisingly; I agree; X claims*
RELATIONAL MARKERS	Make explicit reference to or build relationship with the reader	*Frankly; note that; you can see*
PERSONAL MARKERS	Make explicit reference to author(s)	*I; we; my; mine; our*

Hyland (2005, 49) organizes these two dimensions in a model describing each metadiscursive category involved in them (see Table 5.2).

As Hyland (2005) points out, bearing in mind this distinction between the organizational and the interpersonal dimensions, it is important to notice that metadiscourse is a ubiquitous aspect in everyday language, and it constitutes one of the key features in which people communicate in different genres and settings. For this reason, studies on metadiscourse have suggested its importance in different genres, for instance in casual conversation (Schiffrin 1980), in school textbooks (Crismore 1989), in oral narratives (Norrick 2001), in postgraduate dissertations (Swales 1990) and in slogan headlines (Fuertes-Olivera et al. 2001). As a consequence, Hyland stresses the importance of considering metadiscourse integral to the context in which it is produced, and indeed, as linked to the norms and expectations of a particular cultural and professional community. By saying

Table 5.2 Synthesis of Hyland's 2005 taxonomy of metadiscourse

CATEGORY	FUNCTION	EXAMPLES
INTERACTIVE	***HELP TO GUIDE THE READER THROUGH THE TEXT***	***RESOURCES***
TRANSITIONS	Express relations between the main clauses	*In addition; but; thus; and*
FRAME MARKERS	Refer to the discourse acts, sequences or stages	*Finally; to conclude; my purpose is*
ENDOPHORIC MARKERS	Refer to information in another part of the text	*Noted above; see Fig.; in Section 2*
EVIDENTIALS	Refer to information from other texts	*According to X; Z states*
CODE GLOSSES	Elaborate propositional meanings	*Namely; for example; such as; in other words*
INTERACTIONAL	***INVOLVE THE READER IN THE TEXT***	***RESOURCES***
HEDGES	Withhold commitment and open dialog	*Might; perhaps; possible; about*
BOOSTERS	Emphasize certainty or close dialog	*In fact; definitely; it is clear that*
ATTITUDE MARKERS	Express writer's attitude to proposition	*Unfortunately; I agree; surprisingly*
SELF-MENTIONS	Make explicit reference to the author(s)	*I; we; my; me; our*
ENGAGEMENT MARKERS	Explicitly build relationship with reader	*Consider; note; you can see*

that effective metadiscourse is critically dependent on the rhetorical context, he proposes a "pragmatics of metadiscourse" (Hyland 1998, 439) that is strictly related to the ideas of discourse community and to the genres that develop within it. Metadiscourse becomes a valuable pattern to distinguish discourse communities and to determine the relationship among their members and the genres they produce.

This aspect has a considerable weight in this research which aims to understand the role of metadiscourse employed by lawyers to construe their own discourse in courtroom. In fact, legal professionals can be described as a discourse community, and the analysis of metadiscursive elements proves to be a valuable means to describe the persuasive way in which they communicate with witnesses during the witness examination. As highlighted by Fuertes-Olivera et al. (2001), assuming that metadiscourse is context-dependent and that it is linked to the norms and expectations of a particular setting and genre, it can be used to fulfill different pragmatic functions such as "informing" and "manipulating" that reflect the principal actions performed by counsels in their questions.

In his latest more extensive research, Hyland (2005) develops his methodological model of metadiscourse further, stressing once more its role in the creation of social engagement. He highlights the way in which these linguistic features are used as "bridge" between the writer, the audience and the text. Metadiscourse enables the writer to project him or herself in the text by signaling his or/her attitude towards both the content and the audience of the text. Indeed, language conveys information about the world, presenting it through the organization of the text itself and engaging readers in the understanding of it (interactive plane). According to Hyland, writing is interactive, in the sense that discourse features help the writer to communicate his or her text effectively to the potential audience, which is defined as "the writer's awareness of the circumstances which define a rhetorical context and the ways that the current text is related to or aligned with other texts" (Hyland 2005, 12). Metadiscourse is therefore an important link between a text and its context. The context involves the audience, and it is possible to say that metadiscoursal resources are used by the writer to "co-produce" the text with the audience. In the same way, lawyers employ metadiscourse to create a relationship with their audience, and this is multi-layered and complex in public inquiries.

Hyland (2005) also analyzes more clearly the connection between genre, discourse community and metadiscourse. The notion of genre has proved to be a valuable tool over the last twenty years in exploring language in context and in seeing texts as social actions. The notion of discourse community completes the concept of genre, being the source of it, and conveys the idea that people normally use language to communicate with individuals that are members of the same social group (Hyland 2005, 139). As a consequence, being part of a discourse community involves a number of contextual factors that are relevant to the production and interpretation of spoken and written texts. According to Hyland, the definition of a discourse community offers an understanding of how meaning is produced in interaction and to observe metadiscourse as socially situated. As regards this last point, he focuses in particular on disciplinary communities and on the norms that individuals need to acquire in order to get competence in a specialized language. Hyland argues that the choice of the metadiscourse strategies is strictly linked to the shared knowledge of a particular discourse community, and indeed, to understand its pragmatic use, metadiscourse must be observed in the genres and communities which give it meaning (Hyland 2005, 143). Metadiscourse thus offers a framework for understanding communication as social engagement, as it signals the attitude towards the content and the audience of a text. The present work focuses on this perspective, and intends to analyze how metadiscourse is used by lawyers as an argumentative strategy to build up effective questions in courtroom.

As evidenced by the literature review of metadiscourse studies above, the majority of the research in this field has focused on written discourses, and only few have analyzed oral discourses (for example, Schiffrin 1980; Norrick 2001;

Swales 2001). Moreover, the literature has highlighted a gap in the studies about the use of metadiscourse in the courtroom setting, and for this reason, the present research would like to broaden the scope of analysis by describing the metadiscursive features of the lawyer–witness interaction during the oral genre witness examination.

The Corpus

The analysis is carried out on a corpus of witness examination transcripts collected from the official websites of three public inquiries established in England, Scotland, and Northern Ireland:

1. the Cullen Inquiry, concerning the "Dunblane massacre," a multiple homicide committed in a primary school at Dunblane, Scotland on March 13, 1996, chaired by Lord Douglas Cullen;
2. the Bloody Sunday Inquiry, dealing with the killing of civilians due to a shooting caused by British soldiers during a peaceful march in Derry, Northern Ireland on January 30, 1972, chaired by Lord Saville of Newdigate;
3. the Shipman Inquiry, concerning the homicide of 15 patients carried out by Dr. Harold Shipman at Market Street, Hyde, near Manchester, England, chaired by Dame Janet Smith.

Specifically, the corpus is composed of five days of transcripts for each public inquiry, giving a total of 507,346 tokens. As the main interest of this chapter concerns the questions posed by the lawyers, both during Examination-in-Chief and Cross-Examination, the corpus has subsequently been tagged by means of the software Note Tab Light, which enables the user to select by hand parts of text that can be used separately in a quantitative analysis. Three tags have been chosen to identify three smaller sub-corpora concerning questions:

a. <QST> (Question), including all the questions posed by the lawyers and by the chair of the inquiry;
b. <DE QST> (Direct Examination Question), including the questions posed during Examination-in-Chief;
c. <CE QST> (Cross-Examination Question), including all the questions posed during Cross-Examination.

This type of tagging allows the subdivision into sub-corpora, and at the same time, leaves all the data available in their entire form for a more complete analysis.

Methods

The analysis principally involved a quantitative observation of the data by means of corpus linguistics tools, and in particular by means of *WordSmith Tools*, a suite of programs for text analysis and manipulation. *WordSmith Tools* enables the user to identify and study patterns of lexis in texts which are not easily found otherwise.

As regards the choice of the metadiscursive elements to be researched in the corpus, the present study has integrated Hyland's 1998 model to Hyland's 2005 one, considering both the textual and the interpersonal dimensions.

After having defined these preliminary categories, as a first step we focused on the wordlists of the sub-corpora <DE QST> and <CE QST> to determine the most frequent metadiscursive resources in them. We also checked two-word, three-word and four-word clusters wordlists in order to identify composed items such as code glosses that are usually two-, three- or even four-word expressions (for example, *in other words*) that cannot be not be detected by a simple wordlist.

The second step regarded the investigation of the keywords of the sub-corpora, and we observed the keyness of the metadiscursive elements in the corpus to verify their saliency in the Examination-in-Chief sub-corpus as well as in the Cross-Examination one. In order to find out keyness, at first each sub-corpus wordlist was compared to the BNC Spoken List. The choice of this reference corpus was determined by the nature of the data, which are transcriptions of oral exchanges between counsels and witnesses. Moreover, we also made keywordlists within the corpus itself by comparing each sub-corpus wordlist with the other (the <CE QST> List versus <DE QST> List) to identify peculiarities in the use of the metadiscursive elements due to the different phase of the examination. Looking at the three keywordlists obtained, we detected the most significant items for each category mentioned above, and we also chose other metadiscursive resources typical of the public inquiry witness examination (for example, *Tribunal, Inquiry, statement, paragraph, photograph*) that needed to be studied in detail through the observation of their phraseology.

After this preliminary analysis of frequency and keyness, we decided to modify our first classification that integrated Hyland taxonomies by adding some sub-categories and by leaving aside some others in order to meet the needs expressed by the data. The new scheme conceived is set out in Table 5.3.

The third step of the analysis concerned the phraseology of the items selected for their frequency and keyness. To investigate the phraseology of each metadiscursive element, Wordsmith's Concordance Analysis was used. This function of Wordsmith's Tools allows us to study a keyword in context in order to find recurrent clusters in a corpus. Thus, this step of the analysis consisted of the observation of the concordance lines of every item in both sub-corpora in order to discover the most frequent clusters. The data have been analyzed considering first clusters of three words and then clusters of four words to determine the more significant collocations.

Table 5.3 Re-elaborated taxonomy of metadiscourse after the preliminary quantitative analysis of the sub-corpora

TEXTUAL METADISCOURSE			
CATEGORY		**FUNCTION**	**RESOURCES**
Code Glosses		Introduce reformulations and are used to explain or elaborate what has been said for the witness	*which is; that is; for example*
Evidentials		Are metalinguistic representations of other resources used as basis for the examination (e.g. photographs, statements, etc.)	*statement; photograph; document; letter*
Endophoric Markers	***Examination***	Are expressions which refer to other parts of the examination	*question; answer*
	Intra-evidentials	Are expressions which refer to other parts of an *evidential* quoted	*paragraph; page; sentence; section*
INTERPERSONAL METADISCOURSE			
CATEGORY		**FUNCTION**	**RESOURCES**
Self-mention	***Personal***	Direct reference to the legal professional him/herself	*I; me; my*
	Procedural	Reference to the participants in the Inquiry	*we; us*
	Authoritative	Direct reference to the authority	*Tribunal; Inquiry*
Engagement Markers		Are devices that explicitly address to the witness and to his/her action in the testimony	*you; your*
Hedges		Are devices that mitigate the tone of a question used to negotiate meaning with the witness	*would; could; can; may, might; should; wouldn't; couldn't; can't; shouldn't; is it possible that ...; it is right to say that ...; it is fair to say that ...*
Strategic Boosters		Are devices that upgrade the degree of certainty of a question	*oath; truth*

After having determined the most frequent collocation patterns for each textual and interpersonal piece of metadiscourse, we have tried to relate these clusters to the functions they fulfill in <DE QST> and <CE QST>.

Results

Textual Metadiscourse

This section will present the results concerning textual metadiscourse. The linguistic devices analyzed here allow the lawyer to shape and constrain his or her questions to meet the needs of the courtroom setting, and at the same time to produce precise rhetorical strategies. The use of resources in this category enables the legal professional to organize the discourse during the examination in order to convey the propositional information in a coherent and convincing way.

Code glosses *Code glosses* are textual devices that "supply additional information by rephrasing, explaining or elaborating what has been said, to ensure the reader to recover the writer's intended meaning" (Hyland 2005, 52). In the lawyer's questions, they function as reformulation markers and serve the legal professional to introduce a rephrasing either of his or her request (self-reformulation) or of the witness's answer (other-reformulation).

To begin with, it was decided to start the research of code glosses in the corpus by examining the wordlists from simple words to four-word clusters both for the Examination-in-Chief sub-corpus and for the Cross-Examination sub-corpus, keeping as a reference the examples provided by Hyland in his taxonomy (Hyland 2005, 52). The choice of checking the two-word, three-word and four-word cluster wordlists was driven by the fact that code glosses are in most of the cases two-, three- or even four-word expressions, so not detectable in a simple wordlist. After browsing the frequency lists, it was discovered that the presence of code glosses in the two sub-corpora is limited, and frequency is low in terms of their raw frequency and their number of occurrences per thousand words that goes from a minimum of 0.01% to a maximum of 0.03%, as demonstrated in Table 5.4.

Even though the frequency of code glosses is very low in the sub-corpora, it is possible to notice a higher occurrence of these metadiscursive items in the examination-in-chief, in which the search for information as complete as possible is the main purpose.

Starting from *which is*, the most frequent code gloss in the two sub-corpora, it is possible to notice that it occurs 64 times in the <DE QST> sub-corpus (0.03%) and 30 in the <CE QST> sub-corpus (0.03%). The analysis of the most frequent contexts of this item highlighted that *which is* can fulfill two main functions in both sub-corpora, as shown in Table 5.5.

As highlighted by Table 5.5, *which is* can function both as a restrictive and as an expansive code gloss. It is mainly used by legal professionals during the

Table 5.4 Code glosses frequency in the sub-corpora

Code Glosses	Examination-in-Chief <DE QST> Raw frequency (PTW)	Cross-Examination <CE QST> Raw frequency (PTW)
Which is	64 (0.03)	30 (0.03)
For example	49 (0.03)	21 (0.02)
That is	47 (0.02)	28 (0.03)

Note: PTW = percentage per thousand words.

Table 5.5 Functions of WHICH IS

WHICH IS % FUNCTION	EXAMPLES	<DE QST>	<CE QST>
Introducing restrictive rephrasing giving the alphanumerical code of a circumstantial evidence brought into the proceeding	*If I refer you back to your memorandum dated the 9th of June* ***which is D3****, the fourth page of that, [...]*	**40.6**	**33.3**
Preceding a reformulation that makes explicit a detail of the evidence	*Have you ever come across another case of somebody who has died of carcinomatosis* ***which is*** *widespread secondary cancers, as I understand the definition [...]*	**56.2**	**60**

whole examination to guide the witness through the evidence determining his or her preferred pattern of understanding. In both cases, the main purpose of *which is* is to introduce a specification that makes the evidence in the question as clear as possible in order to avoid any ambiguity that could mislead the search for information.

A similar function is performed by *that is*. As a code gloss, this item occurs 47 times (0.02%) in the <DE QST> sub-corpus and 28 (0.03%) in the <CE QST> sub-corpus, and in the majority of cases, it prefaces a specification of a reference that can be a letter, a document, a statement and so on cited in the question, usually with an abbreviation (see Table 5.6).

Table 5.6 Function of THAT IS

THAT IS % FUNCTION	EXAMPLES	<DE QST>	<CE QST>
Introducing a specification of a reference	*Would you have a look at D82L.* ***That is*** *a memorandum dated November 11, 1991 [...]*	**55.3**	**64.3**

The phraseology of *that is* shows that the pragmatic function of this code gloss is exploited to make explicit a reference produced in an abbreviated form for the witness and for the other parts of the multi-layered audience as well. This enables the legal professional to be as clear as possible about a piece of evidence quoted, and at the same time to ask for confirmation of his or her description of it from the witness.

Another very interesting item is *for example,* which presents 49 occurrences in the <DE QST> sub-corpus (0.03%) and 21 in the <CE QST> sub-corpus (0.02%). The analysis of this item and of its principal collocates showed that the main function of for example in both sub-corpora is to introduce a reformulation in which the lawyer makes a presupposition about a piece of evidence given in his or her question (see Table 5.7).

Table 5.7 Functions of FOR EXAMPLE

FOR EXAMPLE % **FUNCTION**	**EXAMPLES**	**<DE QST>**	**<CE QST>**
Introducing a reformulation that makes a presupposition about the evidence	*What happened if somebody who was on one of your registers became house-bound for an unrelated reason,* ***for example,*** *if they became very arthritic or something of that nature and could not actually come [...]*	**92**	**90**

The code gloss for example enables the legal professional to introduce a personal presumption about the evidence, making a detail explicit for the witness, but from his or her own perspective. The presence of the lawyer in this operation represents the main difference with which is and that is, which serves to introduce "impersonal" types of rephrasings.

The data have also shown instances of *for example* performing the function cited above preceded by the transition marker so (10%). In these cases, the code gloss is positioned at the beginning of the question, and the reformulation that follows involves the interpretation of the previous witness answer. The legal professional reinterprets what has been stated by the witness from his or her own perspective.

Evidentials *Evidentials* are "metalinguistic representations of an idea from another source" (Hyland 2005, 51) which guide the reader's interpretation and establish an attribution to a reliable source. While in academic writing the term refers to a community-based literature and provides important support for arguments, in the courtroom setting evidentials are the basis for the whole examination. Evidentials in the witness examination are the metalinguistic realizations of all the documents brought as circumstantial evidence to the inquiry that provide the framework for what will be discussed during the lawyer–witness exchange.

Narrative in the witness examination largely depends on evidential elements, since the narrative line is pursued through visual means such as *statement, photograph* and *letter*, as demonstrated by the analysis of the corpus (see Table 5.8).

Table 5.8 Evidentials frequency in the sub-corpora

Evidentials	**Examination-in-Chief <DE QST>** Raw frequency (PTW)	**Cross-Examination <CE QST>** Raw frequency (PTW)
Statement	474 (0.15)	202 (0.23)
Photograph	165 (0.09)	46 (0.05)
Letter	132 (0.07)	69 (0.08)
Document	96 (0.05)	59 (0.07)

As with code glosses, it is possible to notice a higher frequency in the use of evidentials in the <DE QST> sub-corpus rather than in the <CE QST> one. The reference to circumstantial evidence represents the point of departure for the witness examination, and that could explain the major presence of these items in the Examination-in-Chief, the first part of the witness examination. Moreover, in the cross-examination, the line of questioning of legal professionals usually aims to contrast what the witness said during the examination-in-chief, reducing the reference to documents.

The main function of these evidentials in both sub-corpora is to provide an objective basis for the ideational content on which the lawyer can build up his or her questions.

Looking in particular at the most frequent clusters of *statement*, it is possible to notice that this item tends to collocate with the words paragraph and contents. The main function of this type of evidential is to take the witness back to what he or she stated in the investigative part of the Inquiry, as shown in Table 5.9.

Table 5.9 Functions of STATEMENT

STATEMENT % **FUNCTION**	**EXAMPLES**	**<DE QST>**	**<CE QST>**
Taking the witness to what he/she stated in the investigative phase of the Inquiry	*Are the contents of your* ***statement*** *true at to the best [...]; the* ***statement*** *that you made [...]; go back to your* ***statement*** *[...]*	**9**	**4.2**
Creating a pattern of discussion for the examination	*In paragraph X of your* ***statement*** *you say [...]; if we go to your* ***statement*** *[...]; you say in your* ***statement*** *[...]*	**10.3**	**7.5**

While the statement is a kind of evidential that is clearly referred to the witness (your statement, the statement you made), letter and document are usually included in the questions to make general reference to a piece of evidence that is shown by the lawyer to the witness. In particular, when the evidential document performs this function, it is often preceded by verbs of seeing such as look at, see and recognize, and by the demonstratives this/that, which clearly demonstrate the action of showing. On the other hand, the item *letter* is frequently followed by a specification about date (this/that is a letter dated/of), sender (this/that is a letter from) or receiver (this/that is a letter addresses to) or topic (this/that is a letter which) (see Table 5.10).

Table 5.10 Function of DOCUMENT and LETTER

FUNCTION	EXAMPLES	<DE QST>	<CE QST>
DOCUMENT% General reference to a piece of evidence shown to the witness	*Look at/See/Recognize a/Refer to this/that **document***	**42.3**	**45**
LETTER % Specifying evidence	*This/that is a **letter** dated/of*	**15.2**	**0**
	*This/that is a **letter** from*	**13**	**14.5**
	*This/that is a **letter** addressed to*	**0.8**	**10.2**
	*This/that is a **letter** which/about*	**4.54**	**4.3**

A last very interesting evidential that we find second-ranked in respect to its frequency in the sub-corpora is *photograph*. Even though this element does not fall within the classical definition of evidential given by Hyland, the analysis proved that this item is used by legal professionals as a reference to materials displayed during the examination and discussed in the exchange with the witness. Like the other evidentials, *photograph* identifies circumstantial evidence that provides the basis for the construction of the ideational content. This element is more frequent in the Examination-in-Chief (165, or 0.09%, versus 46, or 0.05%), and it serves the lawyer to introduce visual evidence. It tends to occur with verbs of seeing such as look at or see followed by demonstrative adjectives that accompany the act of showing. Moreover, it also tends to occur with references to a precise detail of the image, thus focusing the witness's attention on what will be central in the question (for example, to the left corner, to the bottom side) (see Table 5.11).

Generally speaking, it is thus possible to say that the main functions fulfilled by evidentials in the public inquiry witness examination is to provide an objective basis that can be both written (*statement, document, letter*) or visual (*photograph*) for the ideational content to be discussed in the examination and on which the lawyer can build up his or her questions.

Table 5.11 Functions of PHOTOGRAPH

PHOTOGRAPH % FUNCTION	EXAMPLES	<DE QST>	<CE QST>
Presenting a visual evidence	*Look at this/that* ***photograph*** *...* *Can you see this* ***photograph*** *...*	**31**	**45**
Focusing on a detail to be discussed	*To the bottom side /left corner of the* ***photograph*** *...*	**15.1**	**43.4**

Endophoric markers *Endophoric markers* are expressions which refer to other parts of a text in order to facilitate the reader's comprehension and to support argument by referring to earlier material. In the case of the witness examination of the public inquiry, the data has shown two groups of endophoric markers fulfilling two different functions:

1. **examination endophoric markers**, referring to other parts of the examination;
2. **intra-evidential endophoric markers**, referring to parts of a document quoted (*evidential*).

The *examination endophoric markers* that we found in the two sub-corpora in reference to the first function are related to the question–answer structure of the examination, and they are indeed question and answer. The frequencies of these items in <DE QST> and in <CE QST> are represented in Table 5.12.

Table 5.12 Examination endophoric markers frequency in the sub-corpora

Examination Endophoric Markers	**Examination-in-Chief <DE QST>** Raw frequency (PTW)	**Cross-Examination <CE QST>** Raw frequency (PTW)
Question	122 (0.06)	95 (0.11)
Answer	47 (0.02)	46 (0.04)

As the data show, the occurrence of the two items is higher in the Examination-in-Chief than in the Cross-Examination. However, if we look at the normalized frequencies, we discover that the presence of these types of endophoric markers concerning other part of the examination is more significant in the Cross-Examination. This is because the aim of the second part of the witness examination is to contrast what the witness said during the Examination-in-Chief, thus making reference to the questions posed by the previous lawyer or to the answers previously given by the witness him or herself.

The items *question* and *answer* frequently tend to occur with past-tense verbs and with direct reference to who posed the question or to the number of the question or of the answer, as shown in Table 5.13.

Table 5.13 Functions of QUESTION and ANSWER

FUNCTION	EXAMPLES	<DE QST>	<CE QST>
QUESTION % Linking the question to a previous question turn	*You were asked a* ***question*** *...* *You said in* ***question*** *from X* *Referred to* ***question*** *Y* *Look at the* ***question*** *you were asked*	**16.4**	**25.5**
ANSWER % Linking the question to a previous answer turn	*In* ***answer*** *to question X you said* *You told in* ***answer*** *to question X* *In* ***answer*** *to Y you explained/ indicated*	**39**	**31.3**

Moving on to the second group of endophoric markers, they are intra-textual references to part of documents that are used in the legal professionals' questions as evidentials and for this reason they have been called intra-evidential endophoric markers. These items are used to specify a *paragraph*, *page*, *sentence* or *section*[2] of an evidential source in order to avoid ambiguity and to identify the part that will be discussed in the questions. The frequency of these elements in the sub-corpora is reported in Table 5.14.

Table 5.14 Intra-evidential endophoric markers frequency in the sub-corpora

Intra-evidential Endophoric Markers	**Examination-in-Chief <DE QST>** Raw frequency (PTW)	**Cross-Examination <CE QST>** Raw frequency (PTW)
Paragraph	435 (0.23)	213 (0.24)
Page	296 (0.15)	143 (0.16)
Sentence	40 (0.02)	29 (0.03)
Section	35 (0.02)	35 (0.04)

The most frequent items are *paragraph*, *sentence*, *page* and *sentence*, and they are all referred to the statement previously given by the witness. Moreover, they all tend to occur with their reference number in the statement (in paragraph/page/sentence X) in 90% of cases, or more generally with ordinal numbers that indicate

2 Intra-evidential endophoric markers chosen after having scanned the wordlists of the sub-corpora.

their sequential position in it (first/second and so on, paragraph/page/sentence). These intra-evidential endophoric markers serve the legal professional to select a particular part of the evidential to be central in his or her questions and to guide the witness through the document quoted, thus helping his or her understanding.

Unlike the other elements, the item *section* does not refer to the witness statement, but to a general document or act discussed in the examination. This intra-evidential endophoric marker presents the same clusters of the other ones, and tends to collocate in 90% of the cases with its reference number in relation to the document (in section X of Y) or with sequential markers such as next, last, and previous that are used to lead the audience through the discussion of the piece of evidence quoted.

Interpersonal Metadiscourse

In this section, the results concerning interpersonal metadiscourse will be presented. The linguistic features analyzed here allow lawyers to express themselves and to engage the witness in the discourse realizing different rhetorical strategies. These items contribute to establishing and maintaining the relationship between the legal professional and the witness, while also giving the counsel's perspective about the information brought in the examination. This category involves interactional and evaluative aspects of metadiscourse, and expresses both the lawyer's attitude and his or her commitment to the propositional content and to the witness.

Self-mention In written discourse, *self-mention* is often referred to the degree of explicit presence of the writer in the text, measured by the frequency of first-person pronouns and possessive adjectives. The presence or the absence of explicit author reference is generally as a result of a conscious choice by writers to adopt a particular stance and a contextually situated authorial identity (Hyland 2001).[3]

In the witness examination, the presence of the legal professionals in their questions can be very important to create effective rhetorical strategies. This is particularly true for the Cross-Examination, in which lawyers exert their power to control both the form and the ideational content of their questions. In fact, after preliminarily consulting the keyword list of the <CE QST> sub-corpus in comparison with the <DE QST> sub-corpus, the data have proved a higher keyness of self-mentions in the cross-examination (see Table 5.15).

As a next step, the analysis focused on the wordlists of the two sub-corpora in order to find other self-mention items, and the most frequent elements are represented in Table 5.16. As it is possible to see from the data, self-mention in lawyers' questions can be divided into three groups, considering the different referential realizations:

3 Cited in Hyland (2005), 53.

Table 5.15 Keyness of self-mentions in the sub-corpora

WORD	FREQ.	CE.LST %	FREQ.	DE.LST %	KEYNESS
I	1.108	***1.27***	1.740	***0.90***	77.8
ME	126	***0.14***	121	***0.06***	42.0
WE	478	***0.55***	1.476	***0.76***	42.7
TRIBUNAL	104	***0.12***	53	***0.03***	81.5

Table 5.16 Self-mention frequency in the sub-corpora

Self-mentions	**Examination-in-Chief <DE QST>** Raw frequency (PTW)	**Cross-Examination <CE QST>** Raw frequency (PTW)
I	1740 (0.9)	1108 (1.27)
Me	121 (0.06)	126 (0.14)
My	100 (0.05)	90 (0.10)
We	1476 (0.76)	478 (0.55)
Us	280 (0.14)	142 (0.16)
Tribunal	53 (0.03)	104 (0.12)
Inquiry	167 (0.49)	49 (0.06)

1 **personal self-mention**—*I, me, my*—direct reference to the legal professional him or herself;
2 **procedural self-mention**—*we, us*—reference to the participants in the inquiry;
3 **authoritative self-mention**—*tribunal, inquiry*[4]—direct reference to the authority

Personal self-mention represents the real presence of the counsel in his or her questions. This engagement of the questioner can be realized by different linguistic means, but the most frequent items in the two sub-corpora proved to be the first-person pronouns I and me and the possessive adjective my. Even though I and my present a higher frequency in <DE QST>, their normalized frequency demonstrates that they have a particular saliency in <CE QST>, supporting the thesis of greater control of legal professionals over their questions in the second phase of the examination.

4 This group was created following the analysis of the concordance lines of the two words.

In both sub-corpora, the first-person pronoun *I* tends to occur with metalinguistic markers conveying the speech act of questioning (I ask you …), but also with verbs describing mental processes (I think, I wonder, I understand, I suppose and so on), signaling the personal involvement of the lawyer in the interpretation of the evidence. Moreover, in the cross-examination sub-corpus, it is possible to observe the association of this item with more challenging forms, such as the expression *put to you*, or verbs in the progressive forms that, as argued by Heffer (2005), are typical signs of the combative aspect of trial cross-examinations. In particular, the co-occurrence of *I* with verbs in the progressive forms denotes the explicit subjectivity of the counsel in the interaction (I AM thinking …). Thus, the metalinguistic speech act categories in which the personal self-mention is involved can be described as in Table 5.17.

Table 5.17 Functions of I

***I* %** **FUNCTION**	**EXAMPLES**	**<DE QST>**	**<CE QST>**
Asking	***I*** *ask ...* *Can* ***I*** *ask ...* ***I*** *am going to ask ...* ***I*** *want/would like/may/should/have to ask ...*	**8.5**	**8.3**
Interpreting	***I*** *think ...* ***I*** *suggest ...* ***I*** *suppose ...* ***I*** *understand ...* ***I*** *wonder ...*	**26.4**	**27.1**
Challenging	***I*** *am (not) suggesting/proposing/telling/ putting to you ...* ***I*** *put it to you ...* ***I*** *have to put it to you ...*	**5**	**15**

As far as *me* is concerned, this item creates two different patterns in <DE QST> and in <CE QST>. In the first sub-corpus, in fact, *me* tends to occur with modals plus verbs indicating the verbal action requested from the witness (can/could you tell me …, can/could you explain to me …). On the other hand, in the Cross-Examination sub-corpus, *me* appears to be used with the imperative form of verbs indicating the verbal action requested from the witness (tell me …, help me …, describe to me …), with imperative forms used to introduce a question (let me ask …, let me put …), or with verbs introducing a presupposition of the lawyer (would you agree with me …, take it from me that …). This difference in combativeness is also demonstrated by the possessive pronoun *my*, which in <CE QST> mainly occurs in the expressions *this is not an answer to my question* and you didn't answer my question, thus highlighting the incapacity of the witness in giving the right answer (see Table 5.18).

Table 5.18 Functions of ME

ME % **FUNCTION**	**EXAMPLES**	**<DE QST>**	**<CE QST>**
Requesting a verbal action from the witness	*Can/could you tell* ***me*** *..., can/ could you explain to* ***me*** *...* *Tell* ***me*** *..., help* ***me*** *..., describe to* ***me*** *...*	**23.1** **3.3**	**6.3** **10.2**
Introducing a question	*Let* ***me*** *ask ..., let* ***me*** *put ...*	**3.3**	**13.5**
Introducing a presupposition	*Would you agree with* ***me*** *..., take it from* ***me*** *that ...*	**5.8**	**12.7**

All these items of personal self-mentions denote an "onstage subjectivity" (Heffer 2005: 127) of the legal professional that linguistically marks his or her presence in the examination, especially regarding the Cross-Examination. In this phase, in fact, the data demonstrate a particular concern with the process of signaling the verbal interaction with the witness, thus showing a higher degree of control on the questioning.

Moving on to procedural self-mention, it represents the inclusion of the lawyer in the inquiry participant group. In this case, the counsel uses the first-person plural pronoun *we*, thinking of him or herself as an inquiry member, thus employing an inclusive *we*. The frequency of the items *we* and *us* shows that they occur respectively almost three and two times as often in the <DE QST> sub-corpus as in the <CE QST> sub-corpus. This is because the Examination-in-Chief is conducted by the counsel for the Inquiry, thus being part of the Inquiry itself.

We can be defined as a procedural self-mention because of its collocational profiles. In fact, in both sub-corpora, this item tends to co-occur for almost the 100% of cases with verbs of procedures indicating actions of the primary reality of the courtroom setting (have a look, go back to, focus, see, look at and so on) in their modal form followed by evidentials (statement, photograph, document) or by intra-evidential endophoric markers (paragraph, page, sentence). Thus, it is possible to say that *we* has the function of representing the lawyer as part of the procedures of the inquiry and at the same time to guide the witness into the modus operandi of the courtroom. The main five-word clusters of *we* in the two sub-corpora are represented in Table 5.19.

Authoritative self-mentions represent a shifting reference for legal professionals, who can use these metadiscursive elements to pose their question by referring to the authority that in this case is the *Inquiry* or the *Tribunal*. *Inquiry* and *Tribunal* are the most frequent items of this category found in the corpus.

Table 5.19 Five-word clusters of WE

<DE QST>		<CE QST>	
we have on the screen	52	if we look at the	7
could we have on the	46	if we go over the	4
if we go to the	20	we go over the page	4
we go over the page	15	I think we know that	3
we go to the next	14	I wonder if we could	3
if we look at the	12	if we go on to	3
then if we go to	12	if we look at page	3
go to the next page	11	if we look at paragraph	3
if we go over the	11	this but if we go	3
		we look at paragraph no.	3
		we look at the plan	3

From a quantitative point of view, it is interesting to notice how these two self-mentions are in inverse proportion in the two sub-corpora. In fact, *Inquiry* presents 167 occurrences in <DE QST> and 49 occurrences in <CE QST>, while *Tribunal* shows 53 occurrences in the former sub-corpus and 104 occurrences in the latter one. This numerical difference can be easily explained by the functions they fulfill during the examination. On the one hand, *Inquiry* is used as a procedural shifting reference for the counsel, and can perform both an active and a passive function. When it performs an active function, it tends to occur with verbs that indicate a personification of the institution, describing the actions performed by the representatives in the proceeding (the inquiry has heard, has seen, understands and so on). On the other hand, when this item performs a passive function, it tends to occur with verbs that frame the institution as a receiver of the witness's evidence, which can be both evidentials (you give a statement to the inquiry) or answers given during the testimony (can you tell the inquiry, you told the inquiry).

Moving on to *Tribunal*, we find a different function concerning the cross-examination. In fact, in the second part of the examination, this item is still a shifting reference for the legal professional, but it serves the purpose of hiding the counsel's presumptions behind the authority. It creates a "fictionalized shield" (Caffi 1999, 896) that shifts the responsibility from the lawyer to the authority. In this way, the lawyer de-focuses his or her utterance and at the same time frightens the witness by referring to the institution ruling the proceeding. The authoritative self mention through the use of *Tribunal* has a stronger impact on the witness than inquiry because, even semantically, they prove to be completely different. Indeed, the semantics of *Inquiry* involves an information-seeking process that includes the notions of "search, research, investigation, examination" for "truth, knowledge or information concerning something." On the other hand, the semantics of *Tribunal* is strictly linked to the idea of judging, and it is characterized by its reference to the "judicial authority" that has as a final goal to return a verdict. Moreover, when *Tribunal* is used with this function, it tends to occur with verbs in the progressive forms that create, as mentioned above, a challenging strategy underlining the transitory context-dependent nature of the speech event in contrast with the permanence and universality of the truth (Heffer 2005, 145).

The functions of the authority self mentions *Inquiry* and *Tribunal* in the two sub-corpora are described in Table 5.20.

Table 5.20 Functions of INQUIRY and TRIBUNAL

INQUIRY % **FUNCTION**	**EXAMPLES**	**<DE QST>**	**<CE QST>**
Giving the actions of the representatives in the proceeding (personification → *active function*)	***The Inquiry*** *understands that he was a man who had a somewhat complex medical history, was rather preoccupied with his medication and his health and quite a frequent attender at the surgery.*	**19.1**	**10**
Receiving evidence from the witness (*passive function*)	*You say in your witness statement to* ***the Inquiry*** *that she had other health problems owing to her size but that she did not talk about them a great deal and you say that you expect that she had problems with her heart in particular?*	**58.4**	**46**
TRIBUNAL% **FUNCTION**	**EXAMPLES**	**<DE QST>**	**<CE QST>**
Giving the actions of the representatives in the proceeding (personification → *active function*)	***The Tribunal*** *knows from the timetable that they have been given of the times which the barriers were erected, the best you can do is that that would have been obviously before the march started, somewhere about the middle of the day?*	**77.4**	**66.9**
Receiving evidence from the witness (*passive function*)	*You have now told* ***the Tribunal*** *that the information that you picked up during the course of the afternoon was as a result of you and other people phoning home and collecting together the information that you had received?*	**22.6**	**20.6**
Being an "authoritative shield" for the legal professional and frightening the witness (*hiding behind the authority*)	*Would* ***the Tribunal*** *be right to assume what he was 6 saying was: yes, this is jolly good evidence, but I have got it now on the recording that I have made; is that what that means, or can you ascribe any other meaning to it?*	—	**12.5**

As Table 5.20 shows, the results are equally distributed as regards the functions in the two sub-corpora. The most striking difference concerns only the last function of tribunal, which can only be found in the cross-examination.

Engagement markers In written discourse, *engagement markers* have traditionally been defined as devices that explicitly address readers, either to focus their attention or to include them as discourse participants. These items allow writers either to highlight or to downplay the presence of their readers in the text (Hyland 2005, 53).

In the witness examination, engagement makers are all the linguistic means that are employed by the lawyer to directly engage the witness in his or her questions, and the most frequent elements used in the two sub-corpora are the pronouns you and your, as shown in Table 5.21.

Table 5.21 Engagement markers frequency in the sub-corpora

Engagement Markers	**Examination-in-Chief <DE QST>** Raw frequency (PTW)	**Cross-Examination <CE QST>** Raw frequency (PTW)
You	8598 (4.45)	3969 (4.54)
Your	1467 (0.76)	653 (0.75)

Since the witness examination develops in dialogue form, the presence of reference to the witness in the lawyer's questions is very high. If we compare our corpus to the Spoken BNC Corpus, *you* ranks at second place in the keyword list. This massive presence of the two items is, however, very different in the two sub-corpora. Indeed, their occurrence in the Examination-in-Chief is almost doubled as regards to that in the Cross-Examination. This is because the witness is considered as an evidential source through which the legal professional wants to construe the narrative line of the testimony. Thus, this tendency proves to be stronger in the first part of the examination, in which the witnesses are characters counsels narrate through in order to give authenticity to the story, while following their own professional skills in conveying the evidential points. This allows the examiner to discuss the evidence from an objective perspective, leaving aside his or her subjectivity and preserving the information-seeking aim. On the contrary, in the cross-examination, lawyers narrate despite the witness (Heffer 2005, 210), and are primarily concerned with challenging the witness's telling. Therefore, they demonstrate a higher degree of subjectivity, as we have already seen for self-mentions, and for this reason, they engage the witness in their questions, but privileging their own interpretation of the evidence.

The most frequent item in both sub-corpora is *you*, and it presents three frequent patterns—indeed, it usually co-occurs with: (1) verbs signaling verbal processes (you say, deal, describe, told and so on) in the affirmative form, referring to what the witness tells in his or her statement; (2) verbs indicating mental processes (do you understand …?, do you think …?, do you know …?) in the question form, asking for an interpretation from the person who is questioned; (3) verbs asking for a service from the witness, usually preceded by a modal auxiliary (could you go to…?, could you tell us …? and so on). Even though these patterns are respected both in <DE QST> and in <CE QST>, in the Cross-Examination sub-corpus we find a peculiar aspect of the verbs of speech associated with *you*. Indeed, they are often used in the past tense (you told, you said, and so on) or in the progressive form (you are telling). The past tense and the progressive form perform a similar function: challenging the witness. In fact, the past tense is a marked pattern, and signals a contrast in the witness's telling, while the progressive form focuses on the transitory context-dependent nature of the speech event, in contrast with the permanence of the evidential truth, thus creating a doubt about what the witness is or has been telling during the examination or in the investigative phase. The principal functions of *you* in <DE QST> and <CE QST> are described in Table 5.22.

Table 5.22 Functions of YOU

YOU % **FUNCTION**	**EXAMPLES**	**<DE QST>**	**<CE QST>**
Referring to what the witness tells in his/her statement	*In paragraph 19* ***you*** *say this: "We all began walking south down Rossville Street [...]"*	**6.8**	**1.5**
Asking for an interpretation of the evidence from the witness	*Do* ***you*** *think in fact that you went to the Rossville Street side of that ramp?*	**3.6**	**1**
Asking for a service from the witness	*Can* ***you*** *tell us the nature of such enquiries?*	**1.8**	**3.1**
Challenging the witness	*Are* ***you*** *telling this Tribunal on oath today that you have no recollection of giving that statement in 1972?*	**0.2**	**1.2**

In the Examination-in-Chief, lawyers frequently tend to engage the witness with the pronoun *you* to quote what he or she says in his or her statement (6.8) or to ask for an interpretation from him or her (3.6). On the other hand, the controlling nature of the cross-examination is demonstrated by the fact that the counsels usually engage the witness in their questions mostly to ask for a service from him or her (3.1) or to challenge what he or she said or is saying (1.2).

Moving on to *your*, this item is often preceded by you plus verbal processes and followed by evidentials (you say in your statement …). *Your* reinforces the presence of the witness referred to what he or she stated in the investigative part of the inquiry, signaling the will of the lawyer to take the exact words of the person who testifies in order to produce as objective evidence as possible. This explains why the frequency of this item is higher in the Examination-in-Chief than in the Cross-Examination.

Another recurrent pattern is the occurrence of *your* plus the nouns *recollection* and *knowledge* that is used by legal professionals to attribute the responsibility of what they are telling to the witness, while asking for a confirmation from him or her. The functions of your in the sub-corpora are expressed in Table 5.23.

Table 5.23 Functions of YOUR

YOUR **% FUNCTION**	**EXAMPLES**	**<DE QST>**	**<CE QST>**
Making reference to the evidence produced by the witness in the investigative part of the Inquiry	*You say in* ***your*** *statement that you have no recollection of that interview.*	**13**	**4.4**
Attributing responsibility for what the lawyer is stating to the witness and asking for a confirmation	*Is it* ***your*** *recollection that Shipman had in fact given Mrs Coulthard injections on a fairly regular basis in the course of her illness?*	**4.8**	**10.7**

As it was for you, even with this engagement marker it is possible to notice a difference in its use in the two phases of the examination. In fact, in the Examination-in-Chief the data prove objectivity in reporting the witness's evidence again to be prevalent, while in the Cross-Examination, engaging the witness is mostly used to attribute responsibility to him or her.

Boosters *Boosters* are words such as *clearly*, *obviously* and *demonstrate* that allow the writer to close down alternatives, head off conflicting views and express his or her certainty in what he or she says (Hyland 2005, 52). Therefore, boosters emphasize certainty of the writer/speaker, and in the witness examination they signal an upgrading in the degree of certainty of a question. Lawyers use these metadiscursive devices to strengthen their positions about a piece of evidence in order to lead the witness to a preferred pattern of understanding, and thus to a preferred answer.

The data showed that classical items are not representative of the real functions of boosters in the witness examination. However, we found other strategic boosters—that is to say those items that do fall in the traditional definition of boosters but that enable the lawyer to emphasize the force of their questions in order to control the witness both from the ideational and the relational point of view. Strategic boosters are *oath* and *truth*, and they are typical of the cross-examination since we do not find instances of these items in the Examination-in-Chief sub-corpus, as demonstrated in Table 5.24.

Table 5.24 Strategic booster frequency in the sub-corpora

Strategic Boosters	**Examination-in-Chief <DE QST>** Raw frequency (PTW)	**Cross-Examination <CE QST>** Raw frequency (PTW)
Oath	—	13 (0.01)
Truth	—	15 (0.02)

Oath and *truth* are elements that exploit the power of the unusual legal setting for the witness to increase the control of the lawyer. These items are mainly used by legal professionals to undermine the credibility of the witness, frightening him or her through a reminder of the duties imposed by the legal context. Moreover, they tend occur with verbs in the progressive or in the imperative form and with authoritative self-mentions that amplify their enforcing effect. Table 5.25 shows examples of oath and truth in the Cross-Examination.

Table 5.25 Examples of OATH and TRUTH

Oath	*Are you telling this Tribunal on **oath** today that you have no recollection of giving that statement in 1972?* *It is not entirely candid to this Tribunal to say today on **oath** that you did not see any journalist, is it?*
Truth	*Mr. McGlinchey, I am afraid I must suggest to you that although you swore to tell the whole **truth**, you have not been doing it, not by a long chalk.* *Tell the **truth**.*

As it is possible to observe in the examples quoted above, lawyers employ *oath* and *truth* to increase the intimidating power of their questions, exploiting their authority on the witness and showing the inconsistency of his or her answer. These items transform their requests into accusations, increasing their level of control on the person who is testifying.

Hedges *Hedges* allow writers to mitigate their propositions in order to negotiate meaning with the reader. This is particularly true for face-to-face conversation, in which hedges mitigate the speaker's utterances in order to avoid "face-threatening acts" for their interlocutors.

In the Public Inquiry context, lawyers generally use hedges to mitigate the force of their questions, both from a formal and from an ideational point of view. The most frequent items used to fulfill this purpose are modal auxiliaries (would, could, can, may, might, should, wouldn't, couldn't, can't, shouldn't) and periphrasis that indicate possibility/probability (is it possible that…, it is right to say that …, it is fair to say that … and so on), as shown in Table 5.26.

Table 5.26 Hedges frequency in the sub-corpora

Hedges	**Examination-in-Chief <DE QST>** Raw frequency (PTW)	**Cross-Examination <CE QST>** Raw frequency (PTW)
Modal auxiliaries	3500 (1.82)	1600 (1.83)
Periphrasis of possibility/ probability	2400 (1.22)	1313 (1.5)

The two types of hedges highlighted in Table 5.26 present two different functions considering the objects of their mitigating effect. On the one hand, modal auxiliaries downgrade the illocutionary force of a question, decreasing the impact of the request on the witness. By using these devices, lawyers diminish the level of coercion of their questions, creating a more friendly relationship with the witness. Modal auxiliaries frequently collocate with engagement markers, and signal the cooperative relation the lawyer wants to establish with the witness (see Table 5.27).

On the other hand, periphrasis of possibility/probability mitigates the ideational content of the question and allows lawyers to downgrade the degree of certainty of the presuppositions they make in their requests. Legal professionals give their own point of view on the evidence discussed, but at the same time seek confirmation from the witness. These devices introduce the negotiation of meaning between the counsel and the witness about the lawyer's suppositions (see Table 5.28).

Conclusions

This chapter aimed to describe the role of metadiscourse in counsels' questions during the witness examination, considering in particular the case of Public Inquiries in Great Britain.

Table 5.27 Functions of MODAL AUXILIARIES

MODAL AUXILIARIES % **FUNCTION**	**EXAMPLES**	**<DE QST>**	**<CE QST>**
Creating a cooperative relation with the witness	***Would*** *you like to tell us what those views are?* ***Would*** *you agree with me that the facts must obviously have been much better in your mind at the time?* ***Could*** *you tell us the difference between a rimfire cartridge and a centerfire cartridge?*	**60**	**40**

Table 5.28 Functions of PERIPHRASIS OF POSSIBILITY/PROBABILITY

PERIPHRASIS OF POSSIBILITY/ PROBABILITY % **FUNCTION**	**EXAMPLES**	**<DE QST>**	**<CE QST>**
Negotiating meaning of the lawyer's suppositions	***Is it right that*** *in the ordinary course of events you would have expected to learn of this death within a day or two of it happening?* ***Am I right in thinking that*** *the Hogg & Mitchell factory is the building to which I am now pointing?* ***Is it possible that*** *you heard two or three shots which were in fact fired by another soldier in the Kells Walk area?* ***Is it fair to say that*** *from 1988 onwards you did have fairly regular correspondence with him?*	**15.9**	**7.6**

The study discussed the functions of both textual and interpersonal metadiscourse (Hyland 1998; Hyland 2005) in the realization of lawyers' argumentative strategies to build up effective questions in the two phases of the witness examination: the Examination-in-Chief and the Cross-Examination.

Before presenting the results of the analysis of the corpus, the chapter outlined the theoretical preliminaries in the field of the linguistic analysis of metadiscourse.

Secondly, the methodology for the study of the reformulations in the corpus was presented, highlighting the principal criteria used in the analysis. The presentation of the results regarding the analysis of metadiscourse in the corpus followed the methodological steps defined for the observation of the data. Indeed, at first, the occurrence of the metadiscursive elements in the Examination-in-Chief and in the Cross-Examination sub-corpora was considered, taking into account both their raw frequency and their weighted frequency. The principal clusters of each metadiscourse element were then described, identifying their most frequent collocates and the functions they fulfill. The frequency of these metadiscursive patterns in the corpus was then given.

Table 5.29 summarizes the quantitative distribution of textual and interpersonal metadiscourse in the two sub-corpora.

Table 5.29 Summary of the frequency of metadiscourse in the corpus

TEXTUAL META-DISCOURSE	**Examination-in-Chief <DE QST>** Raw frequency (PTW)		**Cross-Examination <CE QST>** Raw frequency (PTW)	
Code Glosses	160 (0.08)		79 (0.08)	
Evidentials	867 (0.36)		376 (0.43)	
Endophoric Markers	***Examination***	169 (0.08)	***Examination***	141 (0.15)
	Intra-evidential	806 (0.42)	***Intra-evidential***	420 (0.47)
INTER-PERSONAL META-DISCOURSE	**Examination-in-Chief <DE QST>** Raw frequency (PTW)		**Cross-Examination <CE QST>** Raw frequency (PTW)	
Self-mention	***Personal***	1962 (0.2)	***Personal***	1324 (1.41)
	Procedural	1556 (0.9)	***Procedural***	526 (0.7)
	Authoritative	220 (0.5)	***Authoritative***	153 (0.2)
Engagement Markers	10065 (5.21)		4349 (5.29)	
Boosters	302 (0.16)		169 (0.18)	
Hedges	5900 (3.05)		1913 (4.36)	

The results showed that metadiscourse completes the argumentative strategy used by lawyers in order to control the witness's narrative, giving precise means to shape both the formal and the relational sides of their questions. In particular, on the one hand, textual metadiscourse allows the legal professionals to build the structure of their interrogatives and at the same time to control the development of the testimony leading the trajectory of the interaction. On the other hand, interpersonal metadiscourse serves the counsels to have power over the relationship with the witness and to decide to whom to attribute the responsibility for their reformulations.

References

Aedel, A. (2005), "On the boundaries between evaluation and metadiscourse," in E. Tognini-Bonelli and G. Del Lungo Camiciotti (eds.), *Strategies in Academic Discourse*, Amsterdam: John Benjamins, 153–62.

Bhatia, V.K. (1993), *Analysing Genre: Language Use in Professional Settings*, Harlow: Pearson Education—Longman.

Caffi, C. (1999), "On mitigation," *Journal of Pragmatics*, 31, 881–909.

Conley, J. and O'Barr, W. (1990), *Rules versus Relationships: The Ethnography of Legal Discourse*, Chicago, IL: Chicago University Press.

Crismore, A. (1989), *Talking with Readers: Metadiscourse as Rhetorical Act*, New York: Peter Lang.

—— and Farnsworth, R. (1990), "Metadiscourse in popular and professional science discourse," in W. Nash (ed.), *The Writing Scholar: Studies in Academic Discourse*, London: Sage, 118–36.

Crismore, A. Markkanen, R. and Steffensen, M.S. (1993), "Metadiscourse in persuasive writing," *Written Communication*, 10(1), 39–71.

Dahl, T. (2004), "Textual metadiscourse in research articles: A marker of national culture or of academic discipline?", *Journal of Pragmatics*, 36, 1,807–25.

Danet, B. and Bogoch, B. (1980), "Fixed fight or free-for-all? An empirical study of combativeness in the adversary system of justice," *British Journal of Law and Society*, 7, 38–60.

Drew, P. (1985), "Analyzing the Use of Language in Courtroom Interaction," in T. van Dijk (ed.), *Handbook of Discourse Analysis*, New York: Academic Press, vol. III, 133–47.

Fuertes-Olivera, P.A., Velasco-Sacristán, M., Arribas-Baño, A. and Samaniego-Fernández, E. (2001), "Persuasion and advertising English: Metadiscourse in slogans and headlines," *Journal of Pragmatics*, 33, 1,291–307.

Gibbons, J. (1994), *Language and the Law*, Harlow: Longman.

—— (2003), *Forensic Linguistics: Introduction to Language in the Justice System*, Oxford: Blackwell).

Goodrich, P. (1987), *Legal Discourse*, London: Macmillan.

Halliday, M.A.K. (1973), *Exploration in the Functions of Language*, London: Edward Arnold.

—— (1994), *An Introduction to Functional Grammar*, 2nd edn., London: Edward Arnold.

Heffer, C. (2005), *The Language of Jury Trial: A Corpus-aided Analysis of Legal–lay Discourse*, New York: Palgrave Macmillan.

Hyland, K. (1998), "Persuasion and context: The pragmatics of academic metadiscourse," *Journal of Pragmatics*, 30, 437–55.

—— (1999), "Talking to students: Metadiscourse in introductory coursebooks," *English for Specific Purposes*, 18(1), 3–26.

—— (2002a), "Authority and invisibility: Authorial identity in academic writing," *Journal of Pragmatics*, 30, 1,091–112.

—— (2002b), "Genre: language, context, and literacy," *Annual Review of Applied Linguistics*, 22, 113–35.

—— (2005), *Metadiscourse*, London: Continuum Guides to Discourse.

Ifantidou, E. (2005), "The semantics and pragmatics of metadiscourse," *Journal of Pragmatics*, 37, 1,325–53.

Kurzon, D. (2001), "The Politeness of judges: American and English judicial behaviour," *Journal of Pragmatics*, 33, 61–85.

Levi, J.N. (1990), "The Study of Language in the Judicial Process," in J.N. Levi and A.G. Walker (eds.), *Language in the Judicial Process*, New York: Plenum Press.

Maley, Y. (1994), "The Language of the Law," in J. Gibbons (ed.), *Language and the Law*, London: Longman, 3–50.

Markkanen, R., Steffensen, M. and Crismore, A. (1993), "Quantitative contrastive study of metadiscourse: Problems in design the analysis of data," *Papers and Studies in Contrastive Linguistics*, 28, 147–52.

Mauranen, A. (1993), "Contrastive ESP rhetoric: Metatext in Finnish-English economics texts," *English for Specific Purposes*, 12, 3–22.

Mellinkoff, D. (1963), *The Language of the Law*, Boston: Brown & Co.

Newbury, P. and Johnson, A. (2006), "Suspects' resistance to constraining and coercive questioning strategies in the police interview," *International Journal of Speech, Language and the Law*, 13(2), 213–40.

Norrick, N.R. (2001), "Discourse markers in oral narratives," *Journal of Pragmatics*, 33, 849–78.

O'Barr, W.M. (1982), *Linguistic Evidence: Language, Power and Strategy in the Courtroom*, New York: Academic Press.

Schiffrin, D. (1980), "Metatalk: Organisational and evaluative brackets in discourse," *Sociological Inquiry: Language and Social Interaction*, 50, 199–236.

Swales, J.M. (1990), *Genre Analysis: English in Academic and Research Settings*, Cambridge: Cambridge University Press.

—— (2001), "Metatalk in American academic talk," *Journal of English Linguistics*, 29(1), 34–54.

Tiersma, P.M. (1999), *Legal Language*, Chicago, IL: University Chicago Press.

Vande Kopple, W.J. (1985), "Some explanatory discourse on metadiscourse," *College Composition and Communication*, 36(1), 82–93.

Walton, D. (2002), *Legal Argumentation and Evidence*, Pennsylvania, PA: Pennsylvania State University Press.

—— (2003), "The interrogation as a type of dialogue," *Journal of Pragmatics*, 35, 1,771–802.

Woodbury, A. (1984), "The strategic use of questions in court," *Semiotica*, 48(3/4), 197–228.

Chapter 6
Constructing Legal Narratives: Client-lawyers' Stories

Flora Di Donato[1]

In this chapter, I would like to look at some characteristics of legal narratives within judicial proceedings. The underlying research interest is to investigate the contribution of *lay people* in constructing legal meanings. In other words: how the client takes part in the construction of his or her case in collaboration with the lawyer, and how the client's (cultural) representation of the facts is able to affect the way in which a legal story is presented by the lawyer in court.

The chapter is oriented towards a psycho-socio-cultural perspective that considers stories as "a way of world-making" in legal contexts. A major source of inspiration for choosing this approach to the study of legal narratives has been the works by Jerome Bruner—also in collaboration with Anthony Amsterdam (Amsterdam and Bruner 2000). His most important contributions to the Legal Storytelling movement concern some fundamental epistemological aspects.[2] Bruner (1991; 2002) claims that the narrative structures of the mind are the same in the context of the everyday as they are in the context of law: stories in literature and stories in law can accordingly be considered alike, in that both always involve the activity of constructing the reality narrated. In fact, according to his perspective, human beings actively construct social reality through narrative negotiations of daily meanings that are deeply rooted in culture (Bruner 1990).

This study intends to be an application of this type of approach. It focuses on the socio-cultural relations from which (legal) narrations are originated within the legal context. A qualitative analysis of several labor law and family law cases is complemented by interviews with clients and lawyers, thus making it possible to investigate the roles of those actors in constructing the legal facts, as

---

1 Some of the ideas formalized in this chapter have been discussed during participation in two annual meetings: the First National Congress of the ISLL (Italian Society for Law and Literature), Bologna, May 2009, and the Joint meeting "Complexity, Conflicts, Justice: 20 Years of Sociology of Law," held by the Oñati International Institute for the Sociology of Law, July 2009. The chapter is particularly supported by a new data corpus.

2 Professor Jerome Bruner is known as one of the most important psychologists of the twentieth century. Over the last two decades, he has brought cultural psychology to bear on the study of the law in context. For further details on his psychological works, see Di Donato (2009a; 2009b).

well as some of the aspects of the relationship between them. Thanks to several examples, it is possible to trace the development of the legal narratives from the client's representation of the daily facts to the lawyer's legal definition. It starts by referring to some of the pre-existing and most recent studies on legal storytelling and their influence on legal theory. This is followed by a discussion of a "constructivist perspective" applied to the legal discourse, with a focus on the role of human beings in producing legal meanings. Subsequently, this chapter will try to answer two questions: Where do the legal stories come from? Which kinds of violation are able to provoke a legal narrative? The structure of a story will be illustrated, and the results of a qualitative analysis shown. The second section of the chapter will focus on the client's and lawyer's role in constructing the legal story. Emphasis will be given to the client's initiatives within the relationship with the lawyer, as well as the opportunity for him or her to have a "voice" within the judicial proceeding. Finally, I will discuss the findings, highlighting the different characteristics of the lawyer's discourse in relation to the client's.

Storytelling and Legal Studies: A Brief State of the Art

The consideration of stories within judicial proceedings as narratives is typical of a postmodern approach to the study of law that integrates the appeals coming from the world of law with those from the world of literature, literary criticism, philosophy and theory of law. This is the Law and Literature movement,[3] which originated in the United States but has recently become more widespread and recognized in both European as well as Italian cultural, scientific and academic spheres.[4] It is well known that this movement was founded with the aim, on one hand, to give jurists a literary and humanistic sensitivity (*law in literature*), and on the other, to invite jurists to a critical reading of the law through the use of literary techniques for the interpretation of legal texts (*law as literature*). In a more recent phase, it has been orientated towards the consideration of *law as narrative* or *law as narrative construction*.[5] In fact, one of the main purposes of the Law and Literature movement is to bring to the attention of scholars the relationship between the legal text and the narrative process through which the law itself is originated as a legal and human experience.

Since the beginning, the study of legal-judicial narratives has seemed to follow, to a certain extent, an autonomous path, making use in many cases of the

3 For a brief description of this movement, see Minda (1995).

4 For the most recent developments of the Law and Literature movement in Italy, see Mittica (2009).

5 It worth considering, as examples, the works of Cover (1983), Ost (2004), and in a constructivist perspective, Bruner (2002) also in collaboration with Amsterdam (2000). From the same perspective, it also worth considering Di Donato (2008a; 2008b; 2010) and Sherwin (1994).

contribution of social psychology. At the beginning of the 1980s, Bennett and Feldman (1981) carried out a study that introduced for the first time the theory—not without criticism—that the "effective" representation of a case in court depends above all on the storytelling ability of the legal actors (accused, lawyers, witnesses). According to Bennett and Feldman, jurors tend to base their decision on an evaluation of "plausibility" and "coherence" of the stories narrated, as well as considering them on the whole rather than on the verification of the truth of the facts.

In 1989, there was a symposium at the University of Michigan dedicated to Legal Storytelling. It was an event that scholars judged as "significant," considering it to be an indication of the opening of the Law School to a different approach to law. The stories narrated in a trial, in addition to representing the "diversity" (men/women, white/colored), have the power to represent the "reality" to start from different points of view (individual, social, cultural, legal) from which they are informed.[6]

In fact, following the important season of American legal realism, which had the merit of drawing attention to contexts of production of legal decisions, the influence of the Law and Literature movement will be a decisive turning point of legal studies in a more definite direction, represented by a growing interest in understanding the connections between human-daily dimensions of legal problems and the practices of law. The efforts of scholars aim to understand how "daily problems" are translated into legal cases. This deals with the postmodern awareness that the law should consider more definitely the "life of people" it is aimed at. Lawyers are encouraged to personalize client's stories, to tell their story rather than resorting to "typical stories." Judges are invited to consider the context in which the case is constructed and recognize the story that every part presents as "unique." In summary, legal studies have focused more definitively on the narrations used by lawyers and judges, as well as anyone else within the legal system contributing to the creation of legal meanings.[7]

This change of direction in legal studies will also determine the confirmation of a new orientation of studies that will signal the founding of the Lawyering Theory Colloquium (1992), thanks to the support of contributions coming from other disciplines. A significant contribution is due once again to the fruitful association between the theory of law and (social and cultural) psychology.[8] I am referring in particular to the noteworthy work of Amsterdam and Bruner, *Minding the Law*,

6 For the acts of the symposium, see *Michigan Law Review*, 87 (1988/89). See also *Vermont Law Review* (special issue): "Lawyers as Storytellers and Storytellers as Lawyers: An Interdisciplinary Symposium Exploring the Use of Storytelling in the Practice of Law," 18(3) (1994).

7 We could date the narrative "paradigm shift" to the appearance of a collection of essays, "On Narrative" (ed. W.J.T. Mitchell), drawn from *The Critical Inquiry Journal* (1981).

8 See Bruner (1992).

published by Harvard University Press (2000). The book, which is considered a "turning point" in the study of judicial storytelling, considers the law as "a storytelling enterprise thoroughly entrenched with culture." In fact, the aim of the authors is to explore the underlying relationships between the judicial opinions (of the American Supreme Court) and the American culture of which they are considered expressions.

Stories as "a Way of World-making": An Interdisciplinary Approach

Stories and narrations are essential in the context of legal-judicial proceedings as they represent the main tool for organizing and interpreting the pieces of information, fragments of reality that can be *reconstructed* as a coherent order of data—in other words, "facts" (Twining 2006; Taruffo 2009b).

However, to tell a story is not just a way to give a (legal) order to the reality violated by infractions, violations. According to a constructivist epistemological approach, to tell a story (even a legal story) means "to shape reality" within a cultural frame: "knowledge is never 'point-of-viewless'" (Bruner 1991, 3). In fact, starting from Vygostky's ([1934] 1962) concept of the language as a "cultural product," the anti-positivist Bruner's position is that "cultural products, like language and other symbolic systems mediate thought and place their stamp on our representations of reality." Therefore, the narration represents the key to resolving the problem of "the translatability of knowledge from one culture to another" (Bruner 1991, 3).[9] In a constructive-culturalist perspective, the "world" is not defined as simple "reality," but rather the "meaning" that the people attribute to it. It is a non-individual process, carried out within a community whose members can communicate and interact together, assuming a common ground that emerges from the social exchanges (on the basis of scripts, stereotypes, common meanings and so on) (Bruner 1990).[10]

They are the stories, narrated in both daily and institutional contexts (such as legal and judicial ones), making the cultural cohesion and creation of legal meanings possible (Bruner 1990; Bruner 2002). It is a process that is not automatically imposed from "above" by the State and the other institutional representatives (judges, lawyers, professors), but comes from the "bottom" (Cover 1983), from the "ordinary" people (Merry 1992), the human beings, all those people who have an "active" role in the construction of the social and legal reality of which they are part. Naturally, meanings negotiated and given by individuals to their world become patterned, established, objectified in virtue of the rules, the role of the institutions (courts, legal offices, schools, laws, codes and so on). They "bridge"—according to a well-known metaphor by Cover (1983)—between the

9 See also White (1980–81), 10.

10 See also Bruner, "Culture, Mind and Narrative" (unpublished).

starting reality, intended as cultural visions, and the "possible" and "alternative" social and cultural constructions of reality.

Where Do (Legal) Stories Come From?

What are the origins of a (legal) narrative, and what phases does a "human story" pass through in order to evolve into a "legal story"?

The story starts from the moment of the breaking point of a legitimate situation (Amsterdam and Bruner 2000), which can correspond, simply, to a violation of a cultural script which, for example, has to deal with behavior that normally is held or we imagine we must hold when we are at the post office or the restaurant, or that (more probably) can have to deal with the violation of a rule of law. For example, Mister X hasn't stopped at a red traffic light; Mister Y has been unfaithful to his wife; the Company X has given inferior duty to Miss Y, rather than the once set out in the contract.

It is easy to observe that, either in the case of the infraction of a behavior rule, such as "queuing at the post office," or in the case of the violation of a rule of law—like the reciprocal fidelity obligation (set out in Article 143 of the Italian Civil Code)—we are in the presence of meanings that we assume to be prescribing rules in the context of a culture.

Not every trouble that disturbs the legitimate order of reality is able to start a legal narrative (Amsterdam and Bruner 2000, 129–31). As is well known, remarkable violations of the law can be determined only with reference to the rules of law within a specific legal system: the trouble needs to be transformed into a recognizable legal problem.

Let us consider a typical plot of a (legal) story[11] (Amsterdam and Bruner 2000, 113–14):

> 1. *an initial steady state grounded in the legitimate ordinariness of things*: In 1999, a dear friend and colleague, who I meet while working as an intern in an important Neapolitan office, invited me to come and work as a manager of monitoring and accounting of the management of European Funds. He introduced me to the general director of the "territorial agreements" (drawn up between the council and province) and we started to collaborate in managing these funds. In the space of two years, we managed to spend eight hundred million funded by the European Union without wasting any public money. In a very closed environment, we became "market-leaders". We received calls from everywhere [in our region], even from very difficult contexts in the province

11 Nunzio's story: a respected professional who becomes part of a team of experts managing European funds for Italy. Nunzio becomes a victim of mobbing and exclusion from the workplace by his colleagues.

of Naples. It was informally organised, we were four professionals: a general director, an administrative director, I was nominated general coordinator.

2. *that gets disrupted by a Trouble consisting of circumstances attributable to human agency or susceptible to change by human intervention*:
The relationships [among colleagues] that were also highly emotional, at a certain point, started to deteriorate. The administrative director, at a certain point, wanted to take over as the general director (the boss), he was bored with being the number two. In the meantime, a fifth person had entered the group, a woman, who was having an extra-marital affair with number two. This woman saw number two as a way to make rapid carrier progress. Number two loses his head—notwithstanding my insistence and requests for a more sober behaviour—he buys a €50,000 car, holidays, jewellery. In particular, he violates the pact to not make any deals with local politicians.

Last year, on the 24th July, by complete surprise, he called the six partners of the firm together and obtained the unjustified dismissal of number one, being subsequently nominated in his place. I was replaced.

3. *in turn evoking efforts at redress or transformation which succeed or fail*:
On the 25th July as part of my duties as secretary of the meeting held on 24th July, I faxed all the partner agencies, as well as the President of the Board of Administration, a copy of the minutes of the meeting and invited the mayors as well as the President "to give any opinions…with the aim of not prejudicing the rights of the partner agencies". The following day, the President of the Board replied warning me ….

4. *so that the old steady state is restored or a new (transformed) steady state is created*:
The organizational set up was subsequently modified, I was assigned an exclusively internal role, which I was not interested in. I was also asked to be more flexible, to meet the needs of politics. I am also literally asked "to behave". Obviously, I didn't accept. All my duties are subsequently taken away.

5. *and then story concludes […] with a "coda"*:
I do not know how to be dishonest.[12]

The articulation of Nunzio's story, according to the model proposed by Amsterdam and Bruner (2000), highlights how a narration is made up of a particular sequence of events in which human beings are the protagonists who behave as "actors", with "intentions": Nunzio and his colleagues. The events and characters that exist in reality acquire specific meanings within the narrative plot: the protagonists (the antagonists) are described by Nunzio as "number one,"

12 This is the transcript of the story narrated by Nunzio during the interview.

"number two," according their hierarchical position within the professional context and their specific aim of having a successful career. The story is provoked by the violation of the legitimate initial situation. In this case, it is not only the violation of the rules of law, but also the behavior rules among the protagonists (rule of loyalty and correctness in the relationships between colleagues). The narration is an attempt to restore the status quo: the mediation between Nunzio and his colleagues will not be enough; they will have to go to a lawyer.

Narrations and (Social) Relations: A Qualitative Analysis

Nunzio's story, as described above, is part of a much larger corpus of data that deals with labor law and family law cases, analyzed in the first degree. The aim of the research[13] is to describe the stories in terms of socio-juridical relationships within the legal context in order to show that the construction of legal meanings is a normative process permeated by social relations.

The investigation focuses on the analysis of the official documents as well as the transcripts of interviews with clients and lawyers. The analysis is complemented by the client's notes (a written record drafted upon request of the lawyer containing all the information and details of the case for which legal advice is sought). Starting from the results of the research, it seems that the trouble—what provoked the narration—can have its origin within a relationship between two or more interacting actors who do not share the same representation of reality. It can be a case of mobbing,[14] within the professional context—as we see in Nunzio's case—but it can also be a matter of the separation dynamic between spouses, conditioned, if not also determined, by conflict in the enlarged family context. The trouble seems to flow, every time, from a tension or from a conflict between the different intentions of the protagonists of the narrative plot. Specifically in the labor law cases, we deal with the tensions that relate to the definition or redefinition of the roles played by the protagonists, about their hierarchical position within the company context, for instance. All the actors present on the scene can be involved, and normally they are, from the co-workers to the addressees of the professional

13 This research line has been developed since the doctoral work co-tutored by the University of Naples and the University of Neuchâtel during the years 2003–2007; Di Donato (2008b).

14 A typical case of mobbing can be instigated either by the employer (with or without the support of the other co-workers) or by the co-workers themselves, with the latter isolating the unwanted colleague (this being described as *horizontal mobbing*). The collective Italian contract of state dependants of February 28, 2003, art. 6, defines mobbing as "moral or psychic violence in the working environment, effected by the employer or by other employees and characterized by acts, attitudes or behaviors repeated time after time with aggressive, defamatory or oppressive connotations."

services (who can include the company clients as well as the patients of a medical structure).

Several parts of Angela's story are reported below as an example. She was a psychotherapist in a healthcare structure, and was a victim of mobbing carried out by her employer (Example 1) and supported by her co-workers (Example 2):

> (1) My relationship with XXX (employer) worsened [...] from the moment I told him what I didn't like about him [...]—*Angela* writes in a note—I burst into tears in front of the group due to the highly delicate moment with my relationship with him (I felt that he is being vindictive) as well as the fact that I was passed over for promotion, in addition because certain dis-confirmations should not be made in public in front of interns [...]. I think it was at that point that XXX's (employer) revenge started, criticising my professional figure in front of the students ....

> (2) My co-workers—*Angela* writes—underestimate my work with patients, ridiculing the way it is carried out [...]; my co-workers' attacks were so devaluating that they created disappointment and worry among the interns who didn't really understand what was happening among the other members of staff.[15]

In Angela's case, just as in Nunzio's (seen above), the network between the human and professional dimension dominates the whole to the point that the trouble is determinant in complicating the social and professional relationships within the working context.

The network of problematic relationships, extended to a family context, is also evident in the stories of Fernanda and Tiziana, which will be described briefly. They are similar cases of separation crossed by networks of invasive family relationships that have greatly influenced the dynamics within the two couples.

Fernanda's story is described in a brief extract from the memorandum given to her lawyer:

> Our story started about 23 years ago. From the very beginning, I had problems with his family, especially the mother, who did everything to try and create misunderstandings. Armed with a photo of me, she went to fortune-tellers and priests to see whether our love was the result of a curse. Given our age, Nicola's parents, in an attempt to stop us seeing each other, didn't let him us the family car and stopped giving him pocket money. [...] In the summer of XXX, I decided to leave Nicola because I could no longer stand the mother's oppression who

15 Angela's note is taken from the private legal documents in the possession of the legal studio dealing with the case.

> would not accept our relationship and even less our marriage but also because Nicola had not made a decisive stand.[16]

Even in *Tiziana's case*, the interview with her lawyer confirms the bond between family relationships and separation dynamics, so much so as to influence the reconstruction of the story that the lawyer attempted in order to carry out judicial proceedings:[17]

> It seemed as if I was divorcing the family [...]. In particular, there was the hindering presence of the mother who had even interfered in the reconstruction of the events: I asked the clients questions and the mother replied. The whole judicial proceeding was carried out with the continual anger of the mother being expressed due to the fact that in the house where the couple had decided to live—subsequently occupied by the husband—there was still her dowry which seemed to be that of "Princess Diana" [...]. The case was closed with the settlement which included the mother regaining possession of the dowry [...].[18]

Narrations and Representations: The Client's Role

In a constructivist perspective, "much of human reality and its 'facts' are not merely recounted by narrative but *constituted* by it" (Amsterdam and Bruner 2000, 111). Judicial facts are not part of the trial *sub specie* of empirical reality, but as "fact narratives" (Taruffo 2009b), or rather as objects of complex linguistic products resulting from the negotiations-interactions between the actors on the definition of reality (Di Donato 2008b).

The "trial" becomes "the place" where the narratives are presented and compared, "constructed" starting with the "roles" carried out by the legal storytellers.[19]

In this section of the illustration of the research, I want to deal with several profiles that are involved in the role carried out by the "legal actors," as well as the type of activity that is carried out during or in function of the judicial proceeding in order to produce "versions," "descriptions" or "reconstructions" of the judicial facts.[20]

---

16 Fernanda's note was given to me by the client when interviewed.

17 In this case, for reasons of privacy connected to professional and private life of one of the partners, it was not possible to interview the client in person.

18 This is a transcription of an excerpt of the interview with Tiziana's lawyer.

19 The idea of the trial as a form of "social interaction" patterned on the basis of the roles carried out by the actors who intervene in the dispute has been adapted by Abel (1974). The specific relationships between lawyers and client and the use of narratives were investigated by Elmann et al. (2009).

20 The trial procedure has been understood here from a sociological perspective as the "totality of social actions pertaining to the dispute until it is settled by decisions

I am not only referring to "institutional roles," as in the case of the judge (who will not be considered here[21]) and the lawyer, as well as the phases of the judicial proceeding in a strict sense. I will also consider the "informal roles," such as the role carried out by the client in collaborating with his or her lawyer in (re) constructing the judicial facts.

The first stage of constructing the story in the judicial proceeding is represented by the story proposed by the client to his or her lawyer. Examination of several judicial stories—with examples given above—highlights how the client (whose role is completely ignored in classical analysis) under certain conditions (social, cultural, professional) is capable of actively participating in the construction of his or her own case, thus conditioning the results.[22] The client is not a mere information giver in the trial, but is capable of the following roles.

He or she can give detailed information to the lawyer, not only about his or her own professional conditions, but also the general working context as well as the organization of the relationships between the employer and the co-workers, for example in Angela's case:

> The "clan" is headed by XXX (employer)—Angela declares in a note. XXX is the therapist to the five founding professors of the health-care structure, who in turn are therapists to the new associate professors who are therapists to all the students YYY. All the students YYY must choose a professor ZZZ as therapist. This allows XXX to control every single student enrolled.

The client can give information that can relate to the legislative discipline of a specific working sector (this the case of a school headmaster who was well informed on the legislation of his own area), as in Franco's case:

> Apart from the merits and reasons of the case what is required, from my point of view and my reading of the sentence—Franco writes in a note—is merely to ask that the rules of law laid down 31st March be respected, not the ministerial decrees: A SUSPENSION BY THE JUDGE IS NECESSARY TO ALLOW ME TO PRESENT MY APPLICATION FOR HEADMASTER BY NEXT 22nd MAY. OTHERWISE IT IS ALL A WASTE OF TIME!!![23]

---

resolving it in a more or less contingent or conclusive way"; Ferrari (1993).

21 For the specific treatment of the role of the judge in the construction of the facts in the judicial proceeding, see Di Donato (2008b), 183–202; see also Taruffo (2009b).

22 On the active role of the client in the negotiation of the dispute, see Haavisto (2002), 165–246.

23 Franco's story is illustrated in Di Donato (2008b), 145–6.

The client can also take "initiatives"[24]—he or she can ask questions, trying to give an interpretation to his or her own case (Example 1), express doubts and reservations (Example 2), make assertions and assumptions (Example 3), and suggest possible strategies to the lawyer (Example 4), as in Laura's case (victim of mobbing):[25]

> (1) […] can the company, regardless of its assessment of work (whether it's right or wrong), behave like this? Can they act and react in such a way? Can they assent to leave and then throw it back in my face? Isn't this mobbing?
>
> (2) to me XXX's persecution became apparent not just because of two consecutive official medical checks at home in four days of sick leave […], not only from the day and time this communication was sent, but also and especially because the mail didn't say that I'd be XXX but listed just three roles making up the completely undefined position of "XXX" ….
>
> (3) XXX's mail was obviously to cover her/himself […]; it's obvious that their position is and will always be to show that my sick leave was and is the cause of the professional problems that were cause for complaint, and not, which is the case, a consequence […]; the mail message is a falsehood as regards a central point ….
>
> (4) we should take advantage of the situation to "nail" XXX […] I mean underline the fact that Manager XXX asserts that procedure counts for nothing ….[26]

The client can also participate in the execution of strategies, agreed upon with the lawyer, during the phases preceding the trial (from the writing of e-mails to the employer to the registration of conversations), as in Laura's case:

> with the lawyer XXX—*Laura* declares—we decided that the first move was to completely remove this request for my resignation […]. We decided to send this e-mail in which I officially told the head of personal and the managing director that I had been underutilised, that I had mentioned this to my direct superiors and that nothing had changed.[27]

---

24 Haavisto refers to client's *initiatives* as a key tool for the analysis of the client's attempts to participate in the negotiation of the dispute; Haavisto (2002), 170–72.

25 For further details on client's initiatives, see Di Donato (2008a).

26 Examples 1–4 are taken from e-mails written by Laura to the lawyer. Laura's story is illustrated in Di Donato (2008b), 122–45.

27 In particular, see ibid., 126.

The examples highlight how the client, under certain conditions (social, cultural, professional), can be considered a "legal actor" capable of participating and influencing, in collaboration with his or her lawyer, the execution of the legal strategy to the point of the legal claims being accepted.

Nevertheless, from the point of view of the "representation" of the events, the client's story tends to be a "naive representation," at least during the first phase. It is only due to the comparison with the lawyer that he or she can truly and fully represent what is happening, within the professional context, for example in terms of legal violations.

In the cases examined—I am not only referring to cases of mobbing, but in general to a situation that has to do with the violation of the rights—the representation that the protagonist/client has of the trouble is full of emotional meanings. People talk about trauma, drama, abuses, humiliations, betrayal, with the following examples:

> (1) [...] it could be seen that on my face there was something traumatic [...] this person (the employees boss) has told me such incredibly severe things; who could ever have imagined it—*Laura* says during the interview.[28]

> (2) I didn't felt comfortable during the conversation with the President of the Law School—*Nancy* says—I felt abused.[29]

> (3) I feel betrayed as a patient—*Angela* writes—I feel betrayed as a professional: trusting him blindly. I feel humiliated as a person: because he doesn't value what I think or do. I'm attacked whatever I do. In this context, it's not enough to behave differently, they also want you to be convinced. They want you to sell your soul.

The examples highlight that the first signs of the trouble have to do with an emotional perception of the facts from the side of the private citizen—lay people. It is possible to claim that the narration is induced from the representation of the reality that is set on emotional terms. Indeed, emotions do not only relate to the affective dimension, which is not separable from the comprehensive identity of a person, but they are an integral part of its cognitive activity. Probably, they are the mover of it (Nussbaum 2001).

The Transformation of an Everyday Story into a Legal Case: The Lawyer's Role

This section highlights several of the elements of the transformation of the story proposed by the client into a legal story, upon resorting to a lawyer.

28 See ibid., 133.

29 See ibid., 136.

An element is the way in which the emotional dimension of the trouble that provoked the narrative process, starting from the client's story, can become part of the legal narration. Traces of the client's emotions are in the lawyer's claim, where, for example, the dangerous effects provoked by the professional discomfort (that might have been of such seriousness for the psycho-physical health of the worker as to have pushed her to resignation) are illustrated. There are still traces in the part where the lawyer illustrates the context of the client's life, giving consideration to the family and social difficulties (besides the economic ones) that he or she is going through following the dismissal or resignation. Let us consider some examples:

> (1) Those acts, along with the lack of any possible professional prospect and a substantial exclusion of the complainant—*Luciano's lawyer* writes in the claim – provoked in the aforementioned a great personal discomfort [...];[30]

> (2) Dismayed for the character clearly pretentious and illegitimate of such requests—*Stefano's lawyer* writes in the claim—doctor XXX, at the end of the conversation with doctor XXY, was complaining about a deep discomfort, by leaving his own job in advance.[31]

Nevertheless, the typical attitude of the lawyer is to "objectify" the story, asking the client to tell the story by answering questions such as "What's happened?", asking him or her for a narration that possibly considers the indications that have to do with elements such as dates and places, the general organization of the professional context, duties performed, assignments stolen, the indication of witnesses and documents as proof, even the recording of private conversations with the employer, and so on. This therefore leads to all the happenings being re-read omitting evaluations and personal judgments with the aim of defining "Who has done what, how, when, why and where?"

In fact, the statement of facts on the lawyer's part is the central hub of the case construction. The questions of fact, along with the questions of law, represent the key phase of the transformation of "daily events" into "legal stories" through the use of rules of law and procedural rules. In this sense, according to Twining (2006), lawyers use the stories as tools to place fragments of information and single elements of proof within an ordered context that has a significant relevance for the law.

The lawyer, therefore, does not limit him or herself to narrating the client's story, but creates (with the possible collaboration of the client) a new functional story capable of winning the case.

---

30 This is taken from Luciano's lawyer claim (art. 700 c.p.c.). The case is dealt with in more detail in Di Donato (2008b), ch. 6.

31 This is taken from Stefano's lawyer claim (art. 700 c.p.c.).

This is confirmed by Nunzio's story above, as retold by his lawyer, with an extract of the interview (Example 1) and the relative formalization of the legal claims (Example 2):

(1) The whole story was very mechanical and, in particular, based on a series of personal and political interests. I have tried to omit the personal aspect as well as the threats from the reconstruction of the facts, all things that actually happened. Some of the aspects of this case should not be included in the legal claim in order to show the judge that *Nunzio*, prior to being made unable to carry out his job, was already put in a difficult situation for not having succumbed to their pressure.

(2) Suddenly, in June 2008, there were "tensions", of a political and personal nature, between the management of the Agency and this subsequently lead to a series of discussions between the General Director, XXX and the Administrative Director, XXX, in relation to the approval of the budget for the year XXXX, which would have lead to a changing of the roles within the management.

The two brief descriptions that are associated to the "legal story" in Nunzio's case, confirm what Nunzio told in his role as client. In this case, the trouble that causes the legal story is provoked by the "tensions" arising from the context. However, it is worth noting that most of the interview with the lawyer deals with the legal qualification of the story. The lawyer's aim is to obtain damages as well as a series of benefits for his client, including insurance and social security payments. Further extracts follow:

(3) In this case, there is a three year contract which ends in 2009. The relationship is interrupted in September 2008 and in the contract, in the general discipline, it is set out that, upon agreement of the parties, in the case of anticipated annulment the employee will be paid in full.

(4) I have taken this particular aspect of the contract into account in order to decide whether or not "to set off" for a trial in which to establish the existence of a subordinate work relationship in order to ask to either be reassumed or for the payment of damages, along with what this would entail: insurance and social security payments etc. Otherwise, the other possibility is to stick to the clause in the contract that sets out in anticipated annulment that payment is made in full.[32]

The transformation of Nunzio's story into a story that is conventionally acceptable for the law means that the lawyer's main task is to translate the "naive" representation that the client has in terms of legal violations. It is evident the role

32 Passages 3 and 4 are taken from the interview transcript with Nunzio's lawyer.

that White (1990) acknowledges to the lawyer as "mediator" or "translator" among cultural visions and languages, within the legal system.

It is also worth recalling that the "construction of the case" does not conclude in a dynamic narrative among several different representations of reality between lawyer and client.[33] The ability of the lawyer is relevant, at times due to collaborating with the client, in identifying the causal and temporal connections that contribute to giving the events contextual meanings. They are connections that are not pre-defined in nature, and are connected by a relationship of causality that is more often than not a value of mere "probability" (logic or qualitative) rather than of absolute causality, according to a proposal "It is highly likely that behavior x caused fact y" (Taruffo 1992; Taruffo 2009b).

The following extract from a lawyer's claim is a typical example:

> In May 2005, *dr XXX informed* her superior that she would be absent from work in order to undergo infertility treatment *and*, in the same month, *is substituted* on project XXX, without any explanation [...]; in September 2005, *the plaintiff reports* the immediate demotion and *is asked to conclude the working relationship* by resigning.[34]

The "evidentiary outcomes" are also determinant in the construction of the case. In the perspective discussed so far, the use of proof seems to answer the question: "How to convince the judge that the representation of the facts is the most legal plausible and cultural coherent?"

It is well known, being confirmed in the analysis of the cases, that the "evidentiary outcomes" are not used "objectively" and "impartially" by the parties (nor by the judge), but rather as "elements of meaning" that contribute to the construction of a story (Di Donato 2008b) that seems "true," "probable" or "suitable"—according to what is considered to be the "ideal" aim that is assumed as the basis of the trial in the considered aspect[35]—in order to obtain a favorable verdict for the party.

In conclusion, the use of social and cultural psychology has highlighted how the judicial proceeding can be interpreted as the place where meanings are not given, but are the results of a negotiatory process among the socio-legal actors involved—in the first instance, lawyer and client.

Client-lawyer's stories are not arbitrary constructions. The events are shaped by the story that is constructed in the interaction (Ewick and Silbey 1998, 242–4). They find a form of "objectification" (Ewick and Silbey 1998) and "stabilization" (Latour 2002) thanks to the narrative processes that are culturally situated (Bruner 1991; Cole 1996; Engeström 1987).

---

33 For a detailed list of the possible use of stories by litigators, in particular in jury trials, see Alper et al. (2005).

34 See Di Donato (2008b), 171.

35 See Taruffo (2009a).

References

Abel, R.L. (1974), "A comparative theory of dispute institutions in society," *Law and Society Review*, 8(1), 217–347.

Alper, T. et al. (2005), "stories told and untold: Lawyering theory analyses of the First Rodney King assault trial," *Clinical Law Review*, 12(1).

Amsterdam, A.G. and Bruner, J.S. (2000), *Minding the Law: How Courts Rely on Storytelling and How their Stories Change the Ways We Understand the Law—and Ourselves*, Cambridge, MA: Harvard University Press.

Bennett, L.W. and Feldman, M.S. (1981), *Reconstructing Reality in the Courtroom: Justice and Judgment in American Culture*, New Brunswick, NJ: Rutgers University Press.

Bruner, J.S. (1990), *Acts of Meaning*, Cambridge, MA: Harvard University Press.

—— (1991), "The narrative construction of reality," *Critical Inquiry*, 18, 1–21.

—— (1992), "A Psychologist and the law," *New York Law School Law Review*, 37, 173–84.

—— (2002), *Making Stories: Law, Literature, Life*, Cambridge, MA: Cambridge University Press.

Cole, M. (1996), *Cultural Psychology: A Once and Future Discipline*, Cambridge, MA: Harvard University Press.

Cover, R.M. (1983), "The Supreme Court, 1982 Term—Foreword: Nomos and narrative," *Harvard Law Review*, 97, 4–68.

Di Donato, F. (2008a), "Client–lawyer cooperation in the construction of the case," *Cahiers de Psychologie et Education*, Institut de psychologie et éducation de l'Université de Neuchâtel, 44, 23–33, <http://www2.unine.ch/webdav/site/psy/shared/documents/publications/cahiers/Cahier44.pdf>.

—— (2008b), *La costruzione giudiziaria del fatto. Il ruolo della narrazione nel "processo"*, Milan: FrancoAngeli.

—— (2009a), "Conversing in the Garden on psychology, culture, law, and narration: An interview with Jerome Bruner" ("Conversando in giardino su psicologia, cultura, diritto e narrazione. Un'intervista a Jerome Bruner"), *Il Bigiavi: A Multilingual Sketchbook of the ISLL—Italian Society for Law and Literature*, <http://www.lawandliterature.org/area/documenti/Il%20Bigiavi_issue%201-2009.pdf>.

—— (2009b), "Una postilla a Conversing in the garden on psychology, culture, law, and narration: An interview with Jerome Bruner" ("A note on Conversing in the garden on psychology, culture, law, and narration: An interview with Jerome Bruner"), *ISLL Reviews*, <http://www.lawandliterature.org/area/documenti/Di%20Donato%20-%20Postilla%20Intervista%20Bruner.pdf>.

—— (2010), "La costruzione narrativa dei significati giuridici. Il fatto nel processo," *Symposium on Law and Literature—Research Perspectives: Proceedings of the First National Convention of the Italian Society for Law and Literature*, Bologna, 2009, 76–86, <http://www.lawandliterature.org/area/documenti/atti%20-%20I%20convegno%20ISLL%20maggio%202009.pdf>

Elmann, S. et al. (2009), *Lawyers and Clients: Critical Issues in Interviewing and Counseling*, St. Paul, MN: West Thomson Reuters.
Engeström, Y. (1987), *Learning by Expanding*, Helsinki: Orienta-Konsultit Oy.
Ewick, P. and Silbey S. (1998), *The Common Place of Law: Stories from Everyday Life*, Chicago, IL: University of Chicago Press.
Ferrari, V. (1993), "Teorie e metodo nell'analisi sociologica della litigiosità," *Contratto e Impresa*, 1, 342–54.
Haavisto, V. (2002), *Court Work in Transition: An Activity-theoretical Study of Changing Work Practices in a Finnish District Court*, Helsinki: Helsinki University Press.
Latour, B. (2002), *La Fabrique du droit. Une ethnographie du Conseil d'Etat*, La Découverte: Paris.
Merry, S.E (1992), "Culture, power, and the discourse of law," *New York Law School Law Review*, 37, 209–25.
Minda, G. (1995), *Postmodern Legal Movements: Law and Jurisprudence at Century's End*, New York and London: New York University Press.
Mittica, M.P. (2009), "Diritto e Letteratura in Italia. Stato dell'arte e riflessioni sul metodo," *Materiali per una storia della cultura giuridica*, 1, 273–300.
Nussbaum, M.C. (2001), *Upheavals of Thought: The Intelligence of Emotions*, Cambridge: Cambridge University Press.
Ost, F. (2004), *Raconter la loi. Aux sources de l'imaginaire juridique*, Paris: Odile Jacob.
Sherwin, R.K. (1994), "The narrative construction of legal reality," *Vermont Law Review*, 18(3).
Taruffo, M. (1992), *La prova dei fatti giuridici*, Milan: Giuffrè.
—— (2009a), "Cultura e processo," *Rivista Trimestrale*, 63(1), 63–92.
—— (2009b), *La semplice verità. Come i giudici costruiscono i fatti*, Rome and Bari: Laterza.
Twining, W. (2006), *Rethinking Evidence: Exploratory Essays*, Cambridge: Cambridge University Press.
Vygostky, L.S. ([1934] 1962), *Thought and Language*, Cambridge, MA: MIT Press.
White, H. (1980–81), "The Value of Narrativity in the Representation of Reality," in W.J.T Mitchell (ed.), *On Narrative*, Chicago, IL: University of Chicago Press, 3–23.
White, J.B. (1990), *Justice as Translation: An Essay in Cultural and Legal Criticism*, Chicago, IL: University of Chicago Press.

PART II
Power and Control behind Language

Chapter 7
Magical Images in Law

Christine A. Corcos[1]

Nemo videtur fraudare eos qui sciunt, et consentiunt.[2]

Introduction

In their current Las Vegas act, "bad boys of magic" Penn and Teller[3] make the US flag disappear from a flagpole, wrap it in a copy of the Bill of Rights and appear to set fire to it, and then redisplay the document, while Penn proclaims, "The flag is gone but the Bill of Rights remains!" (Penn and Teller 2010). They then end the illusion by "magically" restoring the flag to its pole.

The duo premiered this illusion ten years ago:

> In 2000, in the midst of all their tricks and commentary, they introduced a discussion of flag burning. Instead of making a red silk handkerchief disappear, the duo replaced it with a United States flag that appears to be set on fire. Penn explains as Teller lights the flag, 'The Supreme Court has defined speech very broadly to include many forms of expression and that includes doing anything you want to this flag. And, I mean any-thing. Take a piece of chemically treated tissue paper as tinder, a very eccentric magic wand (the Bill of Rights) and you can do this. And the Supreme Court says it's okay. Because even though the flag

---

1 I profited from discussions with Professors Jessie Allen, Paul Baier, Sydney Beckman, Ray Diamond, John Devlin and Bob Jarvis, and Sara Crasson of Mintz, Levin, Cohn, Ferris, Glovsky and Popeo. Shelley Luke (LSU Law 2006), Marikatherine Sonnier (LSU Law 2006), Joseph Rochelle (LSU Law 2008), H. Vey Laplace (LSU Law 2011), Charles Watkins (LSU Law 2012) and Stephanie Barreras (LSU Law 2012) provided excellent research and editing assistance. Any errors of phrase or thought are my own.

2 "One cannot complain of having been deceived when he knew the fact and gave his consent"; Ulpianus (Ulpian), "On the Edict," *Digest of Justinian* (1985), 50, 17, 145.

3 Throughout his career, Teller has publicized his refusal to speak during performances, although after the duo's shows he greets audience members and can be quite loquacious. Penn and Teller entered the secondary literature of popular culture some time ago. At least two doctoral dissertations discuss their contributions as well as those of other performers; see Harrison (1989) and Kattwinkel (1997).

> is gone, the Bill of Rights remains. We can only do that because we're working in a free country.[4]

The trick is well done, if a little heavy-handedly symbolic, and it emphasizes the similarities between magic and law. In order to make the flag and document reappear "magically," Penn and Teller do and say ritualistic things.

Penn then asks the question:

> Did we burn a flag? Did we symbolically burn a flag? Or did we merely vanish a flag in a patriotic flash of fireworks? It's all of those, it's none of those. It's up to you. Most shows, and movies, and tv are all fake, they're phony, they're fiction. And news and sports are supposed to be real. But Penn & Teller, we like to drive fast, right on down the middle, because sometimes we're showing you and telling the truth as we see it, from the bottom of our hearts. And sometimes we're lying, and cheating, and swindling. And it's up to you to figure that out.[5]

Penn and Teller do not intend their fancy footwork solely as entertainment. They, like all accomplished magicians, engage in a number of principles intended to distract and deceive audience members.[6] By adding "magic words" to their on-stage movement, which employs the cardinal principle of *misdirection*[7]—one

---

4 See Playboy Foundation (2006) and Penn and Teller (2007). "The Supreme Court says it's okay," in *Texas v Johnson* [1989] 491 US 397, because the state sought to punish Johnson for expressing one type of message by burning the US flag while allowing its burning for other means (for example, for disposal once it was damaged). "If we were to hold that a State may forbid flag burning wherever it is likely to endanger the flag's symbolic role, but allow it wherever burning a flag promotes that role—as where, for example, a person ceremoniously burns a dirty flag—we would be saying that when it comes to impairing the flag's physical integrity, the flag itself may be used as a symbol—as a substitute for the written or spoken word or a 'short cut from mind to mind'—only in one direction. We would be permitting a State to 'prescribe what shall be orthodox' by saying that one may burn the flag to convey one's attitude toward it and its referents only if one does not endanger the flag's representation of nationhood and national unity"; ibid., 416–17.

5 Penn and Teller (2007).

6 Richard Wiseman and Peter Lamont list the methods by which magicians commonly deceive audiences: "1) appearance … 2) vanish …3) transposition …4) transformation … 5) penetration …6) restoration …7) extraordinary feats …8) telekenesis …9) extrasensory perception"; see Wiseman and Lamont (1995), 8–25.

7 Wiseman and Lamont acknowledge that magicians disagree concerning the definition of misdirection, but agree that it is "central to conjuring." They note that "In its narrowest sense, it refers to the diversion of the spectator's attention away from a secret action, but it has also been used to refer to the entire field concerning the psychology of deception"; see ibid., 28–9, citing Mulholland (1963), 324. Mulholland himself was both a gifted magician and a CIA operative; see Robinson and Booth (2008), discussing Mulholland's career as a CIA agent in a role that echoed the work of another conjuror,

of the principles known to all magicians, with which they distract the willing, paying, audience, which involves itself intellectually in the performance to see the deception—they create the illusion that they have burned the flag. The magic words have nothing to do with what is really going on behind the scenes (or on the stage); that is, Penn and Teller could accomplish the trick without saying the words (although not without the movements required to hide the flag). Both the audience and the magicians know that the words do not create the result. But the audience wants the magicians to engage in the ritual—the saying of the magic words, and the use of the magic wand—and the magicians oblige, because all of this ritual is part of the spectacle. To return the flag, Penn says the appropriate language and he and his partner engage in the appropriate movements. The trick ends. When the audience leaves the theater, both it and the magicians know the illusions and the performance are over.

One lawyer-magician suggests that lawyers engage in misdirection as well. "Everyone knows that magicians misdirect audiences, that they visually and verbally disguise their dirty work .... Lawyers also engage in verbal misdirection by 'blindsiding' witnesses, focusing attention on strengths and away from weaknesses, substituting jury charm for legal substance, and bobbing and weaving with words to deflect, convince and prevail" (Baird 1989, 24).

Are "magic words" also a form of misdirection and ritual? Is much of required courtroom behavior simply ritual and incantation (Baird 1989, 24)? When judges use "magic words" or "magic formulas" in writing opinions, are they engaging in the same behavior?[8] Do they create anything substantive by using those words that were not there before? Do the words themselves "mean" anything? Or are they simply a distraction, serving as misdirection, and perhaps because of our insistence on them, denying due process to the clients of those who negligently omit them?[9] Do the wizards behind the curtain manipulate the system in some unfathomable way for their purposes while sending the rest of us on self-serving quests for witches' broomsticks?[10] To what extent can we compare the use of

---

Jasper Maskelyne, who worked for the British during World War II. See also Fisher ([1983] 2004).

8 On the history of the Legal Realists' juridical use of the term "magic words" and a detailed analysis of similarities between modern adjudication and ritual magic in other cultures, see Allen (2008) and Allen (2010). The bailiff's cry of "All rise" when the judge enters the room signals not simply that everyone recognizes the authority of the judge's power and office. It is part of the ritual that confirms the majesty of law and order. But do onlookers and parties really need to rise when the judge comes into court? Would the judge have less power if people did not rise, as long as they were quiet and attentive?

9 See Allen (2008), criticizing the rhetorical attack on "magic words" as a failure to consider the complexities of magic's social meanings and its capacity for social transformation, and Allen (2010), tracing the historical sources of the identification of formalistic legal reasoning with magic.

10 Consider the image of the witch's broom in Baum's *The Wizard of Oz*, first published in 1900. For discussion of politics and law in Baum's work, see Erisman (1968)

magic to the practice of law, and make magical analogies to legal practice? To what extent are such comparisons helpful and/or interesting? When parties, jurors, judges, lawyers, witnesses and onlookers leave the courtroom, are what "magic words" and ritual leave behind more "real" than what is on a magician's stage?

I do not intend to make legal formalism the entire subject of this chapter. Others discuss that subject elsewhere in greater depth. Consider, for example, Pierre Schlag's discussion of the law student's first encounter with "magic words" in law study:

> Still another aspect of the juridification of legal thought is the reliance on "magic words." Students, during their first year of law school, learn that in some legal contexts certain words are magic, in that their mere invocation can be guaranteed to induce certain effects upon legal actors. Such words might include "notice," or "possession," or "strict scrutiny." Legal thinkers often exhibit a haughty derision for the magic words—treating them as unfortunate (though perhaps necessary) legacies of formalism. Nonetheless, legal thinkers clearly have their own set of magic words—words like "values" and "rights" and "reason." These are words which, when accompanied with their usual grammar, will simply arrest thought upon impact.[11]

In a few pages, one cannot re-examine such a debate. But what one can begin to do is examine the repeated comparison that exists in the literature between magicians and attorneys, and question why this particular comparison should be so prevalent. Why do we so often see the phrases "magic words," "the rabbit in the hat" and "smoke and mirrors" applied to attorneys and the legal profession? Why do lawyers and judges apply such phrases to themselves and their behavior, and what do they mean to convey by such usages? Do practicing lawyer-magicians put magic into practice in the courtroom in order to translate stagecraft into "practical magic"? If so, how do other members of the legal profession react?

That a magician knows that magic words do not themselves create a particular effect is one thing. That he uses them to create the *illusion* that they do so is quite another. That becomes the substance of the magical effect, even though, without the words, the trick or illusion would still come off. Lawyers also know that words might or might not create a particular legal effect—hence the importance of the phrase "magic words."[12] Words may seem to be interchangeable, but they may not be so. Attorneys and judges spill a great deal of ink over just such issues. They know that magic phrases might create important *illusions*, and in law illusions can become reality. However, if courts or legislatures require magic phrases in order to create effects, then those phrases we must have, and the magic phrases then

---

and Dighe (2002).

11 Schlag (1995), 1,119 (footnotes omitted).

12 Police officers also pay tribute to "magic words"; see Napier and Adams (1998), 11, discussing phrases, techniques and body language to encourage suspects to confess crimes.

become the substance of law. If such "magic phrases" are lacking, then in order for the desired effect to occur, the lawyers drawing up a document must take care to provide for all the other legal requirements. But such outcomes are rare.[13] Thus, we agree that in order to create the legal effect, we must have the particular magic words, even though we might ordinarily think that other words might do just as well (Corcos 2010a).

Finally, some magicians, like Penn and Teller, have a particular interest in the legal meaning of the magical act. When Penn Jillette says that the difference between "burning a flag" on the Las Vegas stage and then restoring it is fiction, and that entertainment generally is fiction, he has a point. But the act is still "real." Penn and Teller "really" make the flag vanish.[14] When Penn discusses the law (and the Supreme Court opinion) that protects the act, he takes us further along a journey into discussion of the comparison between magic and law. Such "burning" and restoring is a magic trick, but it is also real, and it can be speech, just as the real burning of an American flag can also be speech (*Texas* v. *Johnson* 1989, 414).

Law–magic Comparisons

The law–religious magic connection began centuries ago,[15] but the law–secular magic connection emerged fairly recently.[16] We can trace it at least to 1872, and to the publication of attorney/magician Angelo John Lewis's seminal work *Modern Magic* which the London firm of Routledge and Sons commissioned.[17] For the cardinal sin of revealing secrets of conjuring, Lewis, who agreed according to the terms of the contract to take on a pseudonym, received £100 for a 380-page manuscript. Lewis chose the *nom de plume* of "Professor Hoffmann," a name by which he became either famous or infamous, depending on which side of the "Magician's Oath"[18] tangle one chooses to take. Himself an attorney, Lewis

---

13 See *Hatzel and Buehler* v. *Lovisa Construction* (1993), holding that the omission of the words "condition precedent" in a contract did not invalidate the requirement for payment on that contract because all requirements had in fact been met.

14 Since we do not know (or are not supposed to know) how the flag vanishes, we do not know if they burn it; see the discussion later in this chapter.

15 The history of the regulation of religious magic is beyond the scope of this chapter, but see, for example, Pharr (1932), 269–95. For historical and other comparisons, see also Marcovecchio (2010).

16 For a beautifully illustrated history of magic, see Caveney and Steinmeyer (2009).

17 The contract is available online at the link provided in Grossman (2004). According to the contract, "The book [was] to be written under a nom de plume to be agreed on by both parties and the true name of the author not to be published."

18 The "Magician's Oath" is an agreement not to reveal the secrets of magic except to an apprentice or to another magician. See, for example, the *SAM Code of Ethics* (American Society of Magicians 2010). It includes the promise to "Oppose the willful exposure to the public of any principles of the Art of Magic, or the methods employed in any magic effect

(Price 1985, 40–41) presumably saw no conflict between revealing magic tricks and any magician's oath. However, his magician colleagues did not and do not necessarily agree.

In the nineteenth century, the great secular magicians finally began to define their profession. Alexander Herrmann[19] offered the following passage in *The Art of Magic*:

> The magicians of Europe, beginning with Houdin and Cagliostro, have given a great impetus to their art. I regard the magicians of to-day as the best the world has ever produced. The perfection of mechanical contrivances and the possibilities of electricity and chemistry have been wonderful helps in the exercise of the so-called black art. It is well for the magician that such is the case, for the demands upon him for novelty were never greater. I find the spectators at this species of entertainment more numerous and more interested than those of thirty years ago. How to entertain them leads up to the other question, What are the requisites and qualifications of the magician? I could answer the question by a negative definition of what the magician should not be better than to state positively what his art should make him. No one regards the magician to-day as other than an ordinary man gifted with no extraordinary powers. The spectators come, not to be impressed with awe, but fully aware that his causes and effects are natural. They come rather as a guessing committee, to spy out the methods with which he mystifies. Hundreds of eyes are upon him. Men with more knowledge of the sciences than he come to trip and expose him, and to baffle their scrutiny is the study of his life. Long years of training and exercise alone will not make a magician. I could name a hundred men with these qualifications, who started out in the practice of legerdemain within the past thirty years. not one of whom is known now. There must be some natural aptitude for the art ; it must be born in a man, and can never be acquired by rule. He must be alert both in body and in mind; cool and calculating to the movement of a muscle under all circumstances; a close student of men and human nature. To these qualifications he must add the rather incongruous quality of a mind turning on contradictions. With a scientific

---

or illusion." The International Brotherhood of Magicians administers a similar oath to its members. For a copy, see Bowman (2010).

19 Herrmann was notable for assisting at least one woman to break through the magical glass ceiling. His wife Adelaide (née Scarcez) became not just a magician's assistant, but a magician in her own right. After Herrmann's death, she toured with a nephew, Leon Herrmann, then alone until the age of 75. She died in 1928. H.J. Burlingame gives Mrs. Herrmann's maiden name as Sersey; Burlingame (1897), 87. Burlingame notes: "Mme. Herrmann always traveled with her husband and she was with him at the time of his death. The two appeared on the stage together,—Herrmann, as the master of magic, the inscrutable Mephisto, weird and uncanny, while his wife, with her fresh beauty, served as a foil to her husband's supernatural appearance. At a wave from her husband's hand, or a shot from his pistol, she disappeared and reappeared in the most unexpected places …"; ibid., 112–13.

> cause he must produce a seemingly opposite effect to that warranted by order and system. I know of no life requiring such a series of opposite qualities as the magician's. And after the exercise of all these qualities I have named, resulting in the production of the most startling and novel results, the magician has not the satisfaction, like other men, of the enjoyment of his own product. He must be prepared to see it copied by others, or after a short time discovered by the public. Hence the magician must be an inventor, mechanical and scientific. Think of the time, thought, and weary labor given to the production of such tricks as the " cabinet mystery" of the Davenports, the " sealed tent" of the Eddys, the reading of letters in gummed envelopes, and the " second sight" of Houdin. All these are perplexing in their ingenuity, even after the methods of their performance are known. Again, so great are the demands of the public upon the magician that he can no longer use the machinery and mechanical contrivances of his own invention with which he cumbered the stage formerly. For the most part he must perform his wonders with his contrivances so reduced as to be invisible. Formerly he could extract his birds from bags and covered cages, his flowers and fruits from friendly and unsuspicious-looking tables, and his live animals from confederates. Now he must produce all these things from the coats and pockets of the spectators. I have not drawn a very rosy picture of the magician. I did not intend to do so. To the novice entering the life and promising himself ease, indolence, and wealth, I should say, "Don't!" I have often been asked if the pursuit I follow does not become monotonous. By no means. There is an ever-recurring novelty in the life. Even if the tricks performed admitted of only one method instead of a dozen in their performance, there are the same puzzled lookers-on, wondering, tricked, and baffled through the most simple and natural causes. The magician controls them as potently as the orator controls his audience, and the enjoyment of his power is even greater. Monotonous? Never! The life of the magician is one of almost infinite variety.[20]

At the same time, law was emerging as a self-defining profession, (Stevens 1983) establishing generally recognized codes of conduct, core bodies of knowledge and systematized training. Its transformation as a formal branch of learning, with defined modes of training that required university schooling, government-mandated examinations, and legislative and judicial oversight, had not yet begun.[21]

Both attorneys and magicians, who had found employment with the two traditional great users of talent—the Church and the state—now sought

20 Herrmann (1891), 95–6.

21 Attorneys were "called to the bar" early on in some countries, including England, Ireland and Scotland, and studied law in universities (the oldest known university to offer legal training was Bologna), but the system of legal education that we know today was not yet in place.

employment with the private sector.[22] Seeking remuneration, secular magicians decided to pursue it as first a hand-to-mouth existence in the streets, in which they were only partially successful,[23] and eventually as full-blown entertainment in the theaters of the period. Soon magicians, like other performers, were drawing large and appreciative audiences[24] because they successfully relabeled their work as entertainment rather than as deception. The art of secular magic was increasingly respectable. Indeed, the great French conjuror Robert-Houdin chose his costume, traditional evening dress, in order to give his performance credibility. Dressing like one's audience put the magician on a par with it. Moving the performances from the streets to the theaters, and allowing the audiences the luxury of sitting down while one took their money, meant that one had achieved a kind of respectability.

The Lawyer/Magician Analogy[25]

Like magicians, lawyers affect a particular code of dress. Like magicians, they follow a code of conduct. But lawyers had and have the advantage of official gatekeeping, both for their profession and for society at large.[26] Unlike magicians, who have always relied on self-policing to maintain a conjuror's creed,[27] lawyers quickly developed the benefit of their own power and the government itself to bring down of members of their profession who do not uphold the lawyer's oath.

Lawyers themselves often analogize between magic and law.[28] References to lawyers as magicians, as magical beings who can repair impossible situations, abound. In some cases, attorneys imitate magicians. As Howard Nations says in his article "Overcoming juror bias":

22 A number of books detail the rise of the performing magician during the period of the early to mid-nineteenth century, including Jean-Eugene Robert-Houdin (1805–1871). See Caveney and Steinmeyer (2009), Robert-Houdin (2006) and Bailey (2007).

23 Early on, governments tended to discourage magicians, as they tended to discourage other performers, through the use of vagrancy acts; see, for example, Beier (1985).

24 See, for example, Bailey (2007). Bailey, a long-time magician and former President of The Magic Circle, provides an interesting and detailed account of the organization as well as the history of magic and magicians.

25 For more analogies, see Marcovecchio (2010), and particularly with regard to the courtroom, see Trombly (2010).

26 For the history of the legal profession in the United States, see Stevens (1983). For the legal profession in other countries, see generally Abel and Lewis (1988–89).

27 On secular magic norms, see Loshin (2010) and Dougherty (2010).

28 I could find few extended explicit mentions in the literature to the analogy between magic and law dated prior to 2007. However, Weyrauch (1973), comparing "magic and magicians to law and lawyers," and Traynor (1961) are instructive, as is Baird (1989). Corcos (2010a) includes 24 essays explicitly comparing various facets of law and magic.

> Magicians understand the principle of clinging to perceptions. They use this principle to create miracles. They know that if they can fool our senses into perceiving that something is so, we will believe it. Once we believe that something is so, even though it is not, we accept it. In fact, something else is really taking place. But that doesn't matter to our senses. We continue along with a certain belief. We believe the magician's assistant is in the box. This is not so. We are then faced with the surprise ending when we find the magician assistant is gone and is appearing from another point on the stage. Because our reality is based on perceptions, on what we perceive to be true, we have been fooled.[29]

Magicians have conditioned us to expect that when they or their assistants get in the box, something "magical" will happen—probably an inexplicable disappearance of some kind. This impression arises from the "metamorphosis illusion."[30] Penn and Teller (and some other magicians) use this conditioning to their advantage. They guest-tar in the final episode of the television series *Listen Up*.[31] In that episode, Teller stalks series regular Wendy Makkena, who plays Dana. He pops out of a large box in her Vegas hotel room. When she tells him she is happily married, he disconsolately reclaims the flowers he has given her and climbs back in the box. He finds the fact that she is unavailable a "cruel deception."[32] "I get it," she tells Penn. "He's going to disappear and the box will be empty." "No," says Penn. "He just likes to cry in private." Since the hotel room is not a stage (even though the entire routine takes place within a television episode, itself an illusion), Penn and Teller would have no way to prepare such a trick, even though they could—they are, after all, on a television show. They are human beings and secular magicians, not imaginary magical constructs. Sometimes what seems like an illusion is reality, and sometimes what seems like reality is an illusion. The trick is in developing the ability to tell the difference.

Similarly, in their stage show at the Rio Hotel in Las Vegas, Penn and Teller begin their performance by inviting audience members to close their eyes in order to avoid seeing the way in which Teller actually exits the glass box in which we first see him. How does he leave it? If one thinks about it long enough, one will divine the answer—that nothing supernatural, or even amazing is involved. Teller must somehow open the box and climb out. Sometimes a cigar is just a cigar—and

29 Nations (2003).

30 Harry Blackstone, Jr. says of "Metamorphosis": "The final revelation of the magician satisfies [the audience's] expectations and is an effective dramatic climax. If the bag were to be untied and someone else found inside, [the audience] would be surprised, but also somehow disappointed. As many magicians … have discovered, the surprise ending is not always the best ending"; Blackstone (1985), 147.

31 "Last Vegas," *Listen Up* (2005). Actor Jason Alexander, a trained magician, was the star and executive producer; see IMBD (2010a).

32 Coming from a magician, whose stock in trade is lying, this comment is the ultimate irony.

a brilliant magician is just a balding man in a nicely tailored gray suit. Otherwise put, professional (secular) magicians are in the business of deception. Notes magician Jamy Ian Swiss, "I am an honest liar. I am going to lie to you but that's okay. It's my job" (Waldman et al. 1997, 15).

But not all lawyers appreciate or encourage the lawyer–magician analogy. As one practitioner notes:

> In other instances, lawyers try to differentiate themselves from magicians, or distance themselves from the comparison with magicians. It is no secret that the truly great trial attorneys have most often been those individuals who, not only are skilled in the preparation in pursuit of a cause of action, but also, those who can carefully select what cases should be pursued. It is incumbent to remember that we, as trial attorneys, are truly lawyers and not magicians. Causes of action must be built upon creditable facts capable of collaboration either by expert testimony or lay testimony or both. Cases that result in the presentation of bad facts, even in an environment of good law, will result in less than favorable results for the plaintiff.[33]

After all, lawyers are not stage magicians. They do not control all aspects of the "performance." They cannot really "do magic." That is, they cannot always pull victory from the jaws of defeat if to do so means consistently performing legal "miracles" or impossibilities. But unlike magicians, nearly all lawyers consistently and publicly disclaim that ability.[34] That clients also ask them to be "magicians," attorneys view with varying degrees of hostility:[35]

> Acting within this often esoteric area of the law, patent lawyers are called upon to play the roles of chemists, engineers, physicians, and physicists—now, they are also asked to be magicians. That is, patent lawyers are asked to defend—with smoke and incantations when necessary--business-driven decisions having nothing to do with inventing or discovering anything.[36]

Note that this particular commentator probably intends to refer to stage magic, even though he mentions "incantations."

---

33 Hailey (2003).

34 "As I tell my new clients, criminal defense appeal lawyers are not magicians or miracle workers"; Brenner (2010). But see the image on his website (a magician with top hat, rabbit and magic wand). See also the comments of defense attorney Edward D. Tolley in the case of convicted mail bomber Walter Moody, Jr.: "We're lawyers, not magicians"; Montgomery (1991).

35 Courts also reject the comparison. See the section in this chapter on "Magic Words and Magic Acts."

36 *McNeil-PPC* v. *Perrigo* (2003), 1,367–8.

We also see judges described as magicians[37] when commentators reflect on their considerable power. Writes one law professor: "The case for positive rights implicitly presumes that judges are benevolent magicians, willing and able to wave a wand and thereby dispel the sad conditions of poverty" (Cross 2001, 923). Invariably, when the analogy invokes the magician, the comparison denigrates the judge:[38]

> The majority, like the trial judge, has been led astray and has assumed that the patent in suit is on some imaginary "system" for detecting flaws, which has enjoyed commercial success in the hands of Alco and was copied by Westinghouse, thus changing the prima facie obvious invention into a patentable invention. What has happened here is that by a kind of magician's distracting patter, the purpose of which is to keep the viewer from observing what is actually happening, attention has been directed to the patent's claims to the exclusion of its *disclosure*.[39]

In this 1982 article about the Hinckley trial, Watson compares the entire proceeding to an extended "magic show," and the judge to a conjuror in charge of the event:

> The magician (the judge) is the one who makes things happen, but it is his goal to avoid detection while doing so. He accomplishes this by misdirection; that is, by guiding the attention of the audience (the jury and the public) to amusing patter (the psychiatrists). While the audience's attention is engaged thus, he pulls the verdict from his sleeve, ingenuously attributing its appearance to magic. This show would be more entertaining, of course, if it were not such a serious social issue. Now, consider the task of the jury in the Hinckley trial. The judge, with his knowledge, wisdom and power, had declared that the defendant was insane, and by doing so challenged the prosecution to prove otherwise. Since insanity is a mythical animal, this was equivalent to declaring that the unicorn is white, or that 100 angels can dance on the head of a pin, or that invisible fire-breathing dragons cause forest fires—and then challenging someone to prove

---

37 Note that a good many judges are practicing magicians. On the US Court of Appeals for the 9th Circuit, Alex Kozinski and Barry Silverman, and Senior Judge Stephen Trott are all conjurors. Loren A. Smith of the US Court of Claims practices magic, both in and out of court; see Carter (1997) and Smith (2010), 3. For more attorney magicians, see Corcos (2010b).

38 That attorneys come in for criticism should not surprise us. Most societies criticize, satirize or otherwise marginalize lawyers, particularly in popular culture; see, for example, Galanter (2005). Bill Berger (a trial lawyer himself) and Ricardo Martinez wrote a popular book some years ago titled *What To Do With a Dead Lawyer*, Berger and Martinez (1988). People may make jokes about magicians, but they don't *despise* them. I cannot imagine a similar book entitled *What To Do With a Dead Magician.*

39 *Alco* v. *TVA* (1986), 1,505.

> otherwise. Seen in this light, the task of the jury was simple. The prosecution had no chance.[40]

Whether or not what Watson says about psychiatry and the law is accurate is not the issue. What is interesting is the analogy he draws between the role of the magician and that of the judge, or more precisely, between the actions of the stage magician performing to an audience which *expects* to be deceived and the actions of the judge in the courtroom. The public and parties do not *expect* the legal system to deceive them, even though they may think, somewhat cynically, that they may lose a case because an opponent has more money or influence. Certainly, they do not expect their own lawyers to deceive them.

Watson, however, takes the position that such an expectation is naive at best. Note that he is not referring to stage or secular magic. The evocation of the unicorn and angels tells us that. He invokes religious magic, that is, the kind of magic to which one must truly be "initiated" in the sense that clergy mean the term, and that secular magicians do not. This kind of magic has no rational explanation. One can study for years and still never understand the philosophy of this type of magic. Further, we cannot protect ourselves by rational means against religious magic if an evil entity wields it against us, as he suggests is the case here. Instead, we need a champion with stronger magic.

By contrast, one could learn the basis for a secular magic trick. Individuals might theoretically not agree on the philosophy behind the successful psychology of a stage illusion, but that is a different matter.[41] Secular magicians do "initiate" their members into professional associations, but they do not threaten them with bodily harm if they do not follow the rules.[42] Evoking the mythological medieval argument over angels dancing on the heads of pins suggests both that legal arguments are insoluble and also that they are arcane and pointless.[43]

Watson also suggests that "the judge as magician" is in charge of the entire proceeding, and that the proceeding is some kind of pseudoscientific spectacle—that it is an extraordinary claim that cannot be refuted and that illogically places

---

40 Watson (1982). Watson is a psychiatrist; see Watson (2004). Watson does have a point in this article: he is arguing for abolition of the use of psychiatrists as expert witnesses on the question of legal insanity. My interest here is only in his use of the image of the judge as magician.

41 Penn and Teller's routine explaining the seven principles of sleight of hand (palm, ditch, steal, load, simulation, misdirection, switch) is available at various URLs on the net, including Penn and Teller (2009).

42 However, note that The Magic Circle expelled David Devant (born David Wighton) for revealing the secrets of some illusions, and Patrick Page for writing a book that revealed too many secrets; see Steinmeyer (2003), 306.

43 It also recalls the old libel that medieval writers actually occupied themselves with this kind of argument, a question that was long ago laid to rest; see Franklin (1982), suggesting that the dispute was invented by nineteenth century writers, including perhaps Erasmus Darwin, in order to create the illusion that medieval philosophers were pedantic.

the responsibility for proof on the individuals or parties who are not making the claim. But he has misplaced the burden of proof, not only in terms of law, but in terms of science. As scientist Marcello Truzzi explains:

> In his famous 1748 essay *Of Miracles*, the great skeptic David Hume asserted that "A wise man proportions his belief to the evidence," and he said of testimony for extraordinary claims that "the evidence, resulting from the testimony, admits of a diminution, greater or less, in proportion as the fact is more unusual." A similar statement was made by Laplace, and many other later writers. I turned it into the now popular phrase "extraordinary claims require extraordinary proof" (which Carl Sagan popularized into what is almost the war cry of some scoffers).[44]

In another article, Watson continues the analogy:

> The game of law is premised on the notion that a false champion cannot win a contest against a truthful one, a superstition rooted in the mists of mythology.

---

44 See Truzzi (1998). Writers often cite David Hume's writing on miracles, but rarely read him or quote his entire passage on the subject. Here is the relevant section: "A miracle is a violation of the laws of nature; and as a firm and unalterable experience has established these laws, the proof against a miracle, from the very nature of the fact, is as entire as any argument from experience can possibly be imagined. Why is it more than probable, that all men must die; that lead cannot, of itself, remain suspended in the air; that fire consumes wood, and is extinguished by water; unless it be, that these events are found agreeable to the laws of nature, and there is required a violation of these laws, or in other words, a miracle to prevent them? Nothing is esteemed a miracle, if it ever happen in the common course of nature. It is no miracle that a man, seemingly in good health, should die on a sudden: because such a kind of death, though more unusual than any other, has yet been frequently observed to happen. But it is a miracle, that a dead man should come to life; because that has never been observed in any age or country. There must, therefore, be a uniform experience against every miraculous event, otherwise the event would not merit that appellation. And as a uniform experience amounts to a proof, there is here a direct and full proof, from the nature of the fact, against the existence of any miracle; nor can such a proof be destroyed, or the miracle rendered credible, but by an opposite proof, which is superior.[3] The plain consequence is (and it is a general maxim worthy of our attention), 'that no testimony is sufficient to establish a miracle, unless the testimony be of such a kind, that its falsehood would be more miraculous, than the fact, which it endeavors to establish; and even in that case there is a mutual destruction of arguments, and the superior only gives us an assurance suitable to that degree of force, which remains, after deducting the inferior.' When anyone tells me, that he saw a dead man restored to life, I immediately consider with myself, whether it be more probable, that this person should either deceive or be deceived, or that the fact, which he relates, should really have happened. I weigh the one miracle against the other; and according to the superiority, which I discover, I pronounce my decision, and always reject the greater miracle. If the falsehood of his testimony would be more miraculous, than the event which he relates; then, and not till then, can he pretend to command my belief or opinion"; Hume ([1748] 2000).

> In the legendary court of King Arthur, Merlin the magician guaranteed that jousting matches between champions infallibly determined truth and justice. Believing that a contest between champions can determine the truth still requires believing in magic. Absent real magic, the game of law relies on misdirection, illusion, and deception. To this end, wordplay has replaced swordplay for today's semantic warriors, for words are easily twisted into images that correspond equally well to fiction and reality.[45]

Again, Watson collapses religious magic and secular magic (although he makes a pass at differentiating the two—"absent real magic"). He analogizes words and images. He alleges that "the game of law relies on misdirection, illusion, and deception."[46]

Ultimately, while an attorney (particularly a defense attorney) may come perilously close to the line of deception, ho or she may not cross it. His or her job is to defend, as far as possible, but never to lie. The public has difficulty understanding the difference, which may help to account for the truly bad reputation that lawyers have always had in popular culture. The magician, on the other hand, may rest securely in his[47] convictions that deception is acceptable, as long as he reveals it to the audience.[48]

The analogy of the lawyer as magician turns up in tax law,[49] in family law (Lidman and Hollingsworth 1998), in intellectual property law[50] and in many

---

45 Watson (1994), discussing the O.J. Simpson trial.

46 That law is "a game" is not new with Watson. See, for example, Cardozo (1931) and an extended discussion of the "law as game" in popular culture in Corcos (2003).

47 While percentages on the number of male versus female magicians are difficult to obtain, one can easily observe that males have dominated and continue to dominate the profession; see Mendelsohn (2005), stating that of the Society of American Magicians' 9,000 members in 2005, fewer than 800 were women.

48 The admission is crucial. The *misuse* of magic is a "cardinal sin" for some secular magicians, and when they see activities that they believe constitute that misuse, they become incensed. One former magician who has turned to active debunking fulltime is James "The Amazing" Randi; see JREF (2001) and Garrison (1995). I hope to discuss the use of that deception and the dialog that it may engender between lawyers and magicians in future articles.

49 See examples in the writings of Johnston (2000), Picker (2007) and Tierney (1999). Hanna (2005) devotes pp. 742–55 to a comparison of magic and tax law (the "too perfect theory" of magic), and pp. 755–763 to applying this theory to tax. I began my examination of magic and law long before I came across his work, but was pleased to discover it.

50 "Acting within this often esoteric area of the law, patent lawyers are called upon to play the roles of chemists, engineers, physicians, and physicists—now, they are also asked to be magicians. That is, patent lawyers are asked to defend—with smoke and incantations when necessary—business-driven decisions having nothing to do with inventing or discovering anything. Consistent with schemes to prolong the legally-protected period of exclusivity, companies hire highly talented attorneys to perform acts of legal legerdemain

other areas.[51] Such rhetoric emphasizes the image of both lawyer and magician as "miracle worker"—of both professionals as individuals as persons who can perform feats that are unexplainable to the uninitiated lay person, often mystified by the performances these professionals carry out. Both lawyers and magicians have arcane language that they repeat during their mysterious rituals. Both take money for their services. The lawyer, no matter how skilled, cannot promise an outcome. But the skilled magician must do so, if his audience is to leave pleased, gratified and disinclined to request a refund.

An astonishing number of attorneys pursue careers as magicians, apparently seeing a clear parallel between the creation of stories in the courtroom and narrative on the stage.[52] They may also detect the same habits of mind necessary for the successful performance of magic and the successful practice of law.[53]

We must also consider whether a comparison between the magician and the lawyer is entirely apt, to the extent that although what happens is "real", the performer always relies on the result as illusion. Magicians cannot defy the laws of nature, although they use them to advantage.[54] What happens in the courtroom,

---

in order to make modest developments look and feel like inventions, when in reality the purported discovery is nothing more than a creation of an advertising and marketing department"; *McNeil-PPC* v. *Perrigo* (2002), 374. Note the comparison of the judge both to a stage magician—"legal legerdemain"—and arguably to a religious magician—"smoke and incantations." Although the stage magician could use both legerdemain and smoke and incantations, few stage magicians still do so, but the popular image of the stage magician may still linger. See also Dolak (2002).

51 John W. Cooley develops an extended comparison between magicians and mediators in his article "Mediation Magic: Use and abuse," Cooley (1997). Mark Suchman examines magic as an intellectual property construct in preliterate societies in an article in the *Columbia Law Review*, Suchman (1989).

52 Lawyer-magicians exist in nearly every legal regime. Many Spanish lawyers are members of the Spanish national magicians' society: "[Matthew Haicken] joined the Spanish Society of Magicians, and attended weekly meetings. 'A lot of magicians there are lawyers,' Haicken says. 'I think they both have to do with fooling people'"; Rourke (2002). One Chilean lawyer magician is Enrique Gonzales; see <http://bubbles.org/html/adventures/chile/rehearsal2.htm>. Among other lawyers who actively studied the illusory arts were Gary Ouellet, the Canadian lobbyist who worked for magician David Copperfield (see Ubelacker 2002), and Frederick Garland, a Texas legislator (Landis 2010). I list many lawyer magicians at my blog Law and Magic; Corcos (2010b). Daniel Wise writes about more lawyer-magicians; see Wise (1991).

53 Author telephone conversation with Sydney Beckman, April 18, 2006, Baton Rouge, LA. Magicians, of course, do combine the conjuring arts with other professions—notably medicine; see Sokol (2008).

54 Much of the literature about deception is concerned with whether the ordinary individual can detect deception, and if not, whether if the individual fails to do so, he or she can bring an action against the deceiver. The popular and academic press is full of such discussion, and it is gaining in popularity; see, for example, Green (2006). The number of persons who objected to James Frey's presentation of his memoir *A Million Little Pieces*

while it may be "illusion", is necessarily real. We must always be able to tell the difference. The difference between stage blood and real blood is vital, just as the difference between a murder on stage during a play and a murder in real life have entirely different consequences.[55]

Considering again the "woman sawed in half" illusion (and women are almost always the target of this particular trick), commentator Jaq Greenspon points out that:

> In the late '70s, a magician named Richiardi closed his show with an absolutely stunning illusion. He took his young assistant and cut her in half. That's it. There was no resolution beyond it. He would invite the audience to walk up and examine the corpse, entrails and all. For Teller, the smaller and quieter half of Penn & Teller, the brilliance was in leaving the audience with a feeling of intellect and not of horror, despite the viscera dripping across the stage. "It's interesting to see what people say as they walk by," Teller recalls Richiardi saying. "I remember one time a gentleman saying, 'It's a trick.' Of course it's a trick. I couldn't actually kill a woman every night I do the show. But is it well done?" That's the question: How well does the illusion do what it sets out to do? For Teller, this is what he wants to know, and part of the answer reveals where he thinks magic is heading. "Most magicians, like comedians, measure success by the audience's reaction, not how well they're getting their point across. If it gets a big reaction, then it's a good trick. Fuck them. If it does what you want it to, then it's a good trick." For Penn & Teller, a good trick is one where there's a collision between what you see and what you know, the intellectual with the visceral. For other magicians as well, the visceral is becoming more of the point.

---

as fact when the news broke that it was fabricated, for example, suggests that at least some people believe that a book presented as "truth" should be "substantially true," even if they do not formulate their argument in that way and they believe that they have an actionable claim against an author (and perhaps a publisher) who has marketed a book as "true" which is substantially "not true," in that it purports to be a "memoir" or an "autobiography" but is mostly invention. The furor over the *James Frey* case suggests that while the law may be on his side, ethics perhaps are not. Random House recently agreed to make restitution to readers who have their receipts to submit part of the book (p. 163 of the hardcover edition, for example) and sign a statement saying that they would not have purchased the book if they had known that it was not truthful; see Rich (2006).

55 Kurtz (1994). However, any number of plays, movies and novels use the now familiar plot device in which a mysterious someone, usually the killer, substitutes a real murder weapon for a stage weapon, thus doing in an unsuspecting victim. *Columbo Goes to the Guillotine* uses a variation on this trite plot when a magician changes the set-up on the extremely dangerous "guillotine trick" and does in a rival who knows his guilty secret; see "Columbo Goes to the Guillotine," *Columbo* (1999).

> While the reaction is always the point, the storylines have changed; and the modern magician isn't always as interested in the happy ending.[56]

For the magician, "of course it's a trick," and he does not "really" saw the woman in half. However, the lawyer who wants to win a case in court wants to win in reality; film lawyer Billy Flynn's suggestion that "razzle dazzle" is all one needs (*Chicago* 2002) may be attractive in the abstract, but is unlikely to succeed in the long term. Further, the judge might censure the lawyer who indulges in it.[57]

What does happen in the courtroom, however, *becomes and remains real.* Only appellate courts (or perhaps a legislature) can change its effects. To quote Penn Jillette once again:

> When you're watching Psycho, there's that moment when you have a visceral reaction to watching someone being stabbed. And then you have the intellectual revelation that you're not, and that's where the celebration comes in.[58]

What is on the screen is illusion. For Penn, part of the value of the illusion is in the thought experiment, which the First Amendment protects, just as it protects the magic that he practices.[59]

The Stage and the Courtroom: Illusion and Reality

> Pull a rabbit out of your hat. That's the secret both to trial law and life.[60]

Comparisons Between Law and Magic

The comparison between law and magic and between the lawyer and the magician is not really so strange, as some commentators have pointed out (Marcovecchio 2010; Trombly 2010). In addition, in ancient times, the wizard, or the magus, often represented law and order. Fictional wizard characters, too, such as the Wizard of Oz (Baum 1973) and the various wizards (Saruman the White, Sauron, Gandalf the Grey) in J.R.R. Tolkien's *The Lord of the Rings*[61] represent varying types of order amid chaos. Quite often in role-playing games today, the "wizard" character

---

56 Greenspon (2004). Teller himself claims to have "evil thoughts" that drive his illusions; see NPR (2000).

57 See "The Magician Argument" below.

58 Kurtz (1994).

59 See generally such cases as *Burstyn* v. *Wilson* (1952), *Hustler* v. *Falwell* (1988) and other Supreme Court cases that protect the artist's freedom of speech and expression.

60 "Head Cases," *Boston Legal* (2004).

61 Tolkien (1954–56). A wizard like Saruman may represent a type of law and order that, while it is repressive, is still a type of law and order.

represents law and order, or justice. As an example, consider the role played by the wizard who "toads" (or eliminates) Mr. Bungle, the malefactor in the Lambda MOO (MUD Object Oriented online text-based game) Dibbell describes first in his *Village Voice* article "A rape in cyberspace" (Dibbell 1993) and then in his book *My Tiny Life*,[62] an expansion of the *Village Voice* piece.

The struggle between the wizard/magician (that is, the religious purveyor of law and order) and the attorney to control the bases of authority is a very old one. We can compare it to a question that has bedeviled students of jurisprudence for centuries: is the authority for law supernatural or natural in origin? Does the sovereign rule by divine right or by the will of the people? As Ernst Kantorowicz notes in his influential work *The King's Two Bodies*:

> We need only replace the strange image of the Two Bodies by the more customary theological term of the Two Natures in order to make it poignantly felt that the speech of the Elizabethan lawyers derived its tenor in the last analysis from theological diction, and that their speech itself, to say the least, was crypto-theological. Royalty, by this semi-religious terminology, was actually expounded in terms of Christological definitions. The jurists, styled by Roman Law so suggestively "Priests of Justice," developed in England not only a "Theology of Kingship"—this had become customary everywhere on the Continent in the course of the twelfth and thirteenth centuries—but worked out a genuine "Royal Christology."[63]

To what extent can we compare the stage and the courtroom, and to what extent is what happens on stage as "real" as what happens in the courtroom?[64] First, both the magician and the lawyer attempt to control the "performance"—both "practice" in the sense that the magician rehearses his tricks, his patter, the links between his illusions to create a complete performance, and the lawyer rehearses his or her opening and closing arguments, and the arc of the case to the extent that that is possible. No lawyer wants to be surprised at trial, so any attorney attempts to prepare as much as possible for any circumstance that might arise during the proceeding. Similarly, the magician practices over and over, trying to anticipate

62 Dibbell (1998). "Toading," an extreme punishment in the world of the MOO, is "virtual death." The wizard, a player who has complete control over all the characters in the MOO, decides that the player who has created such havoc really must be eliminated because he or she has refused to play by the rules of the game. Rather than wait for the democratic decision of the other members of the MOO, the wizard, who has been quietly "sitting by," as Dibbell describes it, "listening in," disappears, "takes the law into his own hands" and "toads" or kills the player's character so that he or she cannot continue to contravene the rules of the MOO. Like the wizard, the magician has "the power of life and death," if only for the period that the magic show lasts; see Caveney and Steinmeyer (2009), 35–9.

63 Kantorowicz (1957), 16.

64 For a lawyer-magician's view of how to construct "reality" in the courtroom and on stage, see Trombly (2010), 341–2.

whatever might go wrong during a performance. Rehearsal is absolutely necessary (Abowitz 2008). As many guides on magic performance make clear, knowing how to recover from a trick gone awry is what separates the professional magician from the amateur, and what can rescue a performance (Pogue 1998, 309). Note, however, that one of the major differences between the courtroom proceeding and the magic performance is that one lawyer does not control the proceeding. One magician (or perhaps two) *does* control the magic performance.

Second, the extent to which what happens on stage and what happens in the courtroom is "true" differs. What do we mean by "truth"? If we mean by "true" or "truth" something that approximates reality—that the magician on stage "really" saws a woman in half—then of course the magician does not "really" do that. When Penn Jillette discusses the disappearance (the "vanish") of the flag on stage ("Did we burn the flag? Or did we just vanish the flag?"), he is not simply engaging in semantics. He is asking an important question. Does the flag leave the stage permanently? Of course not. But do he and Teller make us think it disappeared, at least for a few minutes? Yes, they make us think so. It vanishes, and when they make us think so, they also induce us to wonder about what would happen if the country disappeared, and if the rights we associate with the country disappeared as well. That is the point of their trick, and the meaning of their illusion.

In a courtroom proceeding, someone "really" wins and someone "really" loses, in the sense that someone prevails in a tort action, for example, or is acquitted of burglary. At law, we obtain some kind of "truth" in the sense that we settle disputes. Even if we do not attain objective truth, we agree on some version of the truth in order to move on with life. But if by "truth" we mean "what really happened" at a particular time in the past, and if we expect the legal proceeding to elicit one version of the truth upon which everyone agrees, then we have not really designed our legal system to do that. No one in the courtroom knows what "really" happened in that sense, except—perhaps—the defendant in a criminal trial if he or she is guilty, for example. The prosecution and the defense present competing theories of what "really" happened to the jury, and the jury chooses one that seems to comport with its view of "reality"—often a default theory if the prosecution has not proven guilt beyond a reasonable doubt.

But a magical performance is different. If a magician "really" saws his beautiful assistant in half, he will probably go on trial for a serious crime. What a magician does when he "saws" his assistant in half is something quite different.[65] He creates the illusion that he has bisected her in order to put her back together. The illusion is

65 Horace Goldin, the American magician who claimed to have originated the "woman sawn in half" illusion, spent a good deal of his life trying to prove it, suing among others P.T. Selbit, the man whom magic historians generally now recognize as having created the illusion, and R.J. Reynolds Tobacco. Ironically, Goldin's attempts to prove that the stage illusion associated with him was in fact his creation cost him a fortune and ultimately ended in failure; see Goldin (1937), *Goldin* v. *Clarion Photoplays* (1922) and *Goldin* v. *R.J. Reynolds Tobacco* (1938).

one of the magician's very best tricks. It vests in the magician the (illusory) power of life and death—the power that judges and juries have in reality.

The magician knows the "truth" because he has constructed it. Like the attorney who writes the brief which he or she presents to the court or the judge who writes the opinion, the magician knows the intricacies of the illusions. In most instances, he offers no explanation of the trick to the audience. He simply performs the trick and allows the audience to wonder, and to speculate endlessly. Some audience members will envision one theory, some another. Nearly all will be incorrect. In this way, magicians safeguard their secrets and encourage a return audience. "How did he do that?" is a cry that earns repeat business for magicians. It works wonders for lawyers as well, but legal analysts make a career out of explaining how lawyers do it, and they breach no oath by explaining the workings of the law to the public.

Fool Me Once: Lawyers' Tricks and Magicians' Illusions

For the attorney, "How did he do that?" will often evoke anger. The very "tricks" that elicit admiration from an audience when performed by a magician cause fury when performed by a lawyer. Again, we often see "magical vocabulary" invoked when lay persons criticize or dislike judicial opinions[66] or attorney behavior.

In examining the analogy between a magician's stage performance and a lawyer's courtroom performance and the control that each maintains over their respective arenas, attorney-magician Peter D. Baird of the Phoenix law firm Lewis & Roca comments:

> Neither lawyers nor magicians traffic in objective reality. In a magic show, the audience never sees reality, the lady does not get sawed in half and the tiger does not vanish into thin air. In the law, there is not a such thing as absolute reality either because every event, crime, accident, contract or statute is subject to as many interpretations as there are witnesses to testify, lawyers to argue and, sadly enough, clients to pay fees.[67]

Yet legal analysts do not risk disbarment if they explain the workings of the court or possible legal theories of the prosecution or defense of an upcoming case to an eagerly listening television audience. Indeed, such people can earn a tidy living by performing such services. By contrast, "exposure," the explanation of just how magicians perform such famous tricks as the "cups and balls" or the "bullet catch," for example, causes violent debate among magicians. Some believe that such "exposure," the explanation of how conjurors complete such tricks or perform illusions, means that many potential audience members will lose interest

66 See, for example, Mason (2010), a Web page criticizing actions and rulings of the 11th Circuit.

67 Baird (1989), 24. Baird's article makes a good many points extremely economically, and is an excellent place to start to explore the issue.

in attending magic performances. Others disagree. Penn and Teller have built much of their fame on their willingness to explain many famous tricks (the "cups and balls" and the "American flag" illusion, though not the "bullet catch," which ends their current Las Vegas show).[68]

What might account for the difference in treatment between an exposure of legal "secrets" and an exposure of magic "secrets"? Even though in US law individuals can represent themselves (though not others) in court, the legal profession itself acts as a gatekeeper for the profession. Using state-administered examinations, it controls the number of individuals who may practice the profession, for example. One cannot simply advertise oneself as an attorney. On the other hand, one need not belong to any particular association, nor pass any examinations, nor attend any school, nor receive any diploma to practice magic. One need only acquire a certain level of proficiency, and if one wishes to become known as a professional, obtain paying clients. If lawyers wish to impose particular standards of behavior on all members of the profession, they can do so in a number of ways, including by statute. If magicians wish to impose professional norms on members of their profession, they must do so through informal means. If lawyers wish to keep private or confidential secrets of their profession, including for example client secrets, they can do so through the passage of ethical or disciplinary rules.[69] By contrast, if magicians wish to keep professional secrets, they can do so through relatively awkward mechanisms such as the rules of professional associations,[70] or through non-disclosure agreements.[71] Yet intellectual property law seems to provide relatively inefficient mechanisms for many US magicians to protect themselves against competition.[72]

In *Hiding the Elephant*, Jim Steinmeyer explains some of the technique behind the magician's performance:

> The success of a magician lies in making a human connection to the magic, the precise focus that creates a fully realized illusion in the minds of the audience. The simple explanation is that seldom do the crude gimmicks in a magic show—those mirrors, threads, or rubber bands—deceive people. The audience is taken by the hand and led to deceive themselves. Jean Robert-Houdin was famous

---

68 For examples of a Penn and Teller demonstration of the "Cups and Balls Trick," see Penn and Teller (2006). The duo have claimed while demonstrating this trick that The Magic Castle asked them to leave the premises when they revealed the secret of the trick. For the "American flag" illusion, see Penn and Teller (2007).

69 For an example of one US jurisdiction's disciplinary rules, see LADB (2010).

70 See the use of expulsion to regulate behavior, as in the case of The Magic Circle's ouster of David Devant in Steinmeyer (2003).

71 Another magician recently sued superstar conjuror Criss Angel over confidentiality, trade secret and royalty issues; see Milligan (2009).

72 Dougherty (2010), Loshin (2010). But see Faust (2010), who suggests that the German consumer at least may find assistance from his or her legal regime.

> for the opinion that a magician is actually just "an actor playing the part of a magician." It was an especially important distinction in separating the loud mountebanks on the street corner making balls appear and disappear beneath three metal cups from Robert-Houdin's elegant Parisian deceptions. Today it serves to remind us that a magic show is a piece of theatre, and the Frenchman's analogy can be extended: A magic effect is a short play that simulates a supernatural occurrence. There is a progression, or an *arc*, to the action. There is a surprise and a resolution, which not only completes the audience's expectations but builds on them.[73]

While Steinmeyer continues the analogy with regard to the magician as actor, I would suggest that one can also make the analogy to some extent between the magician and the lawyer, since the lawyer is also an actor when he or she appears in the courtroom before a jury. But the lawyer is not an "actor playing the part of a lawyer"—the lawyer is really an advocate for the individual he or she represents. Only in the most literal sense might we say that the lawyer is an "actor"—the lawyer "acts" for another. But the lawyer stands in the shoes of that other.[74]

The lawyer must also "move the audience"—the jury. Just as the magician's performance has an "arc," so too does the litigator's. It consists of an opening statement, the presentation of the case in chief and a closing statement, and within that format, the ordering of the witnesses in some manner that the trial lawyer deems most persuasive. The lawyer must pay close attention to the opposing side's presentation, call rebuttal witnesses, measure the audience's (the jury's) reaction to the opposing side's performance (Trombly 2010). The lawyer does not like surprises, unless he or she plans them. The lawyer wants to control the action, and he or she wants the resolution to be favorable to his or her client.

Granted, the comparison is limited. Steinmeyer's actor/magician analogy continues:

---

73 Steinmeyer (2003), 17.

74 The celebrated magician Robert-Houdin is famous for having encapsulated the conjuror's philosophy: "A conjuror is not a juggler; he is an actor playing the part of a magician, an artist whose fingers have more need to move with deftness than with speed"; Robert-Houdin (1878), 43. It is interesting to note Hoffmann (or Lewis), who, as noted above, writes in the editor's preface, "In the work of translation I have aimed at substantial rather than absolute fidelity. My design has been to produce a manual of practical utility, and rather to indicate clearly what the author *meant*, than to reproduce with literal exactness what he has *said*. To that end, I have not hesitated, where it appeared desirable, to supply a word or expand a phrase, and have further added occasional explanatory footnotes;" ibid., vi. It is a curious choice for the common law lawyer, Hoffmann, to choose to be faithful to the "spirit" of the law rather than to the letter, and quite a contrast between the magician and practitioner of common law and the magician from a civil law country. Was Hoffmann paying homage to the great tradition of the glossators of the civil law tradition by also adding explanatory notes? Or did the translator think that, since Robert-Houdin's original work was (then) rare, most people were unlikely to come across the French original?

> A great magic performance consists of a collection of tiny lies, in words and deeds, that are stacked and arranged ingeniously to form the battlement for an illusion. It's a delicate battle of wits—an audience that welcomes being deceived, then dares to be fooled, alternately questioning, prodding, and surrendering. A great magician seems always to play catch-up to their thoughts but secretly must stay two steps ahead—not only solicitous and anticipating, but suggesting.[75]

The magician lies to his audience continually. The attorney may not lie to his or hers. However, the lawyer's presentation necessarily includes illusion. Subject to certain exceptions, the lawyer is not required to show his or her hand to his or her opponent.[76]

Magic Words and Magic Acts

As I discussed previously, words, both written and oral, are a lawyer's stock in trade, and his or her use of certain words is crucial to the creation of valid legal documents. For example, under US law, valid support trusts require the presence of certain "magic" words in order to show the intent of the donor—for example, "health," "support," "maintenance" and "education"—since these set forth the valid reasons for the existence of the trust (Scott and Fratcher 1987). Why does the law insist on these words specifically, rather than allow their synonyms, or phrases that mean substantially the same thing? In his article "No magic words could do it justice," Roger J. Traynor explores the question by contrasting the age-old traditions followed in the interpretation of statutes with the then trend toward the search for "neutral principles" (Traynor 1961). The battle between the Legal Formalists and Traynor's seekers after neutral principles, and then legal cultural relativists, rages on, since the latter two groups tend to maintain, to differing degrees, that magic words are simply a distraction.

Whether or not they intend to make reference to the issues that Traynor discusses, attorneys use the phrase "magic words" every day. Consider the ease with which they employ it in oral and written communication; it continues to enchant both practicing and academic lawyers (Stanley 2005). But the question concerning the necessity of "magic words" is real for lawyers. That is, the existence or absence of the words has real consequences.

Similarly, magicians make frequent and elaborate use of "magic words" in order to distract onlookers from what is really going on. "Sim Sala Bim," "Abracadabra" and "Hocus Pocus" are all words or phrases of conjuration that encourage the audience to believe that something magical will now happen—something

75 Steinmeyer (2003), 17.

76 These exceptions include, for example, for the prosecuting attorney, the disclosure of exculpatory evidence to the defense in a criminal trial; see *Strickler* v. *Greene* (1999), *Brady* v. *Maryland* (1963).

that would not have happened without the invocations. But, for magicians, the words really are not necessary—that is, magicians create the conditions of the performance as well as the words.

While in magic the notion of illusion is quite attractive, in law it carries unattractive risks. The process of drawing up a contract necessitates that the parties involved know with whom they are dealing. Are the parties at the table truly the parties signing the documents, or should the deal go bad somewhere down the road, might one of the parties find itself in the position of attempting to enforce the contract against a holding company, for example? As in the example of the Wizard of Oz, one needs to know whether someone is behind the curtain.[77]

We encounter other uses of magic vocabulary. In such cases they often, but not always, indicate deception, illusion or trickery. The phrase 'illusory appointment" in equity, for example, means a merely nominal appointment in chancery; such an appointment is void.[78] The top law firms in London refer to themselves as the "magic circle" (Lin 2004). The reference is to the establishment of the "magic circle" of practitioners which creates the sacred rule of law, outside of which is chaos (Hefner 2010):

> A circle is characterised by the separation of inside from outside. Inside is order; outside is anarchy. In magic a circle is used as a wall of protection to divide the greater hostile world from the zone of law. The most obvious magic circle is the human body. Humans look upon the inside of their skins as their own property to do what as they see fit. Mystics extend the personal sphere to the aura, a supposed invisible field of energy that is shaped like an egg around the body and that protects the perceived self from hostile psychic "vibrations", just as the body insulates it from extreme heat and cold. Animals have their territorial limit, another kind of magic circle. The border of a country is a magic circle established by a society.[79]

But the premier magicians' association in England is also called The Magic Circle (Magic Circle 2010). In 1998, lawyer-magician Rupert Connell, a partner with the leading London firm of Hobson Audley Hopkins & Wood, and several other members of the Magic Circle's board engaged in a battle for control of the association. The argument seems to have arisen over questions involving the employment of Connell's law firm as legal advisers to the association (Lindsay 1998). This intriguing juxtaposition between lawyers and magicians, each group

77 I am indebted to my former colleagues Alberto Zuppi and Mark Hoch, who have used this analogy when explaining US contract law to non-US-trained attorneys.

78 "Illusory appointment, *chancery practice.* Such an appointment or disposition of property under a power as is merely nominal and not substantial. 2. Illusory appointments are void in equity"; see Bouvier (1852).

79 Tyson (1996).

working in its sphere toward a desired outcome, creates the kind of tension we do not see often.

"I Resemble that Remark!": Trial Tactics and the Use of Magic Vocabulary

On appeal, defendants often challenge convictions based on prosecutorial misconduct based on "disparaging comments," including the magician analogy, "such as calling counsel 'a magician' who was trying to 'trick' the jury" (*US* v. *Bunge* 1994, 32,734, n2). In *State* v. *Nasi*, the defendant challenged his conviction for possession and sale of methamphetamines based on the prosecution's comparison of his counsel to a magician. Indeed, the prosecution's closing statement was extremely long and the analogy extensive. The Washington Court of Appeals took the argument seriously, studying whether the attorney disparaged the opposing counsel's integrity or her tactics: "Courts have generally disapproved this type of argument, but have concluded that reversal is unwarranted where the remarks focus on counsel's tactics, rather than on counsel's integrity" (*State* v. *Nasi* 2005, 831). However, the prosecutor's analogy between the defense counsel and a magician is instructive. Indeed, the appellate court labeled the section in which it discussed the issue "Magician Argument":

> *Magician Argument*
> During rebuttal argument, the prosecutor told the jury a story about his experience during college of working as a musician on a cruise ship. He talked about a magician who also performed a show on the ship. Because he watched the magician's show every night from backstage and from different angles, he was able to see how most of the tricks were accomplished. But he described one particular trick that he could not figure out, even after seeing it performed every night. Finally, the magician showed him how he created the illusion.
>
> The prosecutor then stated:
>
> We have experienced the same thing in this case. We have, in the course of this trial, heard about a magician. Now the first thing that might spring to mind is that it might be Chris Grant, and that somehow, on five occasions, he was able to conjure up a baggie of methamphetamine when the officers weren't looking; that he was somehow able to, either with luck, as Ms. Mann suggested, or maybe just sheer magic, evade searches before and after the buy, five times; maybe sleight of hand, maybe palming it; maybe he practiced how he would hide it in his sleeve and take it out when they weren't looking.
>
> That's not the magician I'm talking about. The magician I'm talking about that has entered the picture has been present throughout the course of the trial but has really entered the picture today.

> That magician is Ms. Mann.
>
> Realize what she has done in her closing argument and, actually, subtly, during the course of the trial. She has pointed over here to the fact that Chris Grant has a bad history, that he's broken his rules, that he was a drug dealer himself, that he has approached the officers to set up the deals. She's pointed over here; look at the differences in these maps about where people might have been parked. She's pointed over here; she said, Detective Maples, you know, how can we tell what really happened with the serial numbers here? She's pointed to the room; how do we even know this was Shane's room. There's no record that he was renting the room at the time.
>
> Time and time again, she's diverted your attention to different places, all of the time taking your attention away from the focus of this case; and that's on what her client did, what the defendant did.[80]

After considering the argument, the court went on to comment:

> "Because calling counsel a magician has negative connotations, we do not encourage the use of this metaphor. To protect the integrity of the adversarial system, prosecutors should be exceedingly careful, when commenting on defense counsel's strategy, not to improperly disparage defense counsel or defense counsel's role." (*State* v. *Nasi* 2005, 839)

Other courts make similar points. In *State* v. *Hargrove* (1999), the trial court ruled that the following remarks made at trial in reference to the defense attorney amounted to prosecutorial misconduct:

> Likewise, if the Defendant's lawyer makes arguments to you which are not supported by the evidence, your duty is to toss those out and not to consider them at all. A Defense lawyer is often like a magician. If you have ever been to a magic show or seen magic on TV, you understand that the art of magic is the art of misdirection.
>
> [Defense Counsel:] Objection, your Honor. I am going to object. The prosecuting attorney is accusing me of being a magician, the art of misdirection. My duty as an attorney
>
> THE COURT: This is just argument at this point.

80 *State* v. *Nasi* (2005), 831.

> [Prosecutor:] A magician makes you look in one place when what's really going on is occurring somewhere else. (Emphasis added). The prosecutor proceeded to argue that certain of defense counsel's arguments were not supported by any evidence. The prosecutor then argued as follows: This is what the Defendant's lawyer is trying to tell as to why you should disbelieve Travis Ralph. But if that's what she believes, if that's what the Defendant's lawyer thinks might have happened, why didn't she ask him? (*State* v. *Hargrove* 1999, 1,321)

According to the *Hargrove* court:

> Courts have generally disapproved of magician-type arguments and have been more likely to reverse where the arguments attacked defense counsel's integrity, as opposed to counsel's tactics. In the instant case, the prosecutor's initial statement comparing defense attorneys to magicians was improper, but was not, by itself, particularly prejudicial. The prosecutor went on to suggest, however, that defense counsel did not believe her own arguments. At that point, the argument became an attack on defense counsel's integrity. When viewed in the context of the overarching "magician" theme, the prosecutor's arguments carried a clear message that defense counsel was being disingenuous, if not dishonest. The arguments were thus misconduct. The question, then, is whether the misconduct warrants reversal. (*State* v. *Hargrove* 1999, 1,323)

While the court in *Hargrove* did not find that the prosecutor's behavior warranted reversal, it signaled disapproval of his conduct: "when viewed in the context of the overarching "magician" theme, the prosecutor's argument carried a clear message that defense counsel was being disingenuous, if not dishonest."

Other courts that have considered the "defense counsel as magician" argument on appeal include the *Crews* court, (*State* v. *Crews* 1996),[81] in which the prosecutor remarked that the defense counsel "acted like a magician" (*State* v. *Crews* 1996, 483). In a Michigan case, a prosecutor referred to defense counsel as "Mr. Copperfield," comparing him to the famous magician,[82] and intending to make an unfavorable comparison—suggesting, although not actually stating, that the defense attorney was intentionally deceiving the jury:

> Next, defendant argues that the prosecutor improperly denigrated defense counsel by referring to him as "Mr. Copperfield," apparently alluding to

81 Still others include US v. *Lopez-Alvarez* (1992), comparing defense counsel to a magician and a squid and comparing prosecutor to the Wizard of Oz. The Wizard of Oz analogy is discussed below.

82 David Copperfield has recently had his own problems with the law; a young woman brought rape allegations against him in 2007; federal investigators closed the case late last year without bringing charges; see Marikar (2010). For David Copperfield's website, see Copperfield (2001).

> magician David Copperfield. The prosecutor also characterized the defense theory of the case as a "grand illusion," and he told the jury that "every illusion has a trick to it." Defendant contends that the prosecutor's remarks were intended to persuade the jury that defense counsel was engaging in deceptive practices. It is improper for the prosecutor to engage in arguments which attack defense counsel. Such arguments undermine the defendant's presumption of innocence and impermissibly shift the jury's focus from the evidence to defense counsel's personality. When the prosecutor argues that defense counsel himself is intentionally trying to mislead the jury, he is in effect stating that defense counsel does not believe his own client. Although the prosecutor's remarks were inappropriate, a new trial is not warranted on this basis. Unlike in *Wise* and *Dalessandro*, the prosecutor never explicitly stated that defense counsel was intentionally lying to the jury. Furthermore, the improper remarks were fairly isolated in relation to the case as a whole. This was a lengthy trial. The prosecutor's closing argument was extensive. With one exception, the prosecutor stopped referring to defense counsel as "Mr. Copperfield" after a side bar which occurred well before the closing argument was half-over. In this context, it is unlikely that the improper remarks influenced the jury's decision. Moreover, defendant's rights were adequately safeguarded. During his rebuttal argument, the prosecutor admitted that he should not have referred to defense counsel as "Mr. Copperfield." He attempted to explain to the jury that the reference was intended to be a comment on the fact that defense counsel's characterization of the evidence was contrary to the testimony admitted at trial. Later, the jury was instructed that arguments of counsel were not evidence. Under these circumstances, we conclude that defendant did not suffer prejudice as a result of the prosecutor's improper remarks. A defendant is guaranteed a fair trial, not a perfect one.[83]

Lawyers do not necessarily confine such arguments to criminal trials. In *Falkowski* v. *Johnson*, plaintiffs' counsel submitted:

> I want to call your attention to some sleights of hand that can occur in a case, because some sleights of hand have occurred here. There is an art of advocacy. Sometimes you notice it and sometimes you don't. A very good magician, you never notice the tricks of hand that he has, but he has them, or he wouldn't be able to perform magic. [Defense counsel], on several occasions, has called your attention to one area to keep you from looking to where he is performing his magic.[84]

Here the defendants moved for a new trial after the verdict, based on, among other things, "extraneous matters introduced by counsel" during his closing argument,

83 *People* v. *Delgreco* (1997), 1997 Mich. App. Lexis 1,544.
84 *Falkowski* v. *Johnson* (1993), 134.

and the judge granted the motion. Note, however, that counsel's reference to defense counsel's "art of advocacy" was a comparison to the magician's art of misdirection, which Wiseman and Lamont explain in their work *Magic in Theory* (Wiseman and Lamont 1995).

Courts have several objections to characterizations of counsel as "magicians." When prosecutors make such comparisons, judges may have to consider whether the defendant's right to a fair trial might be implicated. In addition, when made either by the prosecution or the defense, such statements may contravene the ABA Model Rules, in particular Rule 4.4(a), "In representing a client, a lawyer shall not use means that have no substantial purpose other than to embarrass, delay, or burden a third person, or use methods of obtaining evidence that violate the legal rights of such a person" (Center for Professional Responsibility 2004), and 8.4(d), "It is professional misconduct for a lawyer to engage in conduct that is prejudicial to the administration of justice" (Center for Professional Responsibility 2004).

Courts generally chide prosecutors who use "magician arguments" or magician analogies: "we would note our disapproval of the prosecutor's comments including those analogizing defense counsel to a magician performing magic tricks" (*People* v. *Torres* 1991, 425).

But, as I note above, the use of a magician analogy does not always result in reversal, even though it offends some judges. In another New York case, a dissenting judge found the following inclusion improper in a prosecutor's summation: "Turning to the prosecutor's summation itself, the prosecutor began with a comparison of defense counsel to a "magician" who '[raises] your [*sic*] right hand with the wand, and everybody watches it, and your [*sic*] left hand does the magic'" (*People* v. *Jones* 1984, 565). The dissent would have reversed the conviction on the basis that the prosecutor's closing argument unfairly prejudiced the jury against the defendant by impugning the defense counsel's integrity:

> It is fundamental that counsel, in summing up, should argue only from the evidence and should not seek to prejudice the jury by inflammatory comment. It is equally fundamental that a prosecutor should not present his or her own opinion as to the veracity of the witnesses. The prosecutor's comments here went awry of both these rules. Furthermore, his statement that the jury could not doubt the complainant's story beyond a reasonable doubt tended to confuse the burden of proof, and his personal attack on defense counsel's integrity was most improper. While objection was not made to the majority of the aforementioned remarks, their highly inflammatory and improper nature could well have led the jury to return a guilty verdict under circumstances where proof of guilt was hardly overwhelming. Hence, I would vote to reverse the judgment in the interest of justice and direct a new trial.[85]

85 *People* v. *Jones* (1984), 566.

A plaintiff's attorney making the following argument in *Bird* v. *Glacier Electric Cooperative, Inc.* "rose to the level of misconduct."[86] The attorney referred repeatedly to "white man's magic" in a statement addressed to a jury composed of members of the Blackfeet tribe:

> All this money, such an efficient organization. How can they trust any of their work to the likes of unskilled Indian contractors like these? Certainly the white man's magic is so much better .... I think you have seen a classic defense to castrating the T.E.R.O. laws on the reservation. The first thing you do is say our business is so big and sophisticated that you lowly Indians, you really can't cut the mustard.[87]

In addition, he inserted references to racism, to the white man's treatment of Native Americans during the nineteenth century, and to continuing tribal poverty today. On appeal, the Ninth Circuit held that "Glacier Construction's appeal to racial prejudice in closing argument in its civil case in tribal court offended fundamental fairness and violated due process owed the Co-op" (*Bird* v. *Glacier* 2001, 1,152). Thus, it refused to give effect to the tribal court's verdict in Bird's favor.

What about the magician analogy might strike a court as improper? Judges may not simply believe that jurors might perceive the magician as a deceptive individual and then extend the analogy to the lawyer. Deception is, after all, the magician's stock in trade. It is that the magician does not believe in the truth of the stories (tricks) he tells. By analogy, therefore, neither does the lawyer.

In a 2007 case, however, the defendant-appellant failed to persuade the court that the prosecutor in his criminal trial had improperly characterized defense counsel as a magician, even though she compared him to a magician in her closing remarks:

> You don't deceive someone unless you're you [*sic*] intend to deceive them. When Mr. Fenner did the trick with the nickel, he wanted to deceive you. When a magician, when you pay to go see a magician or a magician comes to a party, or you see a magician, what's his intent? To deceive you. His intent is to show you slight [*sic*] of the hand. These are the things that can be done. Right? That's his intention. It's to deceive you.[88]

The Sixth Circuit held instead that the defendant failed to show why these comments amounted to "deprivation of due process," instead ruling that: "This court has previously held that '[a] prosecutor commenting that the defense is

86 *Settlegoode* v. *Portland Public Schools* (2004), 518, citing "plaintiff's counsel speaking to a jury comprised only of Indian tribal members ... [and citing] 'white man's magic.'"

87 *Bird* v. *Glacier Electric Cooperative, Inc.* (2001), 1,150.

88 *Brown* v. *McKee* (2007), 479.

attempting to trick the jury is a permissible means of arguing so long as those comments are not overly excessive or do not impair the search for the truth'" (*Brown* v. *McKee* 2007, 479–80).

Some judges and lawyers also make use of the "magician with rabbit" analogy as well, in a disparaging way. Consider Judge Ditter's comment regarding the behavior of an attorney appearing before him: "It is not good faith for a lawyer to frustrate discovery requests and court orders with successive objections like a magician pulling another and another and then still another rabbit out of a hat" (*Massachusetts School of Law* v. *American Bar Association* 1996, 1,177). Not only is pulling rabbits out of hats boring, because a good magician does not repeat the same trick no matter how often his audience begs for it (Pogue 1998, 306), it treads on the patience of the court, and suggests that the lawyer has no substance behind his or her objections ("not good faith").

Magical analogies also appear in appellate briefs:

> Yes, the defense had called the government's witnesses liars, skunks, weasels, idiots and sociopaths. "You've heard hours of arguments from four different defense counsel, and they've got excellent lawyers, and they did their level best to convince you that there is not enough evidence here. Well, as I say, they've got excellent lawyers. They're not magicians. They cannot make the evidence in this case simply disappear in a puff of smoke. There is overwhelming evidence here. Overwhelming. And their efforts to act like magicians and their efforts to make that mountain of evidence disappear, quite frankly, was at times downright silly."[89]

Here, the attack made on the prosecutor's statement at trial was that he improperly characterized the defendant's attorneys as magicians, but made the comparison sound, uncharacteristically, like a compliment:

> The Assistant United States Attorney delivering the rebuttal committed forensic misconduct by denigrating defense counsel and his argument. No objection was made, it is surmised, because the forensic misconduct was disguised in the form of seeming compliments to the quality and creativity of the attorneys, especially the attorney representing Marty Lewis.[90]

Some commentators extend the lawyer/magician analogy even further. In his book *The Cartel: Lawyers and their Nine Magic Tricks*, journalist Evan Whitton points to several legal rules, some of procedure, some of substance, that he claims interfere with justice:

---

89 *US* v. *Riggi* (2003), Brief for defendant Martin Lewis, 12; The conviction and sentence were affirmed; see *US* v. *Riggi* (2004). But see *US* v. *Riggi*, 541 F.3d 94 (2nd Circ. 2008), vacating and remanding on some of the counts, and *US* v. *Riggi*, 308 Fed. Appx. 514, 2009 WL 196210 (2nd Circ. 2009), denying an appeal of defendants' guilty plea.

90 *US* v. *Riggi*; Brief (2004), 11.

> Susanna Lobez: The right to silence is magic trick number 4. How does that help a rapist?
>
> Evan Whitton: Well the right of silence is really a brilliant trick: it protects the guilty only. What it does is that the rapist doesn't have to subject himself to the great engine of truth, cross-examination, so the jury can't see the whites of his eyes. Whereas all sorts of things can be done for the victim, and is done to the victim, by the defence lawyer.[91]

Again, whether or not Mr. Whitton is correct about the effect of the right to silence, or whether he even understands its purpose, is not the issue. What is interesting is his comparison of the right to silence to a "magic trick," to deception. He suggests here that if the prosecution had the opportunity to ask questions of "the guilty," the jury could "see the whites of his eyes." That is, the jury could determine for itself his guilt. It could "see" the truth, as if the truth is apparent on the surface—in someone's eyes, in someone's manner, in someone's words. Silence, or failure to disclose, is the equivalent of deception. Refusal to take the stand in one's criminal defense is the equivalent of deception. It is, in this calculation, a magic trick.[92]

The Principles of Magic: The Judge's Use of Magic Analogies[93]

Senior judge Stephen S. Trott of the US Ninth Circuit sometimes uses magical analogies in his opinions. We should not be surprised; he is a practicing magician (Hanna 2005, 741). Note, for example, the following passage from his dissent in *Compassion in Dying* v. *State of Washington*:

> No magician—not David Copperfield, not even Harry Houdini—can produce a rabbit from a hat unless the rabbit is in the hat to begin with. Moreover, if a hat does not contain such an animal, a magician cannot claim that anything he is able to produce from it is in fact a rabbit, no matter how sincere he may be or how great his forensic skills. All of this has something to do with basic physics. But law may not be physics, as Judge Reinhardt's opinion on behalf of our en banc court demonstrates, because, with all respect, he has in fact succeeded in pulling a nonexistent liberty interest out of thin constitutional air, a liberty interest that certainly does not exist in the document itself. I honestly applaud his splendid effort, which is most skillful and elegant, but unfortunately his production is

91 Lobez (1998b).

92 Ibid. Geoffrey Robertson, the noted South African attorney, defends the common law system in a subsequent interview; see Lobez (1998a).

93 For a comprehensive and stimulating analysis of jurisprudential magic, I highly recommend Jessie Allen's "A theory of adjudication: Law as magic" (Allen 2008), in particular pp. 812–30, which is truly an amazing contribution to the literature in its understanding of the basis for and justification of what we interpret as modern legal magic.

> not law either, it is simply constitutional sleight of hand. Maybe some of us or even many of us would like to see this rabbit in the hat because we believe it's a nice rabbit—hope is an ever-present temptress in a world of woe—but *we* do not get to change the Constitution any more than we get to change physics …. I note with great interest that this alleged right is derivatively asserted by persons *other* than the now deceased patients themselves, i.e., their doctors; and this observation fuels my belief that the broad level of generality or abstraction at which Judge Reinhardt casts the issue is inappropriate and misleading. In substance, he slips the rabbit into the hat so he can later produce it as though it was there all the time.[94]

Neither the magician nor the lawyer can create something out of nothing. Neither the judge nor the attorney should create law out of nothing. Certainly, this is part of Judge Trott's point. But he has another one to make. He suggests here that magical rabbitry in the service of the law is in essence deception: "he slips the rabbit into the hat so he can later produce it as though it was there all the time" (*Compassion in Dying* v. *State of Washington* 1996, 1,446). Rabbity deception in magic is fine entertainment, but clients do not hire lawyers to be entertaining, and judges do not expect them to engage in animal husbandry.

Similarly, in *Gray* v. *Klauser*, Judge Trott opines that:

> We attempt to avoid this clear constitutional restriction, however, by claiming that the state-law violation we falsely perceive is so serious that it violates due process, and we do so even as here, when the state courts have definitively examined the issue under state law and declared that no state law violation or lapse has occurred. With all respect to my colleagues, not even legal legerdemain can accomplish such a result. To pull a rabbit out of a hat, the hat must contain a rabbit before the trick starts. Here, Gray's hat has no rabbit, but we pull one out of it at the State's unwarranted expense nevertheless. Dyer was not in there.[95]

Again, if the legal hat does not already contain the blood, fur and guts of a substantial "rabbit," it is "legal legerdemain" to "pull one out." Judge Trott uses many words that we associate with magic in this analogy because he knows that it evokes uneasiness when we apply them to courtroom behavior.

"Objection! Opposing Counsel is Using Magic Tricks to Entertain and Persuade the Jury!"

The lawyer-magician may on occasion be tempted to use his or her abilities in the courtroom to entertain or beguile the factfinder. Few attorneys may actually do

94 *Compassion in Dying* v. *State of Washington* (1996), 1,446–8.
95 *Gray* v. *Klauser* (2002), 664.

so,[96] but one who does is Philadelphia, Pennsylvania litigator Steven Leventhal. In a recent flap over his use of magic tricks to divert the jury, Mr. Leventhal found himself in a dispute with opposing counsel John Dooley. Mr. Dooley filed a motion to prevent Mr. Leventhal from using what Mr. Dooley considered diversionary tactics in his closing arguments: "In a recent construction accident lawsuit, an opposing lawyer asked the judge to ban any such tricks. They settled the case before trial, but Leventhal still filed an objection. He argued for the right to entertain "underpaid, extremely bored" juries—and to make his point" (CBS News 2009). Said Dooley: "'I think you go up there and argue the facts of the case .... I don't necessarily think he should be up there doing magic tricks to win over a jury'" (Dale 2009). For his part, Leventhal notes that such demonstrations are not evidence. They are argument.[97] Leventhal's courtroom battle garnered a great deal of media attention, which even reached across the pond. Noted barrister David Pannick in *The Times* of London:

> Lord Janner of Braunstone, QC, is a member of the real Magic Circle, but many leading lawyers perform all sorts of tricks in court. Mr Leventhal should be allowed to make his points with the use of such illustrative material as he sees fit. So long as he does not try to saw the court usher in half.
>
> Earlier this year Lord Justice Ward gave judgment for the Court of Appeal in a commercial case. He noted that "riding two horses at the same time is always difficult enough: riding them when they are charging in opposite directions is an altogether remarkable feat". He praised the skills of the successful advocate, David Wolfson, whose wizardry made it look as if he had accomplished this astonishing trick on behalf of his client, American Express, appearing "to stay in the saddle notwithstanding some hostile fire from at least this incredulous member of the court". Magic![98]

Leventhal's magic tricks raise the question for attorneys of what constitutes permissible advocacy on behalf of one's client, and what may constitute impermissible action. Is he correct that a magic trick is simply argument—that it is not evidence of anything, thus permissible, for example during opening and closing statements? Would a magic trick be permissible as part of a demonstration

96 Author telephone interview with Kenneth Trombly, January 30, 2007.

97 Author telephone interview with Steven Leventhal, Baton Rouge, LA, September, 2009. Note that since he does them during opening and closing statements, they are not evidence; see *State* v. *Green* (1997).

98 Pannick (2009).

during a case in chief?[99] Would it depend on who performed the trick—the lawyer or an expert witness, and on the reason for which the trick was performed?[100]

Other attorney-magicians might also make use of magic tricks in the courtroom, but these practitioners seem to be relatively few. Most seem to try to steer clear of mixing the law and the actual practice of secular magic, in order to avoid the type of confusion, commentary (and possible resentment) that Leventhal seems to have stirred up.

Penn, Teller and that Vanishing Flag

The *West Wing* episode "In the Room" allows Penn and Teller to expand and explore their vanishing flag and Bill of Rights illusion. The scenes including the pair involve the character Zoey Bartlet, the daughter of the fictional US President,[101] who is having a birthday. Penn and Teller, playing themselves, are entertaining her and her guests at the White House. During her birthday party, Penn and Teller perform their famous vanishing flag illusion (the piece of cloth, Penn says "that [is] nothing but meaning"), apparently setting fire to the American flag while it is concealed in a tube created out of a copy of the Bill of Rights. They then "restore" the flag.

Horrified, Presidential aide Josh demands an explanation, which Penn refuses to provide. Instead, he gives Josh a written statement indicating that "The Supreme Court has ruled that we can do whatever we want with the flag."[102]

Josh responds firmly:

> This statement does me absolutely no good. I need you guys to give me a statement saying exactly what you did last night—preferably that you did not burn a flag. And if you did actually burn a flag, I need you to admit it, and emphasize that you did not clear your act with anyone in the White House before you performed and had you done so, you now realize you would have been explicitly forbidden to burn a flag in the White House, and you now deeply regret the controversy you have provoked and apologize to the President and his family for treating his home with such disrespect.[103]

---

99 The objections raised to his courtroom magic tricks recall the outrage Hamilton Burger often demonstrates at Perry Mason's courtroom behavior. On Perry Mason generally, see Bounds (1996).

100 On qualifying a magician to testify as an expert witness at trial, see Beckman (2010).

101 Josiah "Jed" Bartlet (Martin Sheen); see IMDB (2010b).

102 Sorkin et al. (2004). In spite of Penn's ebullient interpretation of the case, in *Texas* v. *Johnson*, the court does not actually say one can do "whatever" one wants with the flag. But we are discussing a television show, and an interpretation of the law by someone who is a non-lawyer magician, and actually plays one on TV.

103 Sorkin et al. (2004).

Instead of responding to Josh's request, Penn asks one of the other aides, "You tell me, Charlie, did we burn a flag, or did we just vanish a flag in a patriotic flash of fireworks?" Charlie responds, "Don't know."[104]

> Penn: What's the difference?
>
> Josh: There's a big difference politically.
>
> Penn: Why? I mean, what if we burned a flag, not in protest, but in celebration of the very freedoms that allow us to burn a flag, the freedoms that everyone who has ever worked in this magnificent building has pledged to preserve and protect?
>
> Josh: Did you go to law school?
>
> Penn: No. Clown school.[105]

Whether or not Penn's interpretation of *Texas* v. *Johnson* is correct is as interesting as the interpretation that he places on the Supreme Court's "magic words" that allow him and Teller to perform their "magic acts"—that is, that allow them to "burn" (vanish) the flag. They make the argument that they are not "really" burning the flag ("What if we burned a flag, not in protest, but in celebration?"). But they suggest that if they, like Gregory Lee Johnson, burn a real American flag to make a political statement (*Texas* v. *Johnson* 1989), they would have a very strong First Amendment defense. They are performing a truly symbolic act, in their parlance a magical act, because at the end they "recreate" or "restore" the flag. Like the court jesters of old, in this episode they speak truth to power, performing their tricks in one of the most symbolic arenas in America, the White House.[106] Note also Penn's studied juxtaposition of the words "burning" and "patriotic flash of fireworks." For Americans, burning the flag carries a certain political significance, fireworks, particularly on July 4 (Independence Day) another, and since the flag is a symbol of independence, inviting a listener to consider their meaning while one uses them in a magical illusion makes them both even more politically and legally significant.

Charlie's response is also interesting. The "don't know" could suggest that he does not want to commit himself to an answer concerning what Penn and Teller did on stage, that he does not understand enough about the difference between "burning the flag" (the reality) and simply hiding and restoring the flag (the illusion), that he simply does not know how the trick was managed, or something else.

---

104 Ibid. If Charlie wants to know, he can watch the demonstration provided in a Penn and Teller video clip (Penn and Teller 2007).

105 Sorkin et al. (2004). Penn states the truth here. He really did attend clown school; see Fink (2009).

106 Perhaps they are also recalling the actual burning of the White House in during the War of 1812 by British troops. But then again, maybe not.

Penn refuses to tell Josh, the White House aide, whether the duo has "really" burned a flag ("We're not gonna tell you that."). Although he does not elaborate, his argument must be either that revealing the trick is against the magician's oath[107] or that the First Amendment protects both the right to speak and the right not to speak. Given the symbolic meaning of the illusion, I tend toward the latter explanation. Penn emphasizes the ambiguity of the act by refusing to speak and by enjoying the fact that this representative of the government cannot *compel* him to speak.[108] The first argument, that revealing the secret of a trick to a non-magician is against the magician's oath, would be ironic coming from two magicians routinely identified with exposure, and brings us full circle to Jamy Ian Swiss's comment, "I am an honest liar. I am going to lie to you but that's okay. It's my job." The second, the refusal to speak, is simply the other side of the argument: if one has the right to speak, then one certainly has the right to remain silent, or to choose to whom to speak. It also dovetails nicely with the right of the magician to protect his secrets, and to share or not to share his knowledge.

Consider that the First Amendment protects actually burning the flag as a symbolic act, an act of protest. Such an act could serve as such an act, or it could be a milder form of commentary. Penn and Teller could burn the flag, but only in accordance with the holding in *Texas* v. *Johnson*. Yet the reaction of at least one fictional White House staffer seems to be outrage, undoubtedly for political reasons. Many real-life Americans would probably be outraged as well. Pretending to burn the flag is likewise protected under the First Amendment as entertainment, even though it might disturb or outrage onlookers. Real burning, imaginary burning—these would seem to make little difference to the performance, but in fact they might make a great deal of difference, both to the magical performance and to the law, and they make a great deal of difference to the viewer's imagination. If the burning is purely entertainment, is it less offensive or more offensive than if it is political speech?[109]

Conclusion

Magical analogies permeate the law. More careful and considered examination of their use can yield further understanding both of their symbolism and of their importance to attorneys and to magicians, two groups which use such analogies widely but often for different ends. Ultimately, we make law and magic analogies easily, and sometimes without much reflection. Why such comparisons should have arisen at all, why they persist and what the implications of the speech/act

107 He may also be arguing trade secret, but since the pair reveal the secret of the illusion on YouTube, this explanation seems doubtful.

108 I am indebted to Jessie Allen for discussing this point with me.

109 E-mail from J. Allen, August 19, 2010.

divide mean for the magician, the attorney and the audience continue to create an ongoing and fascinating area of investigation.

References

Abel, R.L. and Lewis, P. (1988–89), *Lawyers In Society,* Berkeley, CA: University of California Press.

Abowitz, R. (2008), “A man, a ball, a hoop, a bench (and an alleged thread) … TELLER!”, *Las Vegas Weekly*, November 20, <http://www.lasvegasweekly.com/news/2008/nov/20/man-ball-hoop-bench-and-alleged-thread-teller/>, accessed January 11, 2010.

Alco v. *TVA*, 808 F.2d 1,490 (1987).

Allen, J. (2008), “A theory of adjudication: Law as magic,” *Suffolk University Law Review*, 41, 773–831.

—— (2010), “Magical Realism,” in C. Corcos (ed.), *Law and Magic: A Collection of Essays*, Durham, NC: Carolina Academic Press, 195–207.

Bailey, M. (2007), The Magic Circle: Performing Magic Through the Ages, Stroud: Tempus.

Baird, P. (1989), “Corpus juris hocus pocus,” *Arizona Attorney* (October), 23–4.

Baum, L.F. (1973), *The Wonderful Wizard of Oz*, New York: C.N. Potter.

—— (2000), *The Wizard of Oz*, annotated edn., New York: Norton.

Beckman, S. (2010), “Smoke and Mirrors: The Escamoteur as an Expert Witness,” in C. Corcos (ed.), *Law and Magic: A Collection of Essays*, Durham, NC: Carolina Academic Press, 349–64.

Beier, A.L. (1985), *Masterless Men: The Vagrancy Problem in England, 1560–1640*, London: Methuen.

Berger, B. and Martinez, R. (1988), *What To Do With a Dead Lawyer: At Home, At Work, At Play, On the Go*, Berkeley, CA: Ten Speed Press.

Bird v. *Glacier Electric Cooperative, Inc.*, 255 F.3d 1,136 (2001).

Blackstone, H., Jr. (1985), *The Blackstone Book of Magic and Illusion*, New York: Newmarket Press.

Bounds, J.D. (1996), Perry Mason: The Authorship and Reproduction of a Popular Hero, Westport, CT: Greenwood Press.

Bouvier, J. (1852), *Bouvier's Law Dictionary*, 4th edn., Philadelphia, PA: Printed for the estate of John Bouvier.

Bowman, C. (2010), *Code of the Magician's Secret*, <http://www.life123.com/hobbies/magic-illusion/magic-basics/what-is-the-code-of-the-magicians-secret.shtml>, accessed August 18, 2010.

Brady v. *Maryland*, 373 US 83 (1963).

Brenner, R.A. (2010), *Criminal Defense Lawyers Are Not Magicians or Miracle Workers*, <http://www.ohiocriminalappealslawyer.com/2010/02/criminal-defense-appeal-lawyer.html>, accessed August 23, 2010.

Brown v. *McKee*, 231 Fed. Appx. 469 (2007).

Burlingame, H.J. (1897), *Herrmann the Magician: His Life, His Secrets*, Chicago, IL: Laird & Lee.

Burstyn v. *Wilson*, 343 US 495 (1952).

Cardozo, B.N. (1931), "The Game of the Law and Its Prizes," in *Law and Literature and Other Essays*, New York: Harcourt, Brace, 160–75.

Carter, T. (1997), "The court conjurer," *American Bar Association Journal*, 83(12), 72–5.

Caveney, M. and Steinmeyer, J. (2009), *Magic, 1400s–1950s*, New York: Taschen America.

CBS News (2009), "Lawyer uses magic to make cases disappear," *CBS News*, March 6, <http://www.cbsnews.com/stories/2009/03/06/national/main4850769.shtml?source=RSSattr=HOME_4850769>, accessed August 23, 2010.

Center for Professional Responsibility (2004), *Model Rules of Professional Conduct*, Chicago, IL: Center for Professional Responsibility, American Bar Association.

Chicago (2002), dir. Rob Marshall.

"Columbo Goes to the Guillotine," *Columbo* (1989), dir. Leo Penn.

Compassion in Dying v. *State of Washington*, 85 F.3d 1,440 (1996).

Cooley, J.W. (1997), "Mediation magic: Use and abuse," *Loyola University Chicago Law Journal*, 29, 1–107.

Copperfield, D. (2001), *David Copperfield*, <http://www.dcopperfield.com/>, accessed July 6, 2005.

Corcos, C.A. (2003), "Legal fictions: Media re-creations and interpretations of law and justice," *University of Arkansas Law Review*, 25, 503–633.

—— (ed.) (2010a), *Law and Magic: A Collection of Essays*, Durham, NC: Carolina Academic Press.

—— (2010b), *Lawyer Magicians*, Law and Magic Blog, <http://lpcprof.typepad.com/law_and_magic_blog/>, accessed January 14, 2010.

Cross, F.B. (2001), "The error of positive rights," *UCLA Law Review*, 48, 857–923.

Dale, M. (2009), "Philly lawyer uses magic to make cases disappear," *ABC News*, March 6, <http://abclocal.go.com/wpvi/story?section=news/local&id=6696317>, accessed August 23, 2010.

Dibbell, J. (1993), "How an evil clown, a Haitian trickster spirit, two wizards, and a cast of dozens turned a database into a society," *The Village Voice*, December 23, <http://www.juliandibbell.com/texts/bungle_vv.html>, accessed August 23, 2010.

—— (1998), *My Tiny Life: Crime and Passion in a Virtual World*, New York: Holt.

Digest of Justinian (1985), Philadelphia, PA: University of Pennsylvania Press.

Dighe, R. (ed.) (2002), *The Historian's Wizard of Oz: Reading L. Frank Baum's Classic as a Political and Monetary Allegory*, Westport, CT: Praeger.

Dolak, L.A. (2002), "Trends: Judges increasingly criticize patent counsel," *Patent Strategy and Management* (December), 5.

Dougherty, J. (2010), Now You Own It, Now You Don't: Copyright and Related Rights in Magic Productions and Performances," in C. Corcos (ed.), *Law and Magic: A Collection of Essays*, Durham, NC: Carolina Academic Press, 101–22.

Erisman, F. (1968), "L. Frank Baum and the progressive dilemma," *American Quarterly*, 20(3), 616–23.

Falkowski v. *Johnson*, 148 FRD 132 (1993).

Faust, F. (2010), "Selling Secrets: Legal Problems of the Magic Market," in C. Corcos (ed.), *Law and Magic: A Collection of Essays*, Durham, NC: Carolina Academic Press, 143–58.

Fink, J. (2009), "Staying power is no trickery," *Las Vegas Sun*, April 15, <http://www.lasvegassun.com/news/2009/apr/15/staying-power-no-trickery/>, accessed August 23, 2010.

5 Geo. IV ch. 83 (1824), *An Act for the Punishment of idle and disorderly Persons, and Rogues and Vagabonds, in England.*

Fisher, D. ([1983] 2004), *The War Magician: The Man Who Conjured Victory in the Desert*, London: Weidenfeld and Nicolson.

Franklin, J. (1982), "The Renaissance myth," *Quadrant*, 26, 51–60, <http://web.maths.unsw.edu.au/~jim/renaissance.html>, accessed November 18, 2004.

Galanter, M. (2005), *Lowering the Bar: Lawyer Jokes and Legal Culture*, Madison, WI: University of Wisconsin Press.

Garrison, G. (1995), "Skeptical James Randi finds magic in discrediting deception," *Birmingham News*, July 2, 26A.

Goldin v. *Clarion Photoplays*, 202 AD 1 (1922).

Goldin v. *R.J. Reynolds Tobacco Co.*, 22 F. Supp. 61 (1938).

Goldin, H. (1937), *It's Fun To Be Fooled*, London: S. Paul.

Gray v. *Klauser*, 282 F.3d 633 (2002).

Green, S.P. (2006), *Lying, Cheating and Stealing: A Moral Theory of White Collar Crime*, Oxford: Oxford University Press.

Greenspon, J. (2004), *Now You See It ... Musings on the Future of Magic in Law Vegas*, <http://www.lasvegascitylife.com/articles/2004/11/24/cover_story/cover.txt>, accessed May 2, 2005.

Grossman, J.H. (2004), *Hoffmann's First Book Contract*, <http://www.miraclefactory.net/mpt/view.php?id=59&type=articles>, accessed January 15, 2010.

Hailey, R.D. (2003), "Winning without trial: Remember … We are trial lawyers, not magicians," *AAJ (formerly Association of Trial Lawyers of America)–Continuing Legal Education*, 1, 825–30.

Hanna, C.H. (2005), "From Gregory to Enron: The too perfect theory and tax law," *Virginia Tax Review*, 24, 737–96.

Harrison, M. (1989), *New Vaudeville: Variety Artists in the Contemporary American Theater*, New York: New York University Press.

Hatzel and Buehler v. *Lovisa Construction*, 1993 US Lexis 9,899.

"Head Cases," *Boston Legal* (2004), ABC, October 3.

Hefner, A.G. (2010), *The Laws of Magic* <http://www.themystica.com/mystica/articles/l/laws_of_magic.html>, accessed June 26, 2004.

Herrmann, A. (1891), "The art of magic," *The North American Review*, 153(416), 92–8.

Hume, D. ([1748] 2000), *An Enquiry Concerning Human Understanding*, Kitchener, Ontario: Batoche.

Hustler Magazine Inc. v. *Falwell*, 485 US 46 (1988).

IMDB (2010a), *Listen Up*, <http://www.imdb.com/title/tt0632882/>, accessed August 18, 2010.

—— (2010b), *The West Wing*, <http://www.imdb.com/title/tt0200276/>, accessed May 18, 2010.

"In the Room," *The West Wing* (2004), NBC, December 8.

Johnston, D.C. (2000), "Tax magicians: A special report—Sham shelters for business flourish as scrutiny fades," *New York Times*, December 19, A1.

JREF (2001), "About the Foundation," <http://www.randi.org/jref/index.html>, accessed June 21, 2006.

Kantorowicz, E.H. (1957), *The King's Two Bodies: A Study in Medieval Political Theology*, Princeton, NJ: Princeton University Press.

Kattwinkel, S.E. (1997), *Contemporary Variety Theatre: Using Techniques of Performance To Decrease Performer/spectator Distance*, Austin, TX: University of Texas Press.

Kurtz, S. (1994), "Voodoo and violence," *Reason Magazine*, <http://reason.com/archives/1994/04/01/voodoo-and-violence>, accessed December 2, 2009.

LADB (2010), *Louisiana Attorney Disciplinary Board*, <http://www.ladb.org/NXT/gateway.dll?f=templates$fn=default.htm$vid=ladb:ladbview>, accessed January 15, 2010.

Landis, L.A. (2010), "Lanham, Frederick Garland," <http://www.tshaonline.org/handbook/online/articles/LL/fla33.html>, accessed August 23, 2010.

"Last Vegas," *Listen Up* (2005), CBS, April 25.

Lidman, R. and Hollingsworth, B. (1998), *Rethinking the Roles of Guardians ad Litem in Dissolutions: Are We Seeking Magicians?*, <http://www.wsba.org/media/publications/barnews/archives/dec-98-rethinking.htm>, accessed August 23, 2010.

Lin, A. (2004), "Raises in London may foretell genteel pay war," *New York Law Journal*, May 20, <http://www.law.com/jsp/article.jsp?id=1084824769856>, accessed June 26, 2004.

Lindsay, R. (1998), "Conjurors question Magic Circle advisers," *The Lawyer*, January 13, 3.

Lobez, S. (1998a), *Adventuring Advocates of the Adversarial System*, <http://www.abc.net.au/rn/talks/8.30/lawrpt/lstories/lr980331.htm>, accessed May 18, 2010.

—— (1998b), *Lawyers and their "Magic Tricks": Shaming Juvenile Offenders—HIV Transmission and the Criminal Law*, <http://www.abc.net.au/rn/talks/8.30/lawrpt/lstories/lr980324.htm>, accessed May 18, 2010.

Loshin, J. (2010), "Secrets Revealed: Protecting Magicians' Intellectual Property Without Law," in C. Corcos (ed.), *Law and Magic: A Collection of Essays*, Durham, NC: Carolina Academic Press, 123–41.

McNeil-PPC v. *Perrigo*, 207 F. Supp. 2d 356 (2002).

McNeil-PPC v. *Perrigo*, 337 F.3d 1,362 (2003).

Magic Circle (2010), *Welcome to The Magic Circle*, <http://www.themagiccircle.co.uk/>, accessed August 23, 2010.

Marcovecchio, N. (2010), "Hocus Ipsa Loquitur: The Affinity Between Law and Magic," in C. Corcos (ed.), *Law and Magic: A Collection of Essays*, Durham, NC: Carolina Academic Press, 329–37.

Marikar, S. (2010), "Woman in David Copperfield's rape probe arrested," *ABC News*, January 27, <http://abcnews.go.com/Entertainment/david-copperfields-rape-investigation-vanishes/story?id=9675140>, accessed January 31, 2010.

Mason, M.M. (2010), *Eleventh Circuit, USCA: Trickery Raised to Art Form*, <http://mmason.freeshell.org/trickery/>, accessed May 3, 2010.

Massachusetts School of Law v. *American Bar Association*, 914 F. Supp. 1,172 (1996).

Mendelsohn, A. (2005), "There's no trick to it: Women, minorities turn to magic, *Orlando Sentinel*, January 2, F6.

Milligan, R. (2009), "Production companies for star magician Criss Angel sued for alleged failure to pay royalties for magician's alleged use of confidential and proprietary magic tricks," <http://www.tradesecretslaw.com/2009/07/articles/trade-secrets/production-companies-for-star-magician-criss-angel-sued-for-alleged-failure-to-pay-royalties-for-magicians-alleged-use-of-confidential-and-proprietary-magic-tricks/>, accessed January 15, 2010.

Montgomery, B. (1991), "Moody convicted on all counts," *Atlanta Journal-Constitution*, June 29, A1.

Mulholland, J. (1963), *Mulholland's Book of Magic*, New York: Scribner's.

Napier, M.R., and Adams, S.H. (1998), "Magic words to obtain confessions," *FBI Law Enforcement Bulletin*, 10, 11–15.

Nations, H.L. (2003), "Overcoming juror bias," *AAJ (formerly Association of Trial Lawyers of America)–Continuing Legal Education*, 1, 109–37.

NPR (2000), "Magician and trickster Teller of Penn and Teller," <http://www.npr.org/templates/story/story.php?storyId=1114511>, accessed August 23, 2010.

Pannick, D. (2009), "When lawyers try to make the case for the other side disappear," *The Times*. <http://business.timesonline.co.uk/tol/business/law/columnists/article6143046.ece>, accessed May 18, 2009.

Penn and Teller (2006), "Cups and Balls Trick," <http://www.youtube.com/watch?v=BPyvAtQYVok>, accessed January 15, 2010.

—— (2007), Penn and Teller, "Patriotism," <http://www.youtube.com/watch?v=jF2iX2VG6e4&NR=1>, accessed August 6, 2010.

—— (2009), *Looks Simple*, <http://media.theory11.com/2050-Penn-and-Teller---Looks-Simple>, accessed November 13, 2009.

—— (2010), *Penn & Teller*, <http://www.pennandteller.com/>, accessed August 16, 2010.

People v. *Delgreco* (1997) Mich. App. Lexis 1,544.

People v. *Jones*, 104 AD 2d 565 (1984).

People v. *Torres*, 171 AD 2d 425 (1991).

Pharr, C. (1932), "The interdiction of magic in Roman Law," *Transactions and Proceedings of the American Philological Association*, 63, 269–95.

Picker, R.C. (2007), *Pulling a Rabbi Out of His Hat: The Bankruptcy Magic of Dick Posner*, John M. Olin Law and Economics Working Paper No. 330, 2nd series, Chicago, IL: University of Chicago Press.

Playboy Foundation (2006), *Arts and Entertainment*, Hugh M. Hefner First Amendment Awards for 2006, <http://www.playboyenterprises.com/home/content.cfm?content=t_title_as_division&ArtTypeID=0008B752-BBD0-1C76-8FEA8304E50A010D&packet=00083D82-77CB-1C7A-9B578304E50A011A&MmenuFlag=foundation&viewMe=3>, accessed August 6, 2010.

Pogue, D. (1998), *Magic For Dummies*, New York: John Wiley & Sons.

Price, D. (1985), *Magic: A Pictorial History of Conjurors in the Theater*, New York: Cornwall Books.

Professor Bubbles, *Adventures*, <http://bubbles.org/html/adventures/chile/rehearsal2.htm>, accessed June 7, 2006.

Rich, Motoko (2006), "James Frey and his publisher settle suit over lies," *The New York Times*, September 7, <http://www.nytimes.com/2006/09/07/arts/07frey.html?ref=james_frey>, accessed April 4, 2010.

Robert-Houdin, J.E. (1878), *The Secrets of Conjuring Magic*, London: George Routledge & Sons.

—— (2006), *Comment on deviant sorcier*, Paris: Omnibus.

Robinson, B. and Booth, J.N. (2008), *The Magician: John Mulholland's Secret Life*, Cambridge, MA: Lybrary.com.

Rourke, B. (2002), "Now you see it: Aspiring magician learns the tricks of his trade at Brown Library," *Providence Journal-Bulletin*, August 26, D1.

Schlag, P. (1995), "Law and the post-modern mind: Anti-intellectualism," *Cardozo Law Review*, 16, 1,111–20.

Scott, A.W. and Fratcher, W.F. (1987), *The Law of Trusts*, 4th edn., Boston, MA: Little, Brown.

Settlegoode v. *Portland Public Schools*, 371 F.3d 503 (2004).

Smith, L. (2010), "Law and Magic: An Introduction Out of a Hat," in C. Corcos (ed.), *Law and Magic: A Collection of Essays*, Durham, NC: Carolina Academic Press, 3–12.

Society of American Magicians (2010), *SAM Code of Ethics*, <http://www.magicsam.com/ethics.asp>, accessed December 1, 2009.

Sokol, D. (2008), "Medicine as performance: What can magicians teach doctors?", *Journal of the Royal Society of Medicine*, 101, 443–6.

Sorkin, A., O'Donnell, L., Jr. and Schmidt, L. (2004), "In the Room," transcript.

Stanley, J.F. (2005), "The 'magic words' of s. 554: A new test for formal adjudication under the Administrative Procedure Act," *Hastings Law Journal*, 56, 1,067–93.

State v. *Crews*, 923 S.W. 2d 477 (1996).

State v. *Green*, 343 So.2d 149 (1977).

State v. *Hargrove*, 1999 Wash. App. Lexis 1,321 (1999).

State v. *Nasi*, 2005 Wash. App. Lexis 831 (2005).

Steinmeyer, J. (2003), *Hiding the Elephant: How Magicians Invented the Impossible and Learned to Disappear*, New York: Carroll and Graf.

Stevens, R.B. (1983), *Law School: Legal Education in America From the 1850s to the 1980s*, Chapel Hill, NC: University of North Carolina Press.

Strickler v. *Greene*, 527 US 263 (1999).

Suchman, M.C. (1989), "Invention and ritual: Notes on the interrelation of magic and intellectual property in preliterate societies," *Columbia Law Review*, 89, 1,264–94.

Swint v. *City of Wadley*, 85 F.3d 1,440 (1996).

Texas v. *Johnson*, 491 US 397 (1989).

Tierney, T.J. (1999), "Peracchi: Magicians in the Ninth Circuit Court?", *Southern University Law Review*, 26, 197–226.

Tolkien, J.R.R. (1954–56), *The Lord of the Rings*, Boston, MA: Houghton Mifflin.

Traynor, R. (1961), "No magic words could do it justice," *California Law Review*, 49(4), 615–30.

Trombly, K. (2010), "Conjuring and the Courtroom: All I Needed to Know about Trying Cases I Learned by Doing Magic Shows," in C. Corcos (ed.), *Law and Magic: A Collection of Essays*, Durham, NC: Carolina Academic Press, 339–47.

Truzzi, M. (1998), *Anomalistics: On Some Unfair Practices towards Claims of the Paranormal*, <http://www.skepticalinvestigations.org/anomalistics/practices.htm>, accessed April 21, 2006.

Tyson, D. (1996), *New Millennium Magic*, St. Paul, MN: Llewellyn Publications.

Ubelacker, S. (2002), Ex-lawyer worked magic for illusionists," *Hamilton Spectator*, June 11, D10.

US v. *Bunge*, 1994 US App. Lexis 32,734, 41 F. 3d 1,511 (7th Circ., 1994); cert. den'd 514 US 1,030 (1995).

US v. *Lopez-Alvarez*, 970 F. 2d 583 (1992).

US v. *Riggi*, 2003 WL 24154398. Brief for Defendant-Appellant Martin Lewis.

US v. *Riggi*, 117 Fed. Appx. 142 (2nd Circ. 2004).

US v. *Riggi*, 541 F. 3d 94 (2nd Circ. 2008).

US v. *Riggi*, 308 Fed. Appx. 514 (2nd Circ. 2009), 2009 WL 196210.

Waldman, C., Layden, J. and Swiss, J.I. (1997), *The Art of Magic*, Los Angeles, CA: General Publishing Group.

Watson, D.E. (1982), Actually, jury was judging prosecution, not Hinckley: And the judge presided over the whole circus," *Orange County Register*, June 30, <http://www.enformy.com/$ocr0630.html>, accessed August 12, 2004.

—— (1994), "The game of law," *The Orange County Register*, July 24, <http://www.enformy.com/$ocr0724.html>, accessed June 22, 2005.

—— (2004), *Curriculum Vitae*, <http://www.enformy.com/$cv.html>, accessed August 12, 2004.

Weyrauch, W.O. (1973), "Taboo and magic in law," *Stanford Law Review*, 25, 782–807.

Whitton, E. (1998), *The Cartel: Lawyers and their Nine Magic Tricks*, Sydney: Herwick.

Wise, Daniel (1991), "Lawyers, judges learn new tricks as magicians," *New York Law Journal*, April 1, 1.

Wiseman, R. and Lamont, P. (1995), *Magic in Theory*, Hatfield: University of Hertfordshire Press.

Chapter 8
The Construction of Admissions of Fault through American Rules of Evidence: Speech, Silence and Significance in the Legal Creation of Liability

Janet Ainsworth

Law is an inherently normative enterprise (Schlag 1991), and nowhere is that truer than in its normative approach to what may seem to be purely procedural matters such as the rules governing the admission of evidence in court. This chapter examines the way in which unexamined norms of language usage and meaning implicature are embedded within common law legal system through an examination of two American rules of evidence: one in which the law expressed a normative preference for speaking and consequently penalizes those who instead remain silent, and one in which the law expresses a normative preference for silence and legally penalizes those who instead speak. In both instances, the law's normative approach is empirically baseless and linguistically naive.

The United States, like other common law nations, uses evidence that can be introduced from the English adversarial trial advocacy system as gatekeeping rules, determining the admissibility of testimonial evidence can be introduced in a trial. The overarching standard for admissible evidence requires that it be both reliable—that is, worthy of credibility—and probative—that is, tending to prove some material fact at issue in the case. The emphasis on reliability explains the preference in common law hearsay evidence rules for the testimony of first-hand direct observers over second-hand reports of someone else's observations. The relevance rule, similarly, is grounded in the common law's privileging of testimony that has some tendency, even if slight, to prove a fact that the law deems to be material in resolving the dispute at hand. Evidence rules are seen in law as a gatekeeper ensuring reliability and probative power in admitted testimony. However, a critical examination of how the evidence rules operate exposes the ways in which common law rules of evidence are grounded in assumptions about human nature and behavior that are neither empirically grounded nor, candidly, even anecdotally persuasive as believable accounts of communicative performance.

A few examples suffice to make this point. For example, while ordinarily out-of-court utterances are excluded under the hearsay rules because it is impossible to assess their credibility, statements made by those who believe they are on the point of death are admissible in court as reliable evidence. The theory justifying the admission of this evidence is that deathbed utterances must be reliable because no one who believed they were about to die would willingly do so with a lie on their lips. This justification may once have been persuasive, perhaps, but it is difficult to believe today. Might a person, knowing that death is near, be tempted to take a last opportunity to shade the truth in order to make him or herself look better or to secure last-minute revenge on an enemy? Likewise, what a patient says to a doctor for purposes of obtaining medical treatment is legally considered to be reliable and thus admissible evidence because the law presumes that no one would intentionally lie to a doctor. Yet the law's assumption that such statements are reliable and true flies in the face of what we know about typical patient behavior. Certainly, patients have reason to be less than candid with their doctors about aspects of their behavior—what they eat; whether they indulge in the consumption of alcohol, tobacco and drugs; whether they engage in risky sexual practices; how often they exercise—because they wish to evade potential disapproval of their lifestyle choices. Again, the assumptions behind the rules of evidence appear outdated and naive upon examination. The presumptions underlying the rules of evidence have never been subject to empirical testing by behavioral scientists. Even on non-scientific, commonsense reflection, they seem implausible as a description of actual human motivation and behavior. Despite the strained plausibility of the justifications for these evidentiary rules, the situations described nevertheless lead to admissible testimony on the basis of unexamined beliefs encoded in law about how the "reasonable man" behaves. In other words, the evidence rules acknowledge that the "reasonable man" might lie at times in his life when it is in his interest to do so, but never when he is on the point of Judgment Day. Likewise, the "reasonable man" presumably never evades the truth with his doctor, even when it would expose embarrassing or unflattering aspects of his lifestyle to medical disapproval.

A closer examination of two other evidence rules based on similar unexamined assumptions about behavior and language exposes the implausibility of the behavioral assumptions upon which they are grounded. In the first example considered here, the rules of evidence construe a person's silence in the face of accusation as admissible evidence of admission of wrongdoing, presuming that the "reasonable man" would not remain silent under such circumstances. In the second example analyzed in this chapter, the rules of evidence construe any apologetic language used by a person to constitute admissible evidence of an admission to legal responsibility for the circumstance to which the apologetic language referred. In each case, the law assumes that the linguistic behavior which it constructs as that of the "reasonable man" is an adequate and appropriate basis for considering evidence to be both reliable and probative, and hence admissible in court.

As in other areas of the common law, evidence rules are predicated on beliefs about the behavior—in this case, the linguistic behavior—of what the law traditionally called the "reasonable man." As a general matter, the construct of the "reasonable man" sets the standard in law for legally privileged behavior and activity in the application of substantive legal doctrines, where acting as the law assumes the "reasonable man" would do insulates the actor against both civil and criminal liability. The power of the "reasonable man" construct in law extends beyond the substantive law of torts and criminal law, however, and extends its reach into the procedural realm of evidence law as well. The "reasonable man" has long dominated the common law legal imagination (see, for example, *Vaughn* v. *Menlove* 1837). As described within legal opinions, the "reasonable man" is the embodiment of middle-class values, sensibilities and practices—in the words of one judge, "the man who takes the magazines at home and in the evening pushes the lawnmower in his shirt sleeves" (*Hall* v. *Brooklands Auto Racing Club* 1933, 224). In recent years, the law's "reasonable man" has morphed into the "reasonable person" in an attempt to render the standard more universal and less particularly masculine. Legal scholars have expressed skepticism as to whether this terminology change has effectuated any substantive changes in the behavior expected by the law of this newly gender-neutral "reasonable person" (Bender 1988, 22; Cahn 1992, 1,405). Rather, the use of this gender-neutral standard may well serve only to impose a superficial mask of purported universality onto the unchanged behavioral norms and values incorporated in that original "reasonable man" standard (Graddol and Swann 1989, 110).

The influence of the assumed characteristics of the "reasonable man" in law can be seen in the workings of the rules of evidence at issue here. Specifically, the rules of evidence construe a person's silence in some circumstances as though it were in effect a confession of wrongdoing. Federal Rule of Evidence 801 (d) (2) (B) provides that if a person is confronted with an accusatory statement by someone else under circumstances in which a "reasonable man" would rebut that statement, and instead the hearer remains silent, that silence is admitted as an adoptive admission of the truth of the accusation. Before silence can be taken as a confession, the accused person must have heard and understood the accusatory utterance in question, must have had the opportunity to object to it, and the context must be one in which it would be reasonable to expect that there be a response to the accusation (Wigmore 1904, 102). Once these threshold requirements are met, silence in the face of someone's accusation is treated by the rules of evidence as the legal equivalent to an actual confession to the charge. The presumption behind the rule is that, when faced with an accusation of wrongdoing that is untrue, the "reasonable man" can have only one reasonable response—to explicitly and unequivocally deny it. This evidence rule, then, can be seen to be squarely premised on assumptions about how the "reasonable man" will express himself in situated discourse. The legally constructed "reasonable man" speaks directly, clearly, bluntly and without qualification, hesitation or mitigation (Ainsworth 1993, 302–6, 315–17). He never shrinks from confrontation, regardless of the circumstances. Moreover, he must maintain constant vigilance in his discursive interactions in case someone might use insulting or accusatory language in his presence—vigilance needed so that he spring into action and immediately rebut any implication of wrongdoing on his part.

When articulated in that fashion, the adoptive admission evidentiary rule seems to be based on a caricature of discursive behavior that is unconvincing. Indeed, a handful of courts over the years have suggested that silence in the face of arguable accusation should not necessarily be treated as tantamount to confession (see, for example, *People* v. *Bigge* 1939; *State* v. *Clark* 2008). Nevertheless, the vast majority of American appellate courts have endorsed these supposed adoptive admissions unreflectively. Worse, courts not infrequently apply the adoptive admission doctrine even in cases in which the foundational facts required by the rule for admissibility are highly questionable. The adoptive admissions rule makes no sense unless, at the very least, the party in question has actually heard the supposed accusation. In some cases, however, it is unclear from the evidence adduced at trial that the defendant even heard the statement in question because he may not have been in the room when the supposed accusation was uttered (*Alvarado* v. *State* 1995) or he was in the back seat of a car when a person sitting in the front seat supposedly made an accusation in a conversation with another front seat passenger (*US* v. *Carter* 1985). In other cases, the person who was said to have used accusatory language in the defendant's presence was unable in their courtroom testimony to recall whether or not the defendant remained silent upon hearing the purported accusatory statement, but the adoptive admission was used against the defendant none the less (*Commonwealth* v. *Braley* 2007).

The unfairness of the adoptive admissions doctrine is compounded by the fact that it is often applied in contexts in which the inferential link between the fact of silence and a presumed admission of guilt is extraordinarily unpersuasive as a matter of common sense. For example, in many cases, the supposedly accusatory language is not made in an interaction in which the accused person is a party, but instead merely made within his earshot in a conversation to which he is not a party. Apparently, the law insists that the "reasonable man" must monitor any conversation that happens to be within his hearing, and police it for direct or indirect accusations of wrongdoing, whether he is an addressee of that conversation or not. The "reasonable man" must moreover be particularly alert to ambiguous language that could potentially be interpreted as an accusation against him, especially if someone is using pronouns of ambiguous referential scope such as "we" (*People* v. *Sneed* 1995) or "they" (*People* v. *Riel* 2000) in describing someone's actions. Statements that are ambiguous, if they have any potentially available interpretation that could be construed as possibly accusatory, are especially fraught with the peril of an inadvertent tacit admission of wrongdoing. According to the adoptive admissions rule, innocent-sounding remarks with multiple potential meanings that might conceivably have an incriminating implication must be objected to, or else risk an admission to the incriminating interpretation. For example, in a conversational exchange between two corporate officers, the statement by one of them that "I'll see if we can get anything for this work" was construed to be an agreement that an illegal bid rigging be arranged. Despite the fact that this statement is entirely consistent with an attempt to procure business in a lawful manner, the defendant's failure to anticipate and object to an interpretation of his statement that implied unlawful bid rigging was considered by the court as an admission that he was aware of the illegal nature of the bid (*US* v. *Basic Construction Co.* 1983).

Even a failure to object to innocuous, non-accusatory statements can result in adoptive admissions when, after the conversation has concluded, those statements—innocent in the context in which they were made—turn out to be inculpatory. For example, when a stranger referred to the defendant as "John" to another without objection by the defendant, the court held his lack of protest to be an admission that the defendant went by that name (*State* v. *Wallingford* 2001). In another case, the defendant's failure to object to another person's claim that she usually carried a gun was construed as an admission that not only did she usually carry a gun, but also that she was in possession of a gun at the time of a crime that occurred long after the conversation in question. Apparently, according to this court's analysis, she should have foreseen that failure to object to this characterization of her habitual behavior would constitute an "admission" of a fact concerning a crime that had not even occurred at the time (*State* v. *Browning* 1997). In other words, the law's imagined "reasonable man" is supposed to be alert to the possibility that inaccurate statements made in his presence—however inconsequential they might appear at the time—could turn out to incriminate him for crimes that might occur at some time in the future.

According to this legal doctrine, a "reasonable man" doesn't simply ignore name-calling, but instead must object to it, or be held to have agreed with the characterization. In one such case, when the defendant was called a "butcher," his failure to argue with the name-caller was later held by the court to be an admission of that fact (*State* v. *Gorrell* 1996). Similarly, ducking a rude, point-blank question about impropriety can result in the court construing a refusal to engage with the questioner as adoptive admission of guilt, as when a corporate executive, asked by a reporter at a press conference if the corporation had been "cooking the books," responded by saying, "Next question, please." Although one plausible interpretation of this response is that the executive merely had no intention of engaging the reporter hounding him, the court instead found that his failure to deny the allegation constituted an admission on his part. In the court's view, the "reasonable man" in such a situation would have directly rebutted the reporter's claim without attempting to avoid it (*US* v. *Henke* 2000). Even reacting angrily to an accusation may not be sufficient to avoid the adoptive admission trap, as when a frustrated and angry defendant told an accuser to "shut the f— up." This angry outburst was insufficiently responsive to the accusation, in the opinion of the reviewing court, and actually constituted an admission that the accusation was correct (*State* v. *Gilmore* 1999).

At times, even an explicit denial of an accusation may not be adequate to avoid an imputed adoptive admission if the defendant fails to repeat the denial each time the accusation is made. For example, in one case the defendant was asked if he had committed the crime, and he explicitly denied it. The questioner responded to this denial by telling him that a third party thought that he had done it. Instead of repeating the denial anew, the defendant in this case reacted by turning his head and staring out the window. The court could easily have characterized this response as shock or dismay that someone could think that he had committed the crime, but instead construed it as an adoptive admission because he failed to repeat the denial that he had made just seconds before (*State* v. *Gomez* 2004).

Cases involving recorded telephone conversations pose special problems for appropriate implicated meaning because each conversant's inability to see the other person's facial expressions or body language can give rise to implicature that is not intended, including a false impression of acquiescence to an accusation. For instance, in one such case, a defendant's silence during a recorded jailhouse telephone conversation while a friend read to him a newspaper account of the crime was admitted as an adoptive admission of the facts as set out in the news story, on the theory that the "reasonable man" would have objected during the recitation of the newspaper's version of the crime (*US* v. *Higgs* 2003). In another case involving a recorded jailhouse conversation, the defendant was told by the other party to the conversation that the police had asked that party "twelve times" whether he had seen the defendant shoot the victims, to which the defendant replied, "Oh man, twelve times." From this response, the court concluded that the defendant had admitted to being the shooter because his response did not include a specific denial of that fact. Of course, there was no reason for him have objected in this conversation to the police theory that he was the shooter, because the other party gave no indication that he shared that police belief. In fact, had the defendant done so, it would have been a non-responsive non sequitur in the context of a conversation whose actual topic was the persistence of police questioning of the other party, not the accuracy of the police hypothesis of the defendant's guilt. Apparently, the law's imagined "reasonable man" would express neither shock in the persistence of a false police theory of the case, nor empathy for the police grilling that his friend had undergone, but would instead respond only by explicitly informing the other party that the police were wrong in their suspicions (*People* v. *Davis* 2005).

Merely being quietly present while someone else plans a crime or boasts about past crimes can result in adoptive admissions that one is or was involved in those crimes. In one such case, the defendant nodded his head while someone at a party bragged about having committed crimes. Although the braggart's version of the crimes at no point claimed that the defendant participated in those crimes, the reviewing court found that sitting silently and nodding his head constituted an adoptive admission by the defendant that he, too, had participated in some unspecified way in the braggart's crime spree (*US* v. *Price* 2008). In another case, someone that the prosecution characterized as a racketeering kingpin ordered a third party to commit arson while the kingpin was present in the defendant's home. The defendant did not speak up to object to the kingpin's command to that third party. Remaining silent here was construed to be an admission by the defendant of his own culpability in the arson plot, said the court, since "an innocent man would not let others sit in his house and plan arson" (*US* v. *Manzella* 1986, 545). Apparently, the law's imagined "reasonable man" doesn't fear the physical consequences of confronting powerful criminals who could potentially do him serious harm. In another similar case, a defendant who testified that he could not object because of fear to inaccurate inculpatory statements made by a Mexican Mafia boss in his presence nevertheless was saddled with those statements as adoptive admissions (*Paredes* v. *State* 2004). Power imbalances making objection realistically unavailable are rendered invisible in cases such as these.

Disparities in power between participants in a discursive interaction may inhibit the possibility of a denial of accusatory statements in other contexts as well. In one case, in the course of a court hearing addressing a guilty plea agreement, the judge made statements on the record characterizing the facts of the crime to which the plea was to be entered. In a later matter, that defendant objected to those judicial statements as inaccurate and misleading. He was, however, held to have adopted the misleading details stated by the plea judge because he had not interrupted the plea judge during the plea hearing to object to the judge's characterization of the crime. Apparently, the "reasonable man" doesn't fear jeopardizing a plea bargain and risking a higher sentence by interrupting and contradicting the judge in his description of the offense for which the defendant hopes to get the benefit of his plea bargain (*US* v. *Miller* 2007).

As cases like this show, the adoptive admission rule of evidence maintains that a "reasonable man" not only confronts accusations made directly to him, but must also be alert for any statements that he might overhear made to anyone else that might impugn him, whether explicitly or impliedly, with regard to supposed bad acts that have occurred in the past or that might occur in the future. Unless he defends himself with an uncategorical denial in any of those situations, the law of evidence will treat his silence as the legal equivalent of a confession. Because it is conceptualized as the equivalent of an express confession to the wrongdoing, the adoptive admission is deemed to be sufficient to sustain a conviction even where there is little or no other substantive evidence of guilt of the crime in question (see, for example, *Commonwealth* v. *Braley* 2007; *State* v. *Tolliver* 2001).

The principle behind the adoptive admission rule of evidence can become a particularly insidious trap for anyone who is being investigated by the police on a potential criminal charge. Under the nearly fifty-year-old Miranda rule governing police interrogation in the United States, a person who is arrested must be informed by the police of his constitutional rights to remain silent and to have the assistance of counsel during questioning upon request. He will be reminded that if he chooses to speak, anything he does say can be used against him later in court (*Miranda* v. *Arizona* 1966). The Supreme Court has acknowledged that, having just expressly informed a suspect that he need not respond during interrogation, it would be unfair to then turn around and use silence by the suspect upon being confronted with police accusations as evidence suggesting guilt. Taking a suspect's exercise of the right to silence as an adoptive admission and proof of guilt would completely gut the Miranda rule, turning attempts to exercise the right to remain silent into the functional equivalent of confessions. Therefore, the court has held that, once given Miranda warnings, an arrestee's mere failure to respond to accusatory language by the police cannot be used as an adoptive admission (*Wainwright* v. *Greenfield* 1986). Since the adoptive admissions rule by its own terms requires that the context of the interchange be one in which it would be natural for the accused to affirmatively deny the accusation, it might appear that the adoptive admissions rule could have no application at any point in a Miranda-governed interrogation system, with its guarantees of the right to remain silent. Yet, surprisingly, in a number of American jurisdictions, this is not the case, and a failure to respond to police accusations in certain circumstances runs the risk of inadvertently admitting those allegations by silence.

The Miranda warnings, as the Supreme Court has recently reaffirmed, are part of the cultural fabric of the country (*Dickerson* v. *US* 2000, 443). Reading the Miranda rights to the just-arrested culprit is a stock scene in police dramas on television and in the movies. As a result, there is hardly an American alive who could not recite the famous warning by heart. With that in mind, consider the commonplace situation in which someone is confronted by the police but not read the Miranda rights because the police have not yet made the decision to make an arrest. (Police are free to interrogate suspects without providing Miranda warnings until the point of arrest.) In a situation like this, the suspect might well be aware from his stock of cultural knowledge that he has the right to remain silent, even though the Miranda warnings have yet to be formally given him. If this suspect has had previous police encounters in which he had the Miranda rights read on those earlier occasions, he might be particularly conscious of his right to refuse to answer police questions and to refuse to respond to their accusations. In a pre-arrest context like this, the suspect who stays mute in the face of police accusations could be motivated by his realization that anything he says could be used against him, so that the wisest course may well be is to say nothing at all.

However reasonable this reasoning might be to a suspect, the Supreme Court has nevertheless permitted the prosecution to use evidence of pre-arrest, unwarned silence on the part of a suspect to be used to impeach his credibility if he later takes the stand at trial (*Jenkins* v. *Anderson* 1980). Even post-arrest silence can be used for impeachment as long as the record does not show that Miranda warnings were actually given. Despite the fact that most people already understand that they have the right to remain silent in the face of police accusations, citizens are not justified in relying on the right to remain silent, says the court, unless they can establish that the Miranda warnings had actually been read to them by the time of the police confrontation at issue (*Fletcher* v. *Weir* 1982). Failing that, silence in the face of police accusations can be used as impeachment; that is, to attack the defendant's credibility if he takes the stand to testify in his defense. The prosecutor will be permitted to argue that an innocent person would not have refused to answer police questioning, and further, that the jury should now disbelieve his testimony in court because he failed to tell his story to the police during their investigation.

This line of argument would be clearly unlawful if the defendant had been arrested and Mirandized prior to his refusal to answer police questions, and is only allowed in a pre-arrest interrogation because of the fiction that persons only become aware of their right to remain silent upon the reading of Miranda rights.

One question that the Supreme Court has not yet decided is whether a person's silence in the face of police questioning can be used not merely to impeach—to suggest that his trial testimony should not be believed—but as an adoptive admission that would constitute substantive evidence of guilt. Since adoptive admissions are treated in law as if they were explicit confessions, can silence in the face of police accusations be treated as though it were a confession to the truth of those allegations? If that were the case, then making the mistake of asserting one's right to silence too soon—before the formal reading of Miranda rights—could be a disastrous choice for the unwary. Believing that remaining silent is the safest choice when confronted with police accusations of wrongdoing, the person opting not to cooperate would inadvertently be adopting the truth of those accusations, and in effect unintentionally confessing to them.

In the absence of controlling Supreme Court case law, lower federal appellate courts have been divided in answering the question of whether silence in the face of police accusations can be used as substantive evidence of guilt via the adoptive admission doctrine. The Fourth, Fifth, Eighth and Eleventh Circuits have all ruled that silence in the face of police accusations by arrestees who have not yet been read Miranda warnings can be used by prosecutors as substantive evidence of guilt; the Seventh, Ninth and DC Circuits, on the other hand, have held that it is constitutionally impermissible to use that silence as affirmative proof of guilt. A similar split in the circuit courts exists on the related question with respect to police accusations made prior to any arrest, with the First, Sixth, Seventh and Tenth Circuits determining that silence in the face of police accusations cannot be used as substantive evidence of guilt, whereas the Fifth, Ninth and Eleventh Circuits have concluded that before arrest, a person who refuses to respond to police accusations does so at peril of adopting any allegations by silence (Skrapka 2006, 374–87; Ryan 2007, 908–13). Thus, despite the knowledge of virtually all Americans that they have the right to remain silent when confronted by the police, exercising that right in many American jurisdictions leads to the possibility that such silence will be construed as a confession—a possibility almost certainly not anticipated by the person who naively believes that Americans have the constitutional right to remain silent when questioned by the police.

As this analysis shows, the rules of evidence can have the effect of turning a person's silence into "speech" by presuming that the "reasonable man" would speak to rebut a direct or even inferential accusation of wrongdoing if it were untrue, such that it is fair to construe silence—the failure to respond—as though it were actually a confession to the accusation. In essence, because the law's imagined "reasonable man" would speak to confront an accusation, all citizens have the legal duty to speak, enforced by the law's construal of silence as the equivalent of an admission of criminal guilt or civil liability.

In other situations, however, the "reasonable man" is constructed under the law as someone who would not speak, and the person who instead chooses to speak is penalized under the evidence rules. One such case occurs when a person says something that sounds as though it might be an apology. Evidence law construes utterances such as "I'm sorry" as admissions that the speaker is at fault for the negative circumstance being commented upon. As such, "I'm sorry" becomes admissible against the speaker as a declaration against interest under Federal Rule of Evidence 804 (b) (3), and can be interpreted as a confession of fault. In other words, the law's imagined "reasonable man" never says "I'm sorry" unless he intends to admit being at fault.

Evidence law's interpretation of apologetic language as an admission of wrongdoing betrays the law's impoverished conceptualization of the pragmatics of such language. "I'm sorry" is language that can bear a multitude of meanings, depending on context (Lakoff 2003; Blum-Kulka et al. 1989; Fraser 1981). In some circumstances, "I'm sorry"—or language like it—can of course be fairly construed as a confession of wrongdoing, coupled with an expression of remorse on the part of the speaker for the transgression. This confession-plus-remorse interpretation is the construction that the law's "reasonable man" invariably gives to apologetic language. However, confession-plus-remorse is by no means the only interpretation that can be given to apologetic language. Saying "I'm sorry" can, in some contexts, be an expression of empathy completely devoid of any connotation of fault for the negative situation that provoked the expression. For example, when someone says "I'm so sorry" upon hearing of another's recent bereavement, there is no question that "I'm sorry" is not meant to be an admission of responsibility for the death. Instead, it serves to build and reinforce interpersonal relational ties by an empathetic acknowledgement of the pain suffered by the addressee as a result of the bereavement.

"I'm sorry" can, in other contexts, be interpreted as an expression of non-empathetic regret, again without any implication of responsibility for wrongdoing on the part of the speaker, as when the speaker tells a former lover, "I'm sorry I ever met you." In yet another context, someone might say "I'm sorry" even though the speaker does not truly acknowledge fault in an attempt to defuse a hostile or violent situation. In fact, in a dangerously violent confrontation, a weaker party might have little recourse other than to desperately attempt to placate the stronger party by the use of apologetic language, regardless of whether the apologizer was actually assuming responsibility for the negative situation. Even in contexts unmarked by marked power disparity, saying "I'm sorry" can be an effective discursive strategy to short-circuit an argument when a more substantive response would only serve to prolong an unpleasant interchange. In that kind of situation, "I'm sorry" serves as a useful linguistic resource to smooth over interpersonal disputes without necessarily accepting full responsibility for being in the wrong.

Despite the pragmatic richness of apologetic language and its myriad of interpretable meanings, the law of evidence always permits the construal of language such as "I'm sorry" to be an admission that the speaker is at fault and thus potentially legally liable. The "reasonable man" is careful to avoid apologetic language unless he intends to admit that he is at fault. He cannot contemplate the more nuanced social uses of apology because the law's "reasonable man" assumes that language is nothing more than a referential vehicle of propositional communication, and thus he ignores its use as a mechanism for maintaining and repairing social relationships (Ainsworth 2008, 14–15).

Apologies are avoided whenever possible by the legally imagined "reasonable man" not only because they expose him to legal liability, but also because apologies are seen as language of weakness. Apology puts the speaker in a vulnerable position with respect to the person apologized to. The admission of fault inherent in apology puts the apologizer in a one-down position through that very acknowledgement. Worse yet, from the point of view of the apologizer, is the possibility that the addressee might rebuff the apology and choose not to accept the offered expression of regret. Because the addressee of an apology has that unilateral power to reject an apology, those who might potentially apologize have a keen appreciation that their act of apology puts them at risk of serious face-threat (Goffman 1967, 5–45). When the person apologized to fails to accept the apology unconditionally and instead delivers a reproach to the apologizer, the apologizing party may feel forced to adopt a defensive, self-justifying response in order to mitigate the face-threat inherent in that reproach (Hodgins and Liebeskind 2003). Not surprisingly, then, powerful persons may opt to avoid the face-threat inherent in apology in the first place. Those who are powerful will tend not to apologize even when in the wrong; those who lack power may end up having to apologize despite not being in the wrong.

Here again, it is the presumptively "normal" linguistic behavior of the "reasonable man" that leads the rules of evidence to the default presumption that apologetic language be construed as admission of fault. The "reasonable man"—seen as self-regarding, autonomous, and individualistic—does not need to use language like "I'm sorry" to maintain or repair his relationships or in finding emotional solidarity with others for their misfortunes and tragedies. Nor is he concerned with placating those who may be more powerful than he is, or finding discursive methods to resolve disputes and reduce interpersonal tensions. The only use of apologetic language for the law's "reasonable man" is—when absolutely necessary—to admit wrongdoing. This cramped and impoverished conceptualization of the social meanings potentially available for apologetic language in the law results in insurance companies advising their policy holders never to say "I'm sorry" when they are in an accident (Robbenolt 2005, 1,012). In fact, according to the language found in some insurance contracts, insurers actually have the right to void coverage and refuse to pay policy holders who use such apologetic language after an accident (Bartels 2000, 153).

That the law treats apologetic language as an admission of fault giving rise to potential legal liability has other unfortunate consequences. For example, doctors have long understood the legal danger that apologetic language can present in cases of bad patient outcomes. Apologetic language is, of course, pragmatically ambiguous in such cases. It might be a true acknowledgement that the doctor has acted negligently and caused unnecessary harm to the patient. On the other hand, it also could quite plausibly be an act of emotional solidarity with a fellow human being—an empathetic expression recognizing the suffering of the patient, even if that suffering has come into being without any fault at all on the part of the doctor. Under the rules of evidence, however, apologetic expressions by medical personnel made to patients or their families—whether intended as merely sympathetic or as actually acknowledging some degree of responsibility for the harm—could be used as evidence against them in malpractice litigation. As a result, doctors and other medical workers have long been cautioned to avoid any kind of empathetic language in their communications with afflicted patients and their loved ones, and above all, to refuse to admit the possibility of mistake or misjudgment on their part (Taft 2005a, 58).

The traditional avoidance of language smacking of apology by doctors and other medical workers is not a costless discursive strategic, however. Losing the opportunity to connect on a human level with patients through expressions of empathetic solidarity makes the doctor–patient relationship more bureaucratic—less fully human—than it would otherwise be. Nor does it even turn out to fulfill its ostensible purpose of avoiding legal liability. Partly as a result of perceived physician stonewalling, those who suffer unexpectedly poor medical outcomes often file lawsuits out of frustration in an attempt to find answers to what happened and why. Those who suspect that they or their loved ones may be victims of medical mistakes are often motivated as much by a desire to know the truth behind their tragedies as by the pursuit of monetary compensation for the harms themselves. (Taft 2005a, 77–8; Robbenolt 2005, 1,015–17). Ironically, doctors' silence in the face of bad patient outcomes—a strategy designed to reduce the possibility of liability through avoiding admissions of fault—actually has the unintended consequence of promoting lawsuits. Because of this, there is currently a growing trend to create an exception to the rule that apologies be admissible as admissions of fault in the context of medical malpractice cases. More than half of American state legislatures have in the last few years passed special exceptions to the evidentiary rule construing apologetic language as admissions of fault when the apologetic language was used by medical personnel faced with bad patient outcomes (Todres 2006, 686). In such states, doctors can freely use apologetic language with their patients without worrying that their words will come back to haunt them in any potential future trial. This special exception to the application of the evidence rule in the context of medical malpractice cases has indeed appeared to have had its intended result of reducing overall doctor liability. In the words of one of the doctors who has been a major proponent of legislation insulating medical apologies from legal consequences: "Nothing is more effective in reducing liability" (Taft 2005a, 63).

Based on the success of the legislative move toward preventing doctor apologies from being used as evidence of fault in court, one might ask whether this represents a more general trend toward breaking the legal link between apology and liability. Might it even mean that the law's "reasonable man," with his abhorrence of apology, is losing his grip over the rules of evidence? This seems unlikely, upon further examination. The laws barring the use in malpractice cases of arguably apologetic language used by doctors has not led to a more general questioning of the proposition that apologies should be interpreted as admissions of fault. Rather, the legislative move to insulate doctors' apologies from use at trial has been promoted as part of a package of laws designed to make it harder for patients to sue their doctors—including shortening the time limits for filing suits, restricting compensation for lawyers who represent injured patients, and capping compensable damages for pain and suffering regardless of the severity of the injury (Todres 2006, 693–6). Thus, the doctors' apologies being protected under these new laws are not being excluded from use at trial because of the law's recognition that apologies are pragmatically variable in their implied meaning. Nor are these laws being enacted out of a desire to promote empathy, or to maintain human relationships, or to mitigate power imbalances. Instead, these laws are being promoted as an instrumental means to reduce the frequency of medical malpractice litigation, to limit patients' ability to obtain compensation for their harms, and to free doctors from the consequences of admitting mistakes.

Tellingly, in some states, not only are empathetic apologies excluded from evidence, but even specific admissions of acts of malpractice by medical personnel are also barred from use at trial (Taft 2005b, 602). Apologetic language of this latter sort—articulating factual responsibility for harm caused, acknowledging fault and expressing regret for the harm— is much closer to the kind of canonical apology that unambiguously confesses responsibility for the unjust suffering of another (Smith 2008, 140–42). Those sorts of apologies are exactly the kind of apologetic expressions that legitimately ought to give rise to legal consequences. Yet, in its enthusiasm for reducing medical malpractice liability, the law now refuses to give legal effect to precisely the kinds of apologies that linguistic analysis would confirm actually do support an implicature of admission of fault.

In both the evidentiary rule on adoptive admissions and the rule construing apologies as admissions, legal liability is created through the use of normative presumptions about the linguistic practices of the "reasonable man"—when he would speak and when he ought to instead keep silent. Despite the lack of empirical support for these normative presumptions, evidence law persists in enforcing these "reasonable man"-based standards even in factual circumstances that raise serious doubt about their applicability—privileging discursive practices that accord with the "reasonable man" construct, and penalizing those that do not. In that way, evidence law both constructs and mediates its own discursive paradigms through its role as gatekeeper of admissible evidence in trials. As part of larger normative and ideological systems, evidence law, like law more generally, both reflects existing power relations and serves to maintain, reinforce and amplify those hierarchies.

References

Ainsworth, J.E. (1993), "In a different register: The pragmatics of powerlessness in police interrogation," *Yale Law Journal*, 103, 259–322.

—— (2008), "'You have the right to remain silent' ... but only if you ask for it just so: The role of linguistic ideology in American police interrogation law," *International Journal of Speech, Language, and Law*, 15, 1–21.

Bartels, W.K. (2000), "The stormy seas of apologies: California provides a safe harbor for apologies made after accidents," *Western State University Law Review*, 28, 141–57.

Bender, L. (1988). "A lawyer's primer on feminist theory and tort law," *Journal of Legal Education*, 38, 3–37.

Blum-Kulka, S., House, J. and Kaspar, G. (eds.) (1989), *Cross-cultural Pragmatics: Requests and Apologies*, Norwood, NJ: Ablex.

Bucholtz, M. (1999), "Bad Examples: Transgression and Progress in Language and Gender," in M. Bucholtz, A.C. Liang and L.A. Sutton (eds.), *Reinventing Identities: The Gendered Self in Discourse*, New York: Oxford University Press, 3–24.

Cahn, N.R. (1992), "The looseness of legal language: The reasonable woman standard in theory and in practice," *Cornell Law Review*, 77, 1,389–446.

Fraser, B. (1981), "On Apologizing," in F. Coulmas (ed.), *Conversation Routine: Explorations in Standardized Communication Situations*, Berlin: Mouton de Gruyter, 259–71.

Goffman, E. (1967), "On Face-work: An Analysis of Ritual Elements in Social Interaction," in *Interaction Ritual*, New York: Anchor Books, 5–45.

Graddol, D. and Swann, J. (1989), *Gender Voices*, Cambridge, MA: Blackwell.

Hodgins, H.S. and Liebeskind, E. (2003), "Apology versus defense: Antecedents and consequences," *Journal of Experimental Social Psychology*, 39, 297–316.

Lakoff, R.T. (2003), "Nine ways of looking at apology: The necessity for interdisciplinary theory and method in discourse analysis," in D. Schiffrin, D. Tannen and H. Hamilton (eds.), *Handbook on Discourse Analysis*, Malden, MA: Blackwell, 199–214.

Robbenolt, J.K. (2005), "What we know and don't know about the role of apologies in resolving health care disputes," *Georgia State Law Review*, 21, 1,009–27.

Ryan, M.E. (2007), "Do you have a right to remain silent? The substantive use of pre-Miranda silence," *Alabama Law Review*, 58, 903–18.

Schlag, P. (1991), "Normativity and the politics of form," *University of Pennsylvania Law Review*, 139, 801–932.

Skrapka, M. (2006), "Silence should be golden: A case against the use of a defendant's post-arrest, pre-Miranda silence as evidence of guilt," *Oklahoma Law Review*, 59, 357–402.

Smith, N. (2008), *I Was Wrong: The Meaning of Apologies*, Cambridge: Cambridge University Press.

Taft, L. (2005a), "Apology and medical mistake: Opportunity or foil?", *Annals of Health Law*, 14, 55–94.
—— (2005b), "On bended knee (with fingers crossed)," *DePaul Law Review*, 55, 601–15.
Todres, J. (2006), "Toward healing and restoration for all: Reframing medical malpractice reform," *Connecticut Law Review*, 39, 667–737.
Wigmore, J.H. (1904), *Evidence in Trials at Common Law*, vol. 4, Boston, MA: Little, Brown.

Cases Cited

Alvarado v. *State*, 912 SW2d 199 (Tex. Ct. Crim. App. 1995).
Commonwealth v. *Braley*, 867 NE2d 743 (Mass. S. Jud. Ct. 2007).
Dickerson v. *US*, 530 US 428 (2000).
Fletcher v. *Weir*, 455 US 603 (1982).
Hall v. *Brooklands Auto Racing Club*, 1 KB 205, 224 (1933).
Jenkins v. *Anderson*, 447 US 231 (1980).
Miranda v. *Arizona*, 384 US 436 (1966).
Paredes v. *State*, 129 SW3d 530 (Tex. Ct. Crim. App. 2004).
People v. *Bigge*, 285 NW5 (1939).
People v. *Davis*, 115 P3d 417 (Cal. S. Ct. 2005).
People v. *Riel*, 998 P2d 969 (Cal. S. Ct. 2000).
People v. *Sneed*, 653 NE2d 1,349 (Ill. App. 1995).
State v. *Browning*, 485 SE2d 1 (W. Va. S. Ct. 1997).
State v. *Clark*, 175 P.3d 1,006 (2008).
State v. *Gilmore*, 22 SW3d 712 (Mo. App. 1999).
State v. *Gomez*, 848 A2d 221 (RI S. Ct. 2004).
State v. *Gorrell*, 687 A2d 1016 (NJ App. 1996)
State v. *Henke*, 222 f3D 633 (9th Cir. 2000).
State v. *Tolliver*, 765 NE2d 894 (Ohio App. 2001).
State v. *Wallingford*, 43 SW3d 852 (Mo. App. 2001).
US v. *Basic Construction Co.*, 711 F2d 570 (4th Cir. 1983).
US v. *Carter*, 760 F2d 1560 (11th Cir. 1985).
US v. *Henke*, 222 F3d 633 (9th Cir. 2000).
US v. *Higgs*, 353 F3d 281 (4th Cir. 2003).
US v. *Manzella*, 782 F2d 533 (5th Cir. 1986).
US v. *Miller*, 478 F3d 48 (1st Cir. 2007).
US v. *Price*, 516 F3d 597 (7th Cir. 2008).
Vaughn v. *Menlove*, 132 Eng. Rep. 490 (1837).
Wainwright v. *Greenfield*, 474 US 284 (1986).

Chapter 9
The Construction of Truth in Legal Decision-making

Petrina Schiavi

> "Truth", the proffering of some determinate version of what really happened … [is] a construction produced in and through practical activity. (Pollner 1987, xi)

This chapter is about the construction of "truth" by judges in legal decision-making. It investigates how judges operating within an adversarial system of law are able to "find the true facts" from the competing evidence presented to the court by parties to a dispute. In the process, it identifies the techniques used by judges to explain the phenomenon of conflicting accounts of reality in such a way that the belief in a single reality is not threatened. Fundamental to this analysis is the notion that language plays an integral role in the production and reproduction of social facts and social order.

Where a dispute between parties is heard before a court in an adversarial system of law, at least two competing accounts of reality are presented—the applicant's and respondent's. In addition, there may be additional versions of events related to the court by any witnesses called by the parties. In jurisdictions that use an adversarial system of law (such as Australia, the UK and the USA), the judge is not permitted to undertake any investigations into the facts in dispute before the court. Judges are restricted to deciding the case based solely upon the evidence brought before them by the parties to the case, and such evidence must comply with the requirements of the rules of evidence that apply in that jurisdiction. This is in contrast to the inquisitorial system of law that exists in many European countries, where the judge acts as an independent investigator to the case.

From the judge's perspective, the competing claims of the opposing parties stand in some unknown relationship to the "real" or "actual" state of affairs (Pollner 1987). In determining "what really happened," the judge is faced with a dilemma, for the "real" event occurred independently of the evidence brought before the court by the parties to the dispute. Yet this evidence is the only way the event in question is made "observable" to the judge. As a consequence, the judge's determinations of "what really happened," or the "'truth," must be founded on an anticipation of the formal structure of real things (Garfinkel 1967; Pollner 1987, 30). And so, from this collection of competing claims, judges rely upon certain beliefs about reality to make a "finding of fact" which is the legally authoritative declaration of "what really happened."

This chapter takes as its focus the rulings made by federal judges of the Family Court of Australia between 1976 and 1995 in which allegations of domestic violence were considered as part of the decision-making process. It employs theoretical approaches drawn from the fields of ethnomethodology, the sociological analysis of motivational accounts, and studies of narratives in discourse. Of particular value to the analysis is the work of Garfinkel (1967) in relation to legal decision-making and justification, Sacks' (1979) concept of "membership categorization devices," and Pollner's (1987) analysis of the process of mundane reason and the explanation of conflicting accounts.

Family Court Judgments and Case Reports

The narratives that form the basis of this analysis were drawn from published case reports of judgments of the Family Court of Australia. Central to the judgment is the judge's "finding" of the "facts" of the case, which is the judge's interpretation and resolution of the litigants' testimony of the events relevant to the dispute before the court. This highly condensed account of the judge's construction of the "facts" combines with the authority of the law to become the "truth," the definitive legal reality of the litigants. The judge makes a final ruling by applying his or her interpretation of the relevant law to these "true facts" of the case.

In addition to the obvious and immediate impact of the judge's ruling on the lives of the parties before the court, the judgment published in a case report also has the potential to shape the law into the future. Under the "doctrine of precedent," if a case can be demonstrated to have facts that are consistent with an authoritative case, then a strong legal argument can be made for the new case to be decided in accordance with that authority. Published cases are easily accessible to legal practitioners, and so are more likely to be cited and applied in legal argument in future cases. References to past decisions published in case reports is also a means by which judges and legal practitioners can maintain or challenge certain social issues in a "continuing legal conversation" across time in a way that maintains the authority of legal language in resolving social disputes (see Mertz 1996, 153). Accordingly, published case reports can be seen as especially valuable examples of legal reasoning and the construction of reality. Even though they may not represent a typical cross-section of cases heard before the Family Court, published reports do represent the more influential decisions made by the Family Court.

The case reports selected for this study were in relation to court hearings heard pursuant to the Australian Family Law Act (1975) between 1976 and 1995, and involved a consideration by the court of allegations of violent acts perpetrated by the male respondent against the female applicant. Around 30 case reports were found to have been published over this period that contained references by the judge to an event of violence. Of these reports, 20 were selected that contained at least two paragraphs of description of a violent event. Of these 20 case reports, 10 dealt with disputes around child access or custody, 9 related to restraining orders, and one report concerned an application for common law damages for assault.

The selected case reports were read in detail, with attention paid to instances throughout the texts where conflicting accounts of a violent event were presented to the court by the parties to the case and were then resolved by the judge. From this detailed reading, three stages emerged as fundamental to the way in which judges resolve conflicting accounts of reality into one authoritative version of "the truth." The first stage involves the judge reconciling a mundane belief in a single version of reality with the fact that different versions of reality are presented before the court for resolution. The second stage is where the judge makes a "finding of fact" from the conflicting accounts of reality by constructing a narrative within the judgment of "what really happened." The third stage of the decision-making process relates to the way in which the judge justifies the decision based on the "facts" which were "found." This chapter looks in detail at the first and second stages—the application of "mundane reason" to resolve conflicting accounts of reality and the "finding of facts" by judges.

Mundane Reason and the Resolution of Conflicting Accounts of Reality

Pollner (1987, 23) argues that rather than there being a reality "out there" that is impervious to individuals' social construction of it, an objective reality is advanced and sustained through a process of "mundane reason" supported by certain beliefs and prejudices about the nature of reality. Pollner analyzes these beliefs and prejudices to demonstrate how they effectively protect the process of mundane reason from outside challenges.

The primary function of a judge in the Family Law Court of Australia is to resolve a dispute between two parties. Accordingly, a judge expects that parties to a case will have conflicting accounts of certain sets of events. However, the process of mundane reason used by a judge to resolve conflicting accounts is based on the belief that there is only one objective reality. If, as mundane reason holds, a single, independent "real world" does exist, then logically every person should observe it in the same way. The existence of conflicting accounts of one reality poses a fundamental threat to the key assumption of mundane reason and the judge is faced with a problem. On the one hand, the judge needs conflicting accounts of reality in order to function as a "judge" and resolve the dispute. On the other hand, the process of reason employed by the judge to resolve conflicting accounts is based upon the belief that there is only one objective reality that, presumably, every person should experience in the same way.

According to Pollner (1987), mundane reasoners deal with conflicting accounts of a single reality by explaining a contradiction in one of three ways. First, a mundane reasoner may hold that the observers were experiencing fundamentally different events, objects or scenes (explanation at the level of object). Second, it may be suggested that the observer's experiential or cognitive processes were impaired or distorted in such a way that they had poor vision or were psychologically impaired (explanation at the level of experience). Third, a mundane reasoner may state that the observers were relating the experience in a non-literal method—that is, that they were lying, joking or speaking metaphorically (explanation at the level of account).

The selected case reports were analyzed to identify how judges resolved the dilemma of conflicting accounts of violent events between the parties. The analysis was informed by Pollner's identification of techniques applied in order to protect threats to mundane reason, namely: explanations at the level of object, experience and account. The results of this analysis are discussed in this section.

Explanation at the Level of Object

An explanation of conflicting accounts at the level of object relies upon an assumption that the two parties were observing a different scene, object or event. In none of the case reports included in this analysis did a judge resolve competing accounts of reality by way of explanation at the level of object. This is a somewhat unsurprising result, as a violent act committed by the husband against the wife requires that both parties be present in the same time and space and be engaging with each other. Logic therefore precludes a judge from explaining different accounts of the alleged act of violence by saying that the parties were actually witnessing a different event, or that they were present at different times.

Explanation at the Level of Experience

An explanation of accounts at the level of experience makes reference to the cognitive or experiential processes of the account-giver in order to resolve conflicting versions of events. Explanations at this level may include the claim that the observer "got the version of reality wrong" because he or she had poor vision, poor memory, was hallucinating or had a psychiatric disease. In the case reports analyzed, two types of explanation at the level of experience were found. The most common of these was the judge's reference to the psychological state of the party relating the account. There was also one case where an "appeal to memory" by one of the parties to explain conflicting accounts was considered by a judge, and this is discussed later in this chapter in the context of "lying."

In those instances where the judge appealed to psychological factors as a means of explaining and resolving conflicting accounts of reality, differences emerged in terms of the psychological defects identified in husbands and those identified in wives. The psychological defect most commonly attributed to the husband in this context was the inability of the husband to see the chain of causality of his actions. For example, in one case, the judge concluded that the wife committed adultery because she was seeking solace from her unhappy marriage. The judge said:

> [The husband] lives by a set of standards which he considers right for him and which he can amply justify in his own eyes, and it seems to me that he does not allow that his conduct could in any way have contributed to the rather sad and miserable affair into which his wife entered. (*Gillie and Gillie* 1978 FLC 90–442)

In contrast, the psychological defect most commonly attributed to the wife was a belief that events were actually much worse than they were. In the following example, the judge accepted that the wife was convinced that the events occurred in the way she described, but the judge explained that she only held that belief because she had been subjected to stress and psychological problems:

> In terms of credibility, I find the applicant to be a basically honest witness, prone at time to exaggerate the magnitude of her husband's alleged faults, but in view of her stressful history and her difficulties in coping with it, *I think the degree of their magnitude is real enough to her*. (*J.* v. *J.* 1982 7 Fam. LR 1,011; emphasis added)

The judge's appeal to the psychological state of the parties is used to explain how a party could make a claim about events that "did not really happen." When there was a disjuncture between the events that the husband claimed had occurred and the "true events" as the judge found them, the judge found that the husband "believed" his actions were not as severe or as significant as they were. In contrast, when the wife's account of events was different to the judge's finding of the "true events," the judge typically found that the wife genuinely "believed" that the events were worse than they were. In referring to the psychological state of the party, the judge reconciled anomalies between versions of reality by saying that the parties themselves *believed* their versions to be true, even if they were not aligned with the judge's findings of the "true facts."

Explanation at the Level of Account: Lying, Exaggeration and Truthfulness

The most frequently used technique used by judges for explaining conflicting descriptions of an alleged act of violence in the case reports was explanation at the level of account. In these instances, the judge explained the existence of two competing versions of reality by finding fault with one (or both) of the accounts. This meant the judge could dismiss one (or both) of the accounts as implausible, and so maintain the belief that there can only be one "true" account of events. There were two types of faulty accounts identified by judges. The first was that an account was given by a witness who was "lying," which meant that the judge believed that his or her version of events did not occur at all. The second was the judge's finding that the witness's version of events was an "exaggeration" of the real events. In other words, the judge believed that the basic events did occur, but the witness "added on" extra events for effect. This section explores "lying," "exaggeration" and "truthfulness" in greater detail.

Lying A lie is a false account of the real events. To be able to "find" a lie, a judge must have some notion of the "real events" with which to compare the suspect account. This notion of the "real events" can be constructed through the use of other evidence such as documents or expert evidence which provide some "proof" of the real events, or the judge may refer to his or her own notion of what kinds of events are "believable." A further feature of a lie is that it is a misrepresentation of facts which is calculated and deliberate, and so the demeanor of the witness and the manner in which the evidence is presented to court is also an important consideration.

In the case reports included in this analysis, it was predominantly the husband who was "found" by the judge to have lied about the events. The following extract offers an example of the way in which a judge identifies a lie:

> "I am quite satisfied that ... the husband has deliberately intended to mislead the court. Apart from the evidence from the hospital records, I have had regard to the husband's equivocal answers in relation to this question and his manner of giving them; the husband's failure to provide any supportive or corroborative evidence for his version of events; and the husband's incomplete and implausible attempt to suggest that he was unable to communicate with the hospital personnel. (*In the Marriage of J.G. and B.G.* 1994 FLC 92–497)

All of the elements of a lie are present in the extract. The husband's demeanor and the way he answered questions in the witness box indicated that he was not credible. The husband offered no evidence to support his version of events. Further, the judge's belief as to the approachability of the membership category of "hospital staff" was used to brand as "implausible" the husband's explanation as to why he could not talk with hospital personnel. Overall, the husband was found by the judge to have deliberately given an account of reality that was not true.

In the same case, the husband used an appeal to his memory as an explanation as to why there were inconsistencies between his and his wife's evidence as to how the husband's jaw had been broken. The wife said that the husband told her that the husband's brother, "W," broke the husband's jaw. However, in cross-examination, the husband said that he "did not recall saying that it was [W] who broke his jaw." The judge tested the husband's appeal to his poor memory for its consistency and appropriateness in the circumstances, as is illustrated in the following extract:

> When the husband was confronted in cross-examination with the wife's account ... he said that [W] did not break his jaw. He was then asked whether the wife must be lying and gave the curious answer that he did not recall saying that it was [W] who broke his jaw. He then said that he did not believe that he said that. This seems to be an odd answer if the husband's version is true. If in fact he broke the jaw in the way that he indicated he would surely not have conceivably said that [W] had broken it, and he would have firmly denied that he made such

> a statement, rather than saying that he did not recall making it. (*In the Marriage of J.G. and B.G.* 1994 FLC 92–497)

The judge discounts the husband's version of events on the basis that he found it "odd" that the husband would rely on an appeal to his poor memory as an explanation as to why the his version of events was different to the wife's version of events. The judge noted that a more logical or appropriate response from the husband would have been an outright denial that he made the statement, rather than saying that he "did not recall" making the statement. The husband's appeal to his memory in the circumstances was viewed by the judge as being inappropriate and inconsistent with the actions of a person who was telling the truth. As a result, the husband's claims were viewed suspiciously by the judge, and were seen as indicative of an attempt to mislead the court.

Exaggeration An exaggerated account of events is a form of misrepresentation where the witness has "added on" extra events to his or her account of "what really happened." In general, the judge appeared to view an exaggeration as a less severe form of misrepresentation than an outright lie, and often found that the witness had a reason to exaggerate his or her version of events. There were three main reasons found by the judge to explain why a party had exaggerated their version of events. The first was the incentive of the party to make their case appear stronger than the other party's case. The second was that the witness was attempting to protect his or her family members, while the third reason found by the judge for the use of exaggeration was because the witness was under stress or pressure. It was most often the wife who was found by the judge to have exaggerated her version of events.

It was rare within the case reports that the judge would offer any evidence to support his or her conclusion that the witness had exaggerated his or her version of events. In most cases, the competing claim offered by the opposing party was simply a blanket denial that the events occurred at all, so the judge had no access to an "unexaggerated" version of events against which to compare the "exaggerated" version. It would seem that the judge instead relied upon his or her own preconceived ideas about "how the world is" as a comparison for the witness's versions of events. This is evident in the following extract, where the wife has given evidence that the husband attempted to rape her over a period of several hours. The judge interprets the evidence in terms of his own conception of "rape," and concludes that the wife exaggerated her version of events in order to make the husband's behavior appear more serious than it was. For example:

> As to the alleged rape of her by the respondent, I think that the applicant to some extent exaggerated in her evidence. At one stage she said that he was trying to rape her for the whole of an afternoon, and it seems to me obvious that I cannot accept that allegation in any literal sense. I have no doubt that the applicant was probably harried by the respondent on the occasion in question over a period of some hours, and I think it likely that during the course of time he applied

> forceful persuasion to her in an endeavour to persuade her to have intercourse with him. The applicant was not cross-examined in great detail about the alleged rape .... Therefore I find it somewhat difficult to know precisely what she meant by an attempt to rape. I think that due to the harrying effect of prolonged cross-examination, which caused her to lose some of her ability to respond calmly, she did exaggerate this allegation against the respondent. (*Aly and Aly* 1978 FLC 90–519)

The judge compares the wife's evidence with his own beliefs around what constitutes an event of rape and finds that it is implausible that a man could attempt to rape a woman for a whole afternoon. This finding is notwithstanding the fact that the judge says: "I think it likely that during the course of time he applied forceful persuasion to her in an endeavour to persuade her to have intercourse with him." The judge's own description of events appears to be consistent with attempted rape, but he finds that the allegation of rape is an exaggeration that he could not accept "in a literal sense" as occurring over a whole afternoon. Accordingly, the judge gives precedence to his own notion of the reality of rape as a single act that can occur only over a short period of time, and explains away the wife's evidence as an exaggerated account that was made because she was stressed by the ordeal of cross-examination.

Truthfulness Unlike instances of "lying" and "exaggeration," judges in the case reports rarely described the reasons why they found one party to be "telling the truth." In most cases where the judge accepted one of the parties' version of events as the "truth," the judge simply stated that "I accept the evidence of ...," or "I prefer the evidence of ...." In many cases, the evidence of one party (usually the wife) is consistently preferred by the judge throughout the whole case report. A typical example of the judge's statement in such a case is as follows:

> I find that there was an incident such as she described. Again, the only evidence of it comes from her and it is denied by the respondent but I accept nevertheless that (it occurred). (*J.* v. *J.* 1982 7 Fam LR 1,011)

In cases where there were conflicting accounts and the judge systematically preferred the evidence of one party of that of the other as the true version of events, the judge typically stated that one party had "better credit" than the other party. The word "credit" in this context specifically refers to the credibility of the witness. If a witness has "poor credit," what he or she says is likely to be an unreliable account of the real event, and so he or she is presumably lying about the events or is otherwise altering the facts. Alternatively, a witness with "good credit" will relate to the judge an accurate, unbiased and truthful account of events.

The "credit" of the witness is constructed by the judge and is based primarily on two factors, the witness's demeanor and the consistency of his or her account. "Demeanor" refers to the witness's appearance in court and the manner by which he or she presents the evidence. It is based on the belief that people have a certain appearance when they are lying or telling the truth. "Consistency" operates at a number of levels. Firstly, the witness's account must be internally consistent—that is, there must be no contradictions within the account of reality, and the witness should not make any changes to his or her description of events over the course of the hearing. Secondly, a witness's account must be consistent with other evidence about the same event. This is where corroboration becomes significant, as the witness's account is tested for consistency against other evidence such as documents or the statements of expert witnesses. Thirdly, the account must be consistent with the judge's preconceived ideas about "how things are" in the real world.

In some case reports, the judge found that neither party was telling the 'truth'. In such cases, the judge dismissed one party's version of events as a 'lie' and dismissed the other party's version of events as an 'exaggeration'. The judge then constructed his or her own version of events, based in part on some of the information given to the judge by one or both of the parties.

"Finding the Facts": Constructing One Reality from Multiple Claims

Another means by which conflicting accounts are confronted and resolved in the context of mundane reason is through the use of "idealizations." Idealizations not only function as a framework by which mundane reasoners construct the real world, but also offer a means by which alternative claims to reality can be credited or discredited in order to determine the "true facts" (Pollner 1987, 35). Idealizations encompass such things as consistency, coherency, congruency and determinativeness, and they set out standards for what is acceptable in an intelligible and rational objective world (Pollner 1987, 26). Each account of the event in question must be logically compatible to another in so far as they can collectively be seen as referring to one event that could conceivably exist in the world (Pollner 1987, 37–8). In other words, the mundane reasoner looks for circumstances surrounding the "real event" that may corroborate or discredit a particular account of reality. This might include documentary evidence of the occurrence (such as a medical report on an alleged injury), or the evidence of a third party who was also present at the time.

Preconceived ideas about the nature of events in the real world are also central to the process of resolving conflicting accounts. A mundane reasoner may recall typologies of events or persons that can conceivably exist in the real world and use these as comparisons by which to assess the feasibility of a particular account of reality. For example, Pollner (1987) has observed that a judge in a traffic court accumulates and constructs typologies of archetypal violators and violations, as well as typical police conduct and responses in those circumstances. The judge then refers to these in the process of constructing the "true" set of events. "Membership categorization devices" (Sacks 1979) are also employed in this context to establish what a person making the account might or ought properly know about the event (Pollner 1987, 42). In addition, the membership category confers a certain status to the person describing the events, which then has the effect of placing the purported set of events into a particular mundane order with which it must be reconciled (Pollner 1987, 42).

The process of the resolution of conflicting accounts involves a "politics of experience" whereby one person's claim about or experiences of reality are discounted in favor of an official or accredited version of reality (Pollner 1987, 70). As will be demonstrated in the analysis that follows, the politics of experience plays a fundamental role in decision-making in the Family Court of Australia.

This section looks more closely at the process by which judges transform the competing claims of the parties to a case into one single authoritative account of reality. This single account appears in the case reports in the form of a narrative, and this analysis is limited to the narratives which discuss the violent behavior of the husband. It first examines how the characters are created within the narrative, and then looks at the way in which the actions of the characters are described. Of key interest is the way in which the "reality of violence" is constructed, and the use of idealizations and beliefs by the judge in constructing his or her authoritative account. The final part of this section identifies several techniques which are used within the narrative to either legitimate or condemn the violent behavior in question.

Creating the Characters

In 17 of the 20 case reports analyzed, the judge described the parties at the initial stages of the case report and/or made reference to the parties' personal characteristics at various places within the case report. Once collated, a consistent picture emerged across the case reports of "the man as aggressor" and "the woman as victim." While such consistency might be expected in a collection of cases which all involve instances of violence by the husband against the wife, it is interesting to note that in no cases was the victim of the attack also described as "strong" or "abusive," which may be the case in court cases which relate to episodes of violence between men.

The words used to describe women included: "frightened," "terrified," "quiet," "inarticulate" and "reserved." In contrast, the men were characterized as being "violent," "voluble," "aggressive," "abusive" and "controlling." The judge's opinion of the relative credibility of the parties was also consistent throughout the case reports. Overwhelmingly, the woman was described as "credible" and "truthful," although sometimes "prone to exaggeration," while the man was "not credible," "inconsistent," and often "calculating" and "distorting of the truth."

A distinction also emerged in the way in which the respective mental health of the parties was portrayed. References to women's mental health most commonly took the form of clinical disorders for which they were receiving medication. For example, women were described as "suffering from a nervous disorder," as having been "given medication and electro-convulsive therapy" or "diagnosed with depressive neurosis in the setting of marital disharmony." By contrast, men's mental health—although referred to much more frequently in the case reports—typically took the form of the judge's personal observations rather than reference to a clinical diagnosis. For example, men were described in case reports as having "personality defects," "no grasp of reality" or a "lack of perception and insight."

The category descriptions (Sacks 1979) of the parties remained consistent throughout the case reports even if, in a particular case, custody of the child was awarded to the "aggressive father" or if the "aggressive husband" was found not to have breached the court order restraining him from assaulting the "victim wife." The anomaly of deciding a case in favor of an "aggressive husband" in such cases was resolved by the manner in which the judge made the final ruling. For example, some rulings were made on a point of law, while others were based on a set of facts to which the issue of violence was irrelevant. In most cases, however, the aggressive husband was absolved from moral condemnation for his actions simply by the way in which the violent event was described by the judge in the case reports. These descriptions of violent events in the case reports are the focus of the remainder of this chapter.

"Finding the Facts"

In the case reports, the judge states that he or she is "finding" or "summarizing" the "facts." This use of terminology implies that the events exist independently and in full view in the "real world," and that the judge need simply to discover or observe them. The creative process of the judge in his or her "finding of the facts" is thus obscured even though those very "facts" are fundamentally dependent on the judge's process of "finding" them (Pollner 1987, 26), and reflects Pollner's (1987, 87) observation that mundane inquiry "does not see itself as creating entities but as discovering or reflecting its 'real properties.'"

As discussed above, idealizations are assumptions about the real world that guide mundane inquiry to "find" the real world (Pollner 1987, 27). These include assumptions of such things as consistency, coherency and determinateness, rationality and logic. This section focuses on one of the case reports—*Aly and Aly*—to illustrate the way in which a judge uses idealizations and assumptions about the "real world" to resolve conflicting accounts into one set of "facts."

In *Aly and Aly*, the parties to the dispute were sharing a house even though they had separated. The husband had been issued with a court order restraining him from molesting the wife. The wife claimed that the husband had breached the order and had assaulted her and raped her on a number of occasions. The husband's competing claim was a blanket denial of the wife's claim. The judge says that:

> The husband denied the allegations that he had been guilty of any conduct in the house which was in any way reprehensible and he said that although there

> was some unhappiness caused by the wife's rejection of him to some extent, nevertheless sexual relations between the parties had continued...Further, he said that at all times he had acted in a restrained way and had endeavoured to achieve a reconciliation with his wife by this restraint, by acting reasonably in the home, by maintaining his relationship with the three children, and hoping that the situation between him and his wife would improve. (*Aly and Aly* 1978 FLC 90–519)

The judge is faced with two competing claims of reality and he must reconcile them. He begins by "testing" the wife's claim for consistency. He does this by relying on two assumptions about reality. The first assumption is that if her claim to reality is "true," it will be consistent with other evidence of that event. In invoking this assumption, the judge states in the case report that because the wife's claim was "extremely serious," he "expected" the wife to present evidence, such as medical evidence or evidence from parents or friends, which corroborated her claim that she was sexually assaulted. The judge says that he finds it "surprising" that this evidence was "lacking." As a result, the judge does not accept the wife's allegations because she did not offer any other evidence which "proves" that her claim was consistent with the real events.

The second assumption relied upon by the judge in this case relates to the judge's notion of "how people act in the real world." The judge describes the wife as a "sensitive person," and he believes that no sensitive person would remain living in a house if she was being subjected to the kinds of assaults that were alleged by her. Because the wife's actions are not consistent with the judge's assumption as to how a "sensitive" person in her circumstances would behave, the judge does not believe her claim. After discounting the wife's account of events, the judge then constructs his own version. This version seems to be an attempt to reconcile the wife's claim with the judge's notion of the "real world":

> It could be that the *real truth* of the matter was that the wife was perhaps somewhat reluctant to have intercourse with the husband but nevertheless eventually agreed to have intercourse on these occasions. (*Aly and Aly* 1978 FLC 90–519; emphasis added)

As to the husband's counter-claim, the judge focuses only on the manner in which the husband gives his evidence and his demeanor in the witness box. The judge concludes that there was: "nothing which in any way tended to show that he was not telling the truth when he denied the allegations which the wife made" (*Aly and Aly* 1978 FLC 90–519).

As a consequence, the husband's version of events becomes the substance of the "real events" as the judge forms an opinion that reflects the husband's initial counter-claim:

> I do not say that on all occasions the husband behaved with perfect propriety. It may be that on occasions he behaved in a less than appropriate manner, but in my view he behaved with reasonable restraint, and, speaking generally, behaved reasonably in the household during these months from April onwards. (*Aly and Aly* 1978 FLC 90–519)

The husband's version of events was accepted by the judge because he "appeared" truthful. In contrast, the wife's claim is discounted by the judge because she did not bring forward other evidence to support her claim, and her claim was not consistent with the judge's concept of how things are in the "real world." None the less, the judge uses some elements of both the husband's and the wife's versions of reality to "find" the "true" version of events. The true version of events "found" by the judge is presented in the form of a narrative into which the competing parties are placed as characters. This narrative could be summarized as follows: *The husband had sexual intercourse with the wife. The wife was initially reluctant to have intercourse, but she eventually agreed to it.*

The wife's claim that she was sexually assaulted is transformed by the judge into a narrative in which the wife had "sexual intercourse." The wife's "initial reluctance" meant that the husband was acting "inappropriately" by having sexual intercourse with her. However, his actions become "reasonable" when the judge suggests that the wife "eventually agreed" to sexual intercourse. This version of reality is consistent with the judge's findings about the husband, as well as being consistent with the judge's own concept of "consensual sexual intercourse" versus "rape."

Overall, the narrative "demonstrates" that the husband's actions, while not entirely appropriate, were reasonable. The judge's final ruling at the end of the case report is that the husband's actions did not constitute a breach of the order restraining him from molesting the wife. This conclusion follows logically from the substance of the narrative. Accordingly, the ruling has the appearance of being logical and "correct," and the judge appears to be fair and impartial. The meanings produced by the judge's narrative of the "true events"—in which the judge suggested that the wife "reluctantly agreed" to have sexual intercourse—function in a way that exonerates the husband from the claims of the wife that she was sexually assaulted by the husband.

Violence against Women, and the Family Court

Most violence against women in Australia is perpetrated by men with whom they are in an intimate relationship, so the Family Court of Australia is likely to encounter many women who have been the target of such violence (Graycar 1995, 58). Yet, as Graycar (1995, 58) points out, this violence is often rendered invisible by the Family Court. As she observes, a major issue raised by women who made submissions to the Australian Law Reform Commission's 1994 inquiry into *Equality before the Law* (1994) was that they were not believed by the Family

Court when they spoke about the violence that they had experienced at the hands of their partner.

This chapter has demonstrated how the "facts" of the case are often constructed by the judge in such a way that minimizes the gravity of the violent actions that occurred because the "findings of fact" are premised upon the judge's belief as to how things are "in the real world." This helps to show how a "masculocentric sociocultural context" (Giles-Sims 1983; Walker 1990; Easteal 1995) can filter through legal thought and policy in ways that deny or obscure women's experiences (especially see Wowk 1984). It offers evidential support for a policy recommendation that judicial education of issues around women's lived experiences and violence against women would help to achieve greater equity for survivors of domestic violence who appear before the court. This research also complements other research on the discourse analysis of violence against women in cultural contexts (for example, Tang et al. 2002) and on the breakdown of marital relationships (for example, Hopper 1993) to contribute to a broader understanding of the socio-legal experiences of women as survivors of violence, and social construction of relationships within marriage.

Amendments to the Family Law Act (1975) were implemented in 1995 to seek to address the issue of violence against women in the context of family law disputes, particularly in relation to child custody disputes (Harrison and Sheridon 1995). This research found that the judge's interpretation of the facts to "find the truth" play just as vital a role in shaping the final ruling as do the particular provisions of the Family Law Act. Accordingly, any changes to substantive law in an attempt to increase justice for women before the law may be relatively ineffectual until attention is paid to address and broaden Family Court judges' knowledge about "how the real world is," and this must be an important consideration in any further research.

Conclusion

This chapter explored the ways in which judges create a single "truth" from the competing evidence of the parties to a case. The most significant point to emerge from the analysis was the extent to which judges rely on their own beliefs about "how things are in the real world"—or, to use Garfinkel's (1967) term, "background expectancies"—as a basis for resolving conflicting accounts of reality. Judges rely upon background expectancies as a basis for explaining how competing evidence can exist in the context of mundane reason; as a basis for accepting some evidence, rejecting others and then constructing the narrative of the "true events," and as a basis for justifying the final decision. This has implications for the sociological understanding of legal reasoning and the role of judges in the maintenance of social order.

References

ALRC (Australian Law Reform Commission) (1994), *Equality before the Law: Justice for Women*, ALRC 69, Canberra: Commonwealth of Australia, <http://www.austlii.edu.au/au/other/alrc/publications/reports/69/vol1/ALRC69.html>.

Easteal, P. (1995), "Reconstructing reality," *Alternative Law Journal*, 20(3), 108–12.

Garfinkel, H. (1967), *Studies in Ethnomethodology*, Englewood Cliff, NJ: Prentice-Hall.

Giles-Sims, J. (1983), *Wife Battering: A Systems Theory Analysis*, New York: Guilford Press.

Graycar, R. (1995), "The relevance of violence in family law decision making," *Australian Journal of Family Law*, 9, 58–69.

Harrison, J. and Sheridan, M. (1996), "Family law reform bills update," *Sisters' Say: Newsletter of the Women's Legal Service Inc.* (Brisbane) (January), 3–5.

Hopper, J. (1993), "The rhetoric of motives in divorce," *Journal of Marriage and the Family* (November), 801–13.

Mertz, E. (1996), "Consensus and Dissent in U.S. Legal Opinions: Narrative Structure and Social Voices," in C.L. Briggs (ed.), *Disorderly Discourse: Narrative, Conflict, and Inequality*, New York: Oxford University Press, 135–57.

Pollner, M. (1987), *Mundane Reason: Reality in Everyday and Sociological Discourses*, New York: The Free Press.

Sacks, H. (1979), "Hotrodder: A Revolutionary Category," in G. Psathas (ed.), *Everyday Language: Studies in Ethnomethodology*, New York: Irvington, 7–14.

Tang, C.S., Wong, D. and Cheung, F.M. (2002), 'Social construction of women as legitimate victims of violence in Chinese societies," *Violence Against Women*, 8(8), 968–96.

Walker, L.E. (1990), "Psychology and domestic violence around the world," *American Psychologist*, 54, 21–9.

Wowk, M.T. (1984), "Blame allocation, sex and gender in a murder interrogation," *Women's Studies International Forum*, 7(1), 75–82.

Chapter 10

Hidden Penalties Faced by Non-English Speakers in the UK Criminal Justice System: An Interpreting Perspective

Roxana Rycroft[1]

On January 29, 2010, the number of foreign prisoners in the UK (on remand and convicted) represented 13.7 percent of the total prison population of 83,378, not including juveniles in Secure Training Centres and Local Authority Secure Children's Homes.[2] There are no statistics on the number of non-English speakers (NES) being dealt with by the criminal justice system (CJS); however, it can be safely assumed that their number is far greater when taking into account defendants, people on police bail, people serving community orders as well as witnesses and victims. Likewise, there are no statistics as to the number of foreigners dealt with by the CJS who have little or no English at all, just as we do not know how many British people dealt with by the CJS need interpreters. However, for the purposes of this study, quite apart from philosophical arguments for natural justice, the figure above stands witness to the fact that in a multicultural society such as the UK, interpreters are essential to lawful procedure.

Interpreted communicative events (ICE) have been the focus of much recent research. Traditionally, interpreters have been ascribed the role of invisible communication channels, neutral language conduits and language-switchers—a role poetically conceptualized as that of "bilingual ghosts,"[3] and commonly known as the legal model of interpreting, or the "conduit" role. Its main commandment is that interpreters "shall interpret truly and faithfully what is uttered, without adding, omitting or changing anything."[4] This all-pervasive professional ideology informs

1 Acknowledgment is due to Dr. Prakash Shah, Senior Lecturer at Queen Mary University of London, whose unfailing belief in my work caused this chapter to be written. Many thanks to Dr. Christopher Jackman, former Principal Lecturer, School of Business and Social Sciences, Roehampton University, for his helpful comments on the structure of my arguments.

2 International Centre for Prison Studies, <http://www.kcl.ac.uk/depsta/law/research/icps/worldbrief/wpb_country.php?country=169>.

3 Collado Aís, in Pöchhacker and Schlessinger (2003, 336), quoted in Angelelli (2004), 15.

4 Code of Conduct, National Register of Public Service Interpreters.

the codes and rules of practice of interpreter organizations and training programs whose main concern is to prescribe the "conduit" role to practitioners instead of evaluating interpreting as a situated activity constrained by type of interaction, setting and participants.

A sustained critique of the legal model of interpreting has been leveled by documenting the impact of interpreters on trial proceedings by Hale (1999),[5] and the changed dynamics of interpreted police procedures by Russell (2002), while Angelelli (2004) has gathered empirical evidence of the interpreters' perceptions of their own role in terms of visibility.

The aim of this study is twofold: to raise awareness among the legal profession of specific challenges encountered by non-English speakers in the CJS over the course of ICE, some of them taking place outside courtrooms and police interview rooms; and by canvassing issues that have come to my attention and that of my interpreter colleagues, to further criticize the legal model of interpreting for compounding the aforementioned challenges.

Methodology

This study has emerged from an accumulation of observations over fifteen years of freelance interpreting for the CJS and immigration services in the UK. The observations on which I based my study are quite recent, as my workload and that of my Romanian interpreter colleagues increased dramatically after January 2007, when Romania joined the European Union. My opportunities to observe the conduct of legal proceedings soared accordingly, and I had additional feedback from my colleagues. I believe that my exposure to all stages in the CJS fostered an in-depth understanding of the ways in which non-English speakers are dealt with.

I used a mixture of qualitative research methods in the form of participant observation, and secondary data from published literature. This study is based on observations during police and court proceedings, as well as legal consultations for preparing the case for court.

The following data are used in the construction of the arguments.

Primary data:

a. notes of instances and practices that attracted my attention for illustrating the pitfalls of the legal model of interpreting—I jotted down the salient points of the respective encounters (date, time, setting, people present, purpose and relevant features of encounter) from memory as soon as possible into an ethnographic diary. I coded these encounters by giving them fictitious names, locations and dates.
b. unprompted personal communications from fellow interpreters, included in the study with their authors' consent—they agreed with the contents of the

5 Quoted in Russell (2002).

comments and the context in which they were referred to in the study, and I recorded their consent in the diary. By obtaining respondent validation, I triangulated the data to ensure its reliability and appropriate use.

Secondary data:

a. academic texts relating to the work of interpreters working in legal settings, which were the source of helpful concepts for analyzing the primary data;
b. Internet resources.

Carrying out the research in the course of my job meant that this research has distanced itself from one of the major threats to the validity of my data: reactivity, defined by Hammersley and Atkinson (1995, 130) as "the effects of audience … on what people say and do." It is assumed that non-reactive methods elicit behaviors that occur naturally, therefore circumventing the concern with observer-induced distortions.

Criticisms to the non-systematic means for collecting the primary data can be staved off on two grounds. Firstly, my long-term involvement with legal procedures stands witness to the internal integrity of the study, in the sense that I was at all times aware of usual modes of behavior and their contexts, and therefore could draw valid, context-bound comparisons. Secondly, the connections made between the primary and the secondary data in the course of the study acted as a check on the reliability of the interpretation of the data.

My approach to data gathering could also be criticized for bias. Bias, we are told, is the arch-enemy of objectivity, and research undertaken from a biased perspective can only compromise the results of the study. On the other hand, it is difficult, if not impossible, to achieve a perfectly objective perspective. The political and ideological stances taken in our research are shaped by our identities and life experiences, we are told by Kleinman and Copp (1993), who draw attention to the analytic costs of ignoring the interplay of person with research. There is a strong subjective element in this research. Most of the observations were occasioned by certain instances when I noticed what I felt was a lack of fit between the legal model of interpreting mandate I had and the realities of my work conditions. However, I would argue that this subjectivity is counterbalanced by a rigorous triangulation of data.

The central ethical issues arising from my study are: deception, for using the cover of interpreting to collect data for research, and breach of confidentiality, for exposing sensitive material. Firstly, I started accumulating observations as a matter of personal interest in legal interpreters' predicaments, therefore I did not pose as an interpreter in order to gather data, and the study emerged as a result of my exposure to legal procedures. In addition, I protected the anonymity of all those who provided data by using fictitious names. Secondly, confidentiality protects sensitive legal and personal information capable of causing harm to NES if disclosed. As my study focused on the *manner* in which interpreted CJS encounters played out, not on *contents of cases*, I would argue that the need for confidentiality had been recognized and is an integral part of this study.

One last issue must be addressed: How typical am I as an interpreter? The answer is that I am not, nor could anyone be a typical interpreter. Interpreters cannot constitute a unitary category, as they have situated identities in terms of personality, age, gender, ethnic background, nationality, professional expertise, exposure to various aspects of interpreting, and personal interests. I would argue, however, that the issues I perceive as being part of my work are also encountered by other interpreters and have a particular relevance.

Some Specific Challenges Faced by Non-English Speakers in the UK CJS

Time Constraints

It is perhaps taken for granted that all NES who need a police or court interpreter have the services of one as required, and that the simple presence of an interpreter suffices for legal purposes. However, in my experience and that of my colleagues, this is not always the case. Let us consider three cases.

A.[6] interpreted via video-link for a bail application. Speaking very rapidly, the district judge granted bail with very strict conditions, including a curfew. In turn, A. interpreted very quickly in order to keep pace with the judge's delivery. The defendant was looking very lost throughout. With no time for a post-conference consultation, the defense counsel rushed off without explaining the bail conditions to the defendant.

Sure enough, one week later A. ends up in a different court, this time interpreting face-to-face for the same defendant, newly charged with breach of bail conditions—namely his curfew, of which he was not aware—and by the way, he had breached it by going to his uncle's two doors down the road to celebrate his release. A. explained to the court that in the previous hearing, the defendant was not given the chance to understand his bail conditions, thus substantially deviating from her interpreter's mandate out of moral concern and acting as a witness. However, the prosecution did not withdraw the charge, and the defendant pleaded guilty. Had thc defendant been familiar with the UK justice system and not needed an interpreter, his chances of understanding the fast-speaking district judge would have been greater, regardless of the barrister rushing off. Thus, the price he paid for not speaking English, despite an interpreter being present, included an overnight stay in custody and a conviction for breach of bail. This will immediately impact on his chances of getting bail in the future, as well as skewing the statistics on the criminality of foreigners.

6 Personal communication.

In the second case I turn my attention to,[7] I was interpreting late one night at a police station for a juvenile, in a complicated case. Another Romanian prisoner was brought in, who hardly spoke any English and needed my full assistance for the booking-in procedure. He asked for the duty solicitor, and one was duly called out. So far so good, except that his solicitor happened to turn up just as I was going into consultation with the juvenile and his solicitor and appropriate adult. Two hours later, when I emerged from the consultation room, the prisoner had been interviewed, cautioned and gone. How the interview was carried out and the caution administered remains a perfect mystery to me. To accept a caution, our detained person must have signed a form to confirm he understood the likelihood of being charged if he committed any similar offences, as well as the consequences of the caution in terms of employment and traveling to other countries. He had no way of understanding this form, yet by his signature he assumed responsibility for being aware of its contents. This does not surprise me, as time and time again I see Romanian detainees who, out of long-ingrained deference to authority, would pick up a pen and sign anything when told "Sign here," without requiring any explanations.

In the last example, M.[8] acted as an interpreter in a magistrates' court in three different cases, two of which were in custody. She made initial contact with one of the detained defendants, who specifically requested the assistance of an interpreter and a solicitor. However, his case was heard in the absence of both while M. was commuting between courtrooms and cells in the other two cases.

What explanation can there be for what appear to be breaches of police and court procedures? Interpreter provision is traditionally seen as difficult and resource-intensive, always involving various waiting times for interpreters to arrive—witness the falling faces of court and police officers when they realize an interpreter is needed. Stories abound about London-based interpreters taking up to four hours to arrive at London police stations, and court cases being adjourned for lack of interpreters. However, in each of the examples given, there was an interpreter on the premises, so the costs or the extra time involved would have been negligible.

I would argue that the reason for these three NES being rushed through the system arises out of the changes to Legal Aid, which came into force early on in 2008 and which pay solicitors a set fee per case. My colleagues and I have noticed that solicitors and barristers alike are under pressure to deal with cases very quickly. Duty solicitors at police stations are not willing to wait: they will arrive when everybody is ready for the interview, and leave immediately after the interview, while many court solicitors and barristers represent a panoply of defendants not always in the same court, and being short of time, bounce from one to the other, and as in the above example, sometimes skimp on the explanations given to defendants. Thus, over and above any changes in representation brought

7 Case code PS/29.01.08.

8 Personal communication.

about by Legal Aid, some foreign defendants suffer further legal penalties in terms of curtailed interpreter assistance.

Comprehension Test

Russell (2002) describes the police interview as a major stage in criminal proceedings offering suspects the first opportunity to put forward their version of events leading to their arrest. It constitutes the "main plank in the prosecution case" and "a major piece of evidence for consideration by the jury in reaching their verdict."

The decision about whether an interpreter is needed is usually taken by police officers and is governed by the Police and Criminal Evidence Act (PACE) 1984, which sets out that:

> a person must not be interviewed in the absence of a person capable of acting as an interpreter if:
> a. he has difficulty in understanding English;
> b. the interviewing officer cannot speak the person's own language;
> c. the person wishes an interpreter to be present.

A person may understand English to a certain extent, but Collins and Morris (1996) argue that it may not be sufficient for the purposes of the interview, which involves the ability to comprehend words, concepts, assumptions and legal implications. Thus, under PACE, it falls to police officers as well as court staff to assess the need for an interpreter. Relevant issues arising here include: Who and on what basis assesses the need for an interpreter? Is a reading or a comprehension test to be applied? If so, who is responsible for designing the test, and what does it consist of? What procedures are in place to instruct officers in assessing the level of fluency? Who is the best person in the encounter to evaluate NES' knowledge of English? From what my colleagues and I have seen, the evaluation of someone's knowledge of English is reduced to a variant of "Can you understand me? What is your name and address?"—this is hardly sufficient for legal purposes.

For example, some people have a tendency to say "yes" even when they don't understand what is being said to them. Just to give an example, I have come across many of my compatriots nodding eagerly and saying "yes, yes" to police officers addressing them, then turning to me to ask, "What did he say?" This may be in part a cultural issue of deference to authority, which is strongly instilled in traditionalist Romanian society. I have also come across many Romanians who say they understand what they are told in English, but are unable to explain or repeat the same when asked.

I would argue that people who possess a limited knowledge of English are not the best judges of their own language competency for legal purposes. In any speech situation, the meaning of words is a construct of the social, legal or professional context in which it occurs. Generally speaking, words divorced from their context may come across as meaning something totally different, or maybe make no sense at all, and in understanding this, we are helped by the discipline of pragmatics, which focuses on the study of language in communication and has been defined as "the study of meaning in relation to speech situations" (see Leech 1983, 6, quoted in Petite 2004, 52).

Berk-Seligson (2004) describes the courtroom and police settings as coercive contexts for people who have to answer questions, the police settings arguably even more so than courtrooms due to the absence of a judge who can rein in the behavior of interrogators. And according to Russell (2002), investigative interviews constitute a distinct type of speech event, in the sense that the parties to the dialog have diametrically opposing aims to each other both linguistically (the officer is trained in the art of asking questions, whereas the suspect isn't trained in giving answers) and sociologically (the officer seeks to demonstrate the "guilty mind," whereas the suspect seeks to deny it).

Going back to the discussion of pragmatics against this background, we can see that NES may well be familiar with certain words, but not with the CJS context in which they are used, and therefore run the very real risk of misunderstanding what is being said.

Let us consider one example. Upon my arrival at a police station, it transpired that the NES,[9] who had very limited English, had asked for a solicitor in the mistaken belief that he was actually requesting an interpreter. To the custody sergeant, that was clear enough proof of the suspect's need for my assistance, but unfortunately, that piece of knowledge did not filter through to the interviewing officer. Come the time for the interview, two police officers, the NES and I sit in the interview room and the leading officer asks the NES, "Do you understand me or do you need the interpreter?", to which the answer is, "I understand!" I sit back in my chair suppressing an inner protest. The police officer starts explaining the procedure p-a-i-n-f-u-l-l-y s-l-o-w-l-y, to which the NES nods occasionally, with a look of incomprehension firmly planted on his face. When the police officer gets to "your case will be referred to the CPS," the NES looks even more blank, then nods in assent. I decide to intervene, stop the officer, and ask the NES in English what "refer to the CPS" means. The NES, to my lack of surprise, treats me to the same look of incomprehension and shrugs his shoulders. I then inform the police officers that in my professional capacity, I consider that the suspect not only does not understand what is being said to him, but in addition does not even understand that he doesn't understand, and therefore I will interpret everything, which will mercifully speed things up as well.

I would thus argue that if the NES themselves are unable to decide when and if they need the assistance of an interpreter, the police officers are on even shakier ground when it comes to assessing foreigners' fluency in English. On the other hand, interpreters could be accused of partisanship and scouting for work and being subjective on the matter, so what can be done?

---

9 Case code PS/25.02.2008.

I suggest that a comprehension test be designed to assist with decisions on appropriate level of English. It doesn't have to consist of a standard set of questions, as this would hardly cover the entire gamut of police inquiries, and for reasons of expediency it cannot be time-consuming. I propose a simple procedure, similar to the one already used when explaining the caution,[10] by which police officers test the understanding of the subjects by asking them to either repeat what was said, or explain in their own words the meaning of what was said. This would very quickly show up any lacunae in the subjects' understanding or in their ability to express themselves appropriately.

NES Express Themselves with Difficulty through Interpreters

In my experience, the people who are least able to speak through interpreters are the NES. In order for the interpretation to be effective, the speech must emerge in a tidy fashion, not too fast or low or mumbled or hidden behind hands raised to the face, with interpreter-friendly pauses in the speech flow that do not disrupt the speaker's train of thoughts. This takes practice and patience, and many police officers, and even solicitors, are not quite at ease in interpreted encounters. On many occasions, I had to interrupt the NES' torrent of words due to short-memory overload, and unfortunately, once interrupted, NES tend to forget what they are saying.

Also, because there is less need for me to interrupt the legal practitioners as they tend to have some practice at working through interpreters, NES may suspect me of being oppressive towards them by curtailing their speech, and may therefore get angry or decide the situation is hopeless and become withdrawn—both reactions having their own evidential consequences in terms of an answers being proffered.

Russell (2002, 124) analyzes this situation, from a different angle, in terms of what she calls "an impossible dilemma." The interpreter faced with a NES speaking beyond his or her short-term memory can stop the NES and signal him or her to continue after the interpretation has taken place, thus giving the NES time to consider his or her answer; or the interpreter can allow the NES to finish speaking in the knowledge that some of what is being said will be lost in interpretation. Another reason for interrupting NES—and I have come across many such instances—is to require them not to speak over the interpreter, as overlapping speech renders the tape useless for evidential purposes.

Thus, NES are linguistically constrained and inherently disadvantaged in a CJS context, and unfairness is built into a system that relies on the false premise of the invisibility of the interpreter (more on which later) and the unobtrusiveness of the tape as discussed. As a matter of police and court procedure, NES should be

10 All suspects must be cautioned upon arrest, charge and at the start of taped interviews. The caution sets out the suspects' legal rights to offer explanations or to maintain silence. Its wording is: "You do not have to say anything, but it may harm your defence if you do not mention, when questioned, something which you later rely on in court. Anything you do say may be given in evidence."

made aware of what is involved in interpreted communication events, rather than be thrown in at the deep end and left to get on with it. This could be easily achieved by explaining to NES how they can best express themselves through an interpreter. This explanation could be part of the standard explanation of procedure offered to all police interviewees at the start of interviews, and need only take one minute.

Statement-taking

Fowler (2003) argues that taking a witness statement appears to be one of the most complex cognitive tasks for police officers, regardless of the presence or otherwise of an interpreter. The skills required encompass the ability to listen and interview, possession of a good memory, good note-taking and interpersonal skills, as well as knowledge of the law relating to the incident and the ability to render the account in clear English. Officers receive training in taking statements, but most are not trained to work through interpreters. The interpreter mediates all interactions between the officer and the witness in what is a very complex process. Problems arise when the oral part of the account is over and the statements must be committed to paper.

The statement can be taken down either in English first and then translated to the witness, or in the foreign language first and then translated into English. While the law appears to be silent on which language the statement must be written in first, there are advantages and disadvantages to both methods from various points of view—procedural, linguistic, and most importantly, ownership of control over the statement.

According to Fowler's analysis, taking the statement in English first is the preferable and legally correct approach, because it is the responsibility of the officer to select the relevant parts that must make up the statement. However, in my experience and that of my colleagues, statements tend to be taken in the foreign language first. As Fowler observes, this method presupposes the interpreter to behave in a manner that contravenes the *Code of Practice of the NRPSI* (2002), in that interpreters are not supposed to "enter into discussion, give advice or express opinions or reactions to any of the parties." As the drafter of the statement, the interpreter is pushed into doing all of the above, which constitutes a professional and ethical dilemma, and may have legal consequences for the investigation in terms of facts being omitted or added to the statement.

Unfortunately, things do not stop here, because my colleagues and I have on many occasions been asked to remain in a room with the witness in the absence of the police officer, and to take the statement in Romanian. On one occasion I had to keep calling the officer to come down from the fifth floor to ask him what should or should not go into the statement, with the officer scuttling out of the statement-taking room as soon as feasibly possible.[11] Interpreter R. told me that she was once asked to go to a police station *by herself* and take a statement from the female

11 Personal communication.

victim of an assault. When she protested that she was not allowed to do this, the police officer insisted that he did that all the time and it was procedurally correct. She did take the statement, for what she considered to be compelling reasons, and did her best to structure the account and cover as much ground as possible. However, had another interpreter attended on that occasion, the statement would have been different. The practice of leaving interpreters alone with witnesses for statement-taking purposes puts interpreters in the impossible position of having to abandon their impartiality and become investigation aides. It also shows how little aware police officers can be of their professional obligations, to the point of shifting their responsibility for the investigation to an untrained individual—the interpreter.

Credibility Issues

The change in dynamics brought about by the impact of interpreters in courtrooms has been the focus of much research.

In her study on American court interpreters, Berk-Seligson (1990) shows that they bring a presence that may vary between usurping the power of the attorney to coercing the witness. They are shown to change the image presented by the parties through ignorance of the pragmatics of speech, by introducing alterations (the implication intended by the speakers), such as shifts between active and passive voice (which are directly connected with attribution of blame), using politeness markers, register variation, lengthening the testimony of witnesses, and hedging.

Hale (1997)[12] notices that interpreters tend to raise the linguistic register when defendants address the barrister, and to lower it when the barrister or judge addresses the defendant, while according to Schlessinger (1991),[13] court interpreters tidy up the speech of the interlocutors—a behavior partly driven by the desire to avoid appearing incompetent.

From my experience, I would argue that changing the register down when barristers address defendants is in many cases vital for the avoidance of misunderstandings, since the two parties belong to different linguistic, cultural and social spheres. However, changing the register up when the defendant addresses the barrister is to be avoided because it may introduce alterations to the lexical consistency of the testimony. Lexical consistency is crucial if the person interpreted for is to recognize the original statements in the interpreted version. Mason (1999) has referred to this phenomenon as "ownership of meaning," where interpreters' lexical choices are actually attributed to the parties in dialog, as if they had used that particular term. Lexical deviations are unavoidable against a background of successive statements made to the police (possibly), solicitors and court, where it is likely that the defendant had the assistance of different interpreters for each stage, but they run an inherent risk of impacting adversely on the defendants' credibility

12 Quoted in Russell (2002).

13 Quoted in Russell (2002).

in terms of inconsistency or by portraying the defendant as better educated than he or she purports to be.

Over and above all of these potential challenges to credibility due to interpreter mediation, Romanian and Bulgarian defendants find themselves in a precarious position regardless of whether they use an interpreter or not. My Romanian interpreter colleagues and I have come across an unusual view that keeps being brought up time after time by a number of district judges, and unfortunately some lay benches have adopted this point of view. Upon hearing that the Romanian defendant works, the judge attacks immediately: "But Romanians and Bulgarians are not allowed to work or to look for work, so he/she is in breach of their landing conditions." This is wrong, because certain categories of Romanians and Bulgarians are allowed to work, but the judge never delves into this, and I very rarely heard a solicitor or a barrister to enlighten him, or indeed to seek instructions from the client on whether he or she is entitled to work or not. On a subjective level, district judges entertain a mistaken belief about immigration rules which prejudices their views on issues such as credibility, bail and sentencing. On an objective level, this is an example of how unwarranted penal use is made of immigration restrictions by using this assumed breach as damaging evidence of a defendant's character traits.

Use of Unqualified Interpreters

A major concern is the quality of interpretation in the criminal justice system. As a minimum, interpreters must be qualified and registered as public service interpreters, as stipulated in the National Agreement.[14] To a large extent, the provision of interpreters to courts and police stations is in line with the National Agreement, although we will later consider one example where this is not the case. However, there is no scrutiny of the interpreter services provided to solicitors, who, against a background of blissful ignorance of what constitutes a legally trained interpreter, are not bound by the National Agreement, as well as having to juggle Legal Aid cuts and the interests of their clients. The preparation of the case is crucial to its success, and regardless of qualified interpreters hopefully being instructed by the police and courts, the fact that many defense lawyers use unqualified interpreters in conferences with their clients compromises the quality of evidence and the integrity of the criminal procedure. In support of this argument, Collins and Morris (1996, vii) quote Justice Watkins as saying that "proceedings involving a language handicapped person which are conducted without assistance from an interpreter may be considered to be contrary to natural justice," and they go on to say that in their opinion, "providing an interpreter who is not up to the job may also put justice in jeopardy."

---

14 See <http://webarchive.nationalarchives.gov.uk/20100920143552/http://frontline.cjsonline.gov.uk/_includes/downloads/guidance/race-confidence-justice/National_Agreement_on_Use_of_Interpreters-August_2008.pdf>.

Limitations of the Legal Model of Interpreting

Short History and Critique of Conduit Role

According to Angelelli (2004), the conceptualization of the legal interpreter has relied historically on the Theory of Meaning which came to prominence in the 1970s. This theory argues that interpreting is independent of language and is based on "meaning" construed as existing on its own. The competent interpreter captures the only possible meaning of a given utterance in a source language, and transfers it into a target language. The underlying assumption forming the basis of the code of ethics of professional organizations is that neutrality and accuracy are monolithic, non-negotiable concepts. This simply does not allow for the lack of fit between languages, nor for the participative presence of the interpreter, who in reality often elicits meaning by asking for the information to be clarified, rephrased or repeated.

The theory that meaning has an existence of its own has been under sustained attack from recent interdisciplinary qualitative studies emerging from disciplines like the ethnography of communication and discourse analysis, such as Berk-Seligson (1990), Hale (2004), Fowler (2003) and Biasi (2003),[15] that demonstrate the participatory role of interpreters in ICE. Although lacking an empirical foundation, this theory informs the professional ideology holding interpreters to be "bilingual ghosts" or "conduits"—the idea of the abstract interpreter who acts as a neutral mouthpiece lacking agency in the interpreted encounter—and has been a major influence on interpreter training.

I would like to turn to some of the ways in which, from my experience and that of my colleagues, we as interpreters "stick out" and call attention to ourselves during legal proceedings. These observations are contemporaneous with unrecorded speech events, and provide us with a unique perspective into encounters unavailable for subsequent study.

The Interpreter as the Enforcer of Communicative Rules in the Courtroom

In the defendants' dock, it falls to the interpreter to act as the "gatekeeper" of communication between judge, clerk, solicitors and defendant. More often than not, NES are not familiar with the courtroom ritual, and I find myself in situations where I have to tell the defendant when to speak and not to speak, to explain who the people in the room are, to hear any under-the-breath comments he or she makes and decide if they could constitute instructions and call for the solicitor to approach the dock for further consultation, to tell the NES that the hearing is over and not to worry because the solicitor will visit again in the cells and explain what has happened in the hearing. All of these behaviors fall outside the "conduit"

15 Hale (2004) and Biasi (2003) quoted in Angelelli (2004).

role, but are necessary to give the defendant a fighting chance to understand and actually be present in the proceedings.

Footing

A further factor affecting interpreted legal encounters is the act of interpretation itself, which forces an artificial manner of speaking which has to be mastered by practice. This is related to NES not knowing how to speak through interpreters, and puts pressure on interpreters to correct it.

Footing is a linguistic convention aligning interpreters to the speaker by using the same person as the interlocutor. Its function is to avoid confusions in the ICE as to who is addressing whom and who is speaking about whom, and is particularly important in criminal proceedings concerned with the allocation of culpability.

One of the problems with footing is that it only works if all parties to the ICE are trained in it and use it by addressing each other, not the interpreter. According to Perez and Wilson (2003), Scottish police forces do not offer their recruits any training in using interpreters. To what extent any such training is given to police officers later on in their career, as well as to solicitors and court staff, is a matter for research, as there seems to be no literature about it. From my personal communications with various legal practitioners and court staff who come into contact with NES, there appears to be no training. And in my experience, many police officers, solicitors and virtually all court personnel address the interpreter, thus putting the interpreter in a very difficult position. When this happens, the interpreter may employ one of several strategies:

- Explain the use and implications of correct footing to the English speaking party, and ask them to respect it. This falls outside the remit of the "conduit" role, and amounts to educating the speakers. Even if they take this in good spirit, can they be expected to employ the correct footing throughout the ICE without fail? If not, another strategy has to be employed (see below).
- Intervene to seek clarification as to who is addressing whom and so on. This would lengthen the encounter, and may come across as churlish, especially in the face many repetitions.
- Apply their best judgment and correct the footing themselves. This may be dangerous because of possible misunderstandings on the part of the interpreters, and anyway, even if they always got it right, it would add considerable strain to their workload.
- Stick with the "conduit" role and let matters sort themselves out, because use of wrong footing is not a cultural misunderstanding and therefore interpreters are not mandated to intervene.

All of these strategies are unsatisfactory because they either draw attention to the interpreter or create confusion, and as their use is obscured by the "conduit" role, they are not known or evaluated. They need to be explored and discussed with a view to establishing best practice and incorporating it in interpreter training. On the other hand, if all criminal justice practitioners and employees were trained in working through interpreters, it would lessen the strain on interpreters. I would further argue that it is not fair on interpreters to be compelled to breach their own code of practice in situations where the reality of their working conditions clashes with their prescribed role.

Of course, a major problem with footing is that NES are not familiar with it. To them, it may look as if the interpreter is siding with the other party, especially if they have no English at all and do not understand that the interpreter is speaking for them in the first person as well. To the extent that it happens, it again draws undue attention to the interpreter, and may also amount to a perception of linguistic constraint with its attendant legal implications.

Conflicting Expectations of Court Interpreters

It is important that all court and prison staff are also offered training in working through interpreters, not only to maintain the integrity of footing in all ICE, but to make staff aware of the interpreters' work and harmonize expectations throughout the CJS. The demands made of interpreters outside the courtroom or consultation room show very clearly in my experience the insufficiency of the legal model of interpreting, which only covers ICE for evidential purposes, as well as the court staff's fundamental ignorance of the interpreter's mandate.

Especially since the cuts in Legal Aid, my colleagues and I have been asked to go to the cells on our own to find out from the detained defendants at first hearings if they have a solicitor or if they would like to see one. This happens in a number of magistrates' courts, and it is unacceptable for a number of reasons, of which we are concerned here with the "conduit" role, which presupposes the act of interpreting taking place "face to face," in the presence of both parties in dialog, not the interpreter eliciting information from the defendant in the absence of a court official.

Interpreters are continuously bombarded with questions by defendants and prisoners, such as "Do you think I need a solicitor?", "How should I plead?" or "What sentence do you think I'll get, because you must have seen similar cases to mine?" The list is endless. To send interpreters on their own to the cells undermines their position in the legal proceedings. It exposes them to improper requests for assistance which they must rebut in the absence of any official representative of the very legal proceedings in which they are meant to interpret. This is a further illustration of the interpreters' situated working conditions belying the idealized notion of the "bilingual ghost."

Interpreter Intervention

During legal consultations, I have felt compelled on numerous occasions to clarify immigration and other issues to solicitors and barristers, and on many other occasions I was asked directly my opinion about immigration matters, because, as a fact, criminal lawyers know little or nothing about immigration. Romania has recently joined the European Union, and often there is an overlap between criminal and immigration matters. In my commitment to facilitate comprehension and help clarify aspects of the case that may affect its outcome, I am happy, if asked, to draw on my extensive knowledge of immigration, having worked for the Home Office for over thirteen years. However, this type of intervention comes dangerously close to expert evidence, and is again not provided for in the neutral mouthpiece role ascribed interpreters by the legal profession. Moreover, as Russell (2002, 17) asserts, it is not clear "how much licence should the interpreter accord herself in order to facilitate comprehension between primary participants." The interpreter will be caught between interpreting for *skopos*, or the aim of getting the message across, and "the legal requirement for a "faithful" rendering of the original." It is yet another dilemma, in the sense that whatever the interpreter does or does not do in the circumstances, there will be legal consequences. The interpreters are left to exercise their own judgment as to where to place themselves on the intervention–non-intervention continuum, while the question of how the preparation of the case might have been affected had a different interpreter been instructed in the case shows up the "conduit" role as being nothing more than a legal fiction.

Coping with Dialog Taking Place Partly in English

When NES speak some English, it is very difficult for interpreters to judge when to intervene. The simplest solution seems to be to ask NES to request help when they feel they need it, but this takes us back to the discussion about the comprehension test, where I argued that NES do not always know when they do not understand something. I prefer to interpret everything, which makes things somewhat difficult for NES because they tend to listen to both the English- and their own-language versions and decide when to answer in English or in their own language, or wait for the interpretation and then answer in either English or their own language. I find that in legal consultations with NES who speak a degree of English, the dialog speeds up because of the questioners' impatience to wait for the interpretation when the NES shows understanding of what was said before the interpretation is delivered. In these circumstances, I find myself in the situation described by Russell (2002), namely pushed into simultaneous interpretation due to the denial of space to complete my interpretation, or I stop interpreting altogether and use my judgment as to when to intervene and interpret or ensure that the NES did actually understand.

The Function of the Myth of the "Conduit" Role

If the "conduit role" is a faulty conceptualization of the work of the court and police interpreter, as amply documented in the studies mentioned above, why is it still a belief system so fervently subscribed to? What function does it serve?

Arguing from the perspective of interpreters pushed into working from a mandate at odds with the reality of their work, Angelelli (2004) argues for three possible answers: (1) the notion of invisibility serves interpreters to escape the responsibility for the outcomes of the interaction; (2) invisibility earns the trust of the parties to the ICE, and (3) paying lip-service to the official code of conduct.

However, I wish to argue further that the legal fiction of the "conduit role" serves the legal profession best. The legal process deals in facts, certainties and evidence, and dispenses justice according to findings of truth. Its legitimacy is rooted in its claim to "truth" that by definition cannot be perceived as being relative. To own up to the interpreter's participatory presence in legal encounters is to introduce a wild card that could be perceived to undermine the very basis of the legal process.

Suggestions for Fairer Treatment of NES

The primary data used in this study describes instances in the legal procedure that exemplify a range of events commanding the attention of the legal profession and policy makers. Such instances fall into several categories: breaches of PACE occurring either as a result of bad practice (statement-taking) or lack of designated procedure (comprehension test); curtailment of interpreter provision as a direct effect of cuts in legal aid; lack of awareness on the part of some police officers and court staff as to the role of interpreters and how to work with interpreters; constraints placed by the interpreting process on NES, such as interpreters' impact on the proceedings, and varying degrees of non-English speakers' ability to express themselves in terms of pace and to understand the procedure in terms of footing. Altogether, they paint a stark picture of potential legal penalties incurred by non-English speakers.

Some of the instances leading to the unfavorable treatment of NES in the CJS can be addressed by means of policy recommendations. A comprehension test would reduce the risk of non-provision of interpreters to NES who need one; training programs for police and court officers as well as legal practitioners on working with interpreters would ease the interpreters' workload and lessen their impact on the proceedings. On the other hand, as argued by Angelelli (2004), the findings of the numerous studies on the pitfalls of the legal fiction of the "conduit" role of the interpreter could be used to explore the strategies employed by interpreters in overcoming predicaments, and ultimately inform a realistic model of the participant interpreter role. Policy makers and interpreter trainers alike need to understand that, to the extent that the ideal "conduit" role of the interpreter obscures the realities of the interpreted account for evidential purposes, it could arguably be construed as procedural bias against NES.

References

Angelelli, C. (2004), "Revisiting the interpreter's role: A study of conference, court and medical interpreters in Canada, Mexico and the United States," *Benjamins Translation Library*, 55, 1–125.

Berk-Seligson, S. (1990), *The Bilingual Courtroom: Court Interpreters in the Judicial Process*, Chicago, IL: University of Chicago Press.

—— (2004), "The Miranda Warnings and Linguistic Coercion: The Role of Footing in the Interrogation of a Limited-English-speaking Murder Suspect," in J. Cotterill (ed.), *Language and the Legal Process*, Basingstoke: Palgrave Macmillan, 127–43.

Collins, J. and Morris, R. (1996), *Interpreters and the Legal Process*, Winchester: Waterside Press.

Fowler, I. (2003), "Taking an Interpreted Witness Statement at the Police Station: What Did the Witness Actually Say?", in L. Brunette, G. Bastin, I. Hemlin and H. Clarke (eds.), *The Critical Link 3: Interpreters in the Community*, Amsterdam and Philadelphia, PA: John Benjamins), 46, 195– 209.

Hammersley, M. and Atkinson, P. (1995), *Ethnography: Principles in Practice*, London: Routledge.

Kleinman, S. and M. Copp (1993), *Emotions and Fieldwork*, Newbury Park, CA: Sage Publications).

Mason, I. (1999), "Introduction," *The Translator*, 5(2), 147–60.

Perez, I. and Wilson, C. (2003), "Interpreter-mediated Police Interviews: Working as a Professional Team," in C. Wadensjö, B. Englund Dimitrova and A. Nilsson (eds.), *The Critical Link 4: Professionalisation of Interpreting in the Community*, Amsterdam and Philadelphia, PA: John Benjamins, 79–93.

Petite, C. (2004), *Repair Mechanisms in Simultaneous Interpreting: A Corpus-based Analysis of Interpreters' Deployment of Processing Resources (English/French/German)*, Ph.D thesis, Edinburgh: Herriot-Watt University.

Russell, S. (2002), "'Three's a Crowd': Shifting Dynamics in the Interpreted Interview," in J. Cotterill (ed.), *Language in the Legal Process*, Basingstoke: Palgrave Macmillan, 111–26.

Chapter 11
Language Alternation in Kenyan and Malaysian Courts

Richard Powell and Maya Khemlani David

Introduction

Alternating between two or more languages is an unmarked communication choice for a large part of the world's population. Labov (1971) concluded that this widespread practice is generally unsystematic and rule-free. However, numerous influential studies (for example, Poplack 1981; Gumperz 1992; Myers-Scotton 1999) have indicated that lexicogrammatical, pragmatic and sociocultural factors may constrain speakers' propensity to alternate, even when there are few constraints on their personal proficiency in the languages in question. Such constraints may be reinforced by popular perceptions of language alternation as "broken" (*Utusan* 2004), or indicative of semilingualism rather than bilingualism, or somehow unsuited to formal situations. Further, domain-based macrolinguistic constraints may also add to the limitations of the immediate conversational context (Fishman 1972). There is also some evidence that formality inhibits language alternation—although Jacobson (2001) and David et al. (2009) found this inhibition to be much lower in Malaysia than in other sites they investigated.

Courts of law add further layers of restriction upon language choice, constituting one of the most formal of all sociolinguistic environments, with strict rules of speaking governing who says what to whom and when, often reinforced by official language policies governing which language(s) may be admitted in evidence. Whether for historical and institutional reasons or out of a desire to minimize ambiguity, most legal systems operate monolingually. Many multilingual societies, such as Botswana, prescribe the use of one language for the entire legal system. A smaller number, including Sri Lanka and Switzerland, recognize a number of court languages, but prohibit the mixing of different languages during the same proceedings. Even where there is no official prohibition, social and professional disapproval of mixing languages in formal situations are often reported.[1] Discourse languages that are neither admitted nor tolerated by the court are invariably mediated by an interpreter, and it is the interpreted utterance rather than the original which is recorded. Courtroom code-mixing and code-switching, along with the admission of other languages without translation, are therefore

1 T. Maosa (Tanzanian attorney-at-law), personal correspondence, August 24, 2006.

of great interest for their comparative rarity and the insights they may bring to motivations for code choice.

Aims and Scope of this Study

This study compares language alternation in the courtrooms of two multilingual societies: Kenya and Malaysia. The former is in some ways typical of a great many postcolonial polities where law still functions largely in the medium of the former colonial administration, even though most citizens have limited proficiency in it. While there is little official acceptance of any language other than English in the legal system, code-switching with Kiswahili, the national language and main lingua franca, seems to occur quite frequently in courtroom discourse. Moreover, oral testimony in Kiswahili may be admitted without being translated into English. Malaysia offers us the more unusual case of an officially bilingual legal system. Other cases include Hong Kong, and to a lesser extent, Tanzania. Language planning in the 1980s and 1990s engineered a shift away from English toward the national language, Malay, but many judges continue to accept English, particularly in the higher courts and in commercial and civil matters. Testimony may be heard in either Malay or English without interpretation, and alternation between the two languages is very common.

Kenyan data for this study has been gathered from courtroom observations in a magistrates' court in Central Nairobi (15 hours over ten days in 2009, with some additions from a similar period of observation in 2003). The Malaysian data was obtained from the Sessions Court in Petaling Jaya and the High Court in Shah Alam over three days in 2009, with additional examples from the Altantuya murder trial which took place in Shah Alam during 2008–2009, from Powell's observations in a Kuala Lumpur High Court (in David et al. 2009), and from Noraini Ibrahim's 2006 doctoral thesis on expert testimony. Courtroom data has been supported by documentary evidence (legislation, rules of procedure and so on) about language policy in the respective polities, and further informed by interviews with legal practitioners.

After summarizing the sociolinguistic and sociolegal situations of Kenya and Malaysia, a comparison will be made of the way in which languages are alternated in courtroom interactions in each country, focusing on the following patterns:

1. **lexical code-mixing**, where words from one language are embedded in utterances with a lexicogrammatical matrix largely drawn from another;
2. **code-switching**, in which a speaker juxtaposes clauses and whole sentences in different languages;
3. **code-shifting**, whereby a speaker uses one language with one interlocutor and a different language with another;

4. **non-convergent dialogues**, with two speakers conversing in separate languages and understanding each other without the help of an interpreter.

A second area for comparison is the motivation behind courtroom language alternation. Motivation is a notoriously evasive construct with regard to language alternation. Code-mixes made with local illocutionary intent can be hard to distinguish from habitual and unconscious loanwords. Intersentential code-switching may be significant when used sparingly, yet unremarkable when habitual and frequent. It is rarely possible to identify with any conviction the psychological, cultural, educational or performance-related factors that motivated a particular language choice in any given instance.

However, the courtroom is not a commonplace site of communication. Speakers—both experienced legal practitioners and witnesses appearing in court for the first time—are usually careful about what they say. Unlike in natural conversations, there is rarely more than one person talking at the same time, and the discourse progresses relatively slowly. This makes it reasonable to make intelligent guesses about the way in which speakers choose their words and also their code. In Malaysia, where code-switching is particularly frequent, courtroom interlocutors appear to switch languages not only to increase comprehension (as when lawyers show a preference for English among themselves, but for Malay with witnesses), but also for a number of convergence-, divergence- and performance-related reasons (such as clarification, emphasis, coercion and actual or metaphorical citation; for specific examples, see David 2003). Some of these motivations are apparent in Kenyan courtrooms as well. For example, defence lawyers routinely use English to gain an advantage over police witnesses who are less proficient in it, even after using Kiswahili quite competently in order to accommodate their own witnesses.

Drawing upon courtroom observations and interviews with legal practitioners, this comparative investigation shows how bilingualism in courtroom settings may yield insights into motivations for language alternation in general while shedding light upon the complex nature of legal discourse. Its findings suggest that even though language alternation is often used as a discursive weapon to coerce or isolate courtroom participants, it can also serve to make the workings of the law more transparent without sacrificing the interests of justice.

Sociolinguistic Context of Kenyan Law

Estimates of the number of languages spoken in Kenya range from 34 (Myers-Scotton 1993, 17) to some 60 (Ethnologue.com 2010) (see Table 11.1). Three major language families are represented: the Bantu branch of Niger-Congo, including Kiswahili; Gikuyu (or Kikuyu/Gikikuyu); Nilo-Saharan, which includes Dholuo (Luo) and Kalenjin, and Afro-Asiatic, including Cushitic languages such

Table 11.1 Kenyan languages with over 100,000 reported speakers

LANGUAGE	L1 SPEAKERS	LINGUISTIC GROUP
Gikuyu	7,180,000	Niger-Congo
Dholuo	4,270,000	Nilo-Saharan
Kamba	3,960,000	Niger-Congo
Ekegusli	2,120,000	Niger-Congo
Kimiiru	1,740,000	Niger-Congo
Kalenjin	1,627,000	Nilo-Saharan
Kigiryama	623,000	Niger-Congo
Maasai	590,000	Nilo-Saharan
Lubukusu	565,000	Niger-Congo
Kipsigis	471,000	Nilo-Saharan
Turkana	451,000	Nilo-Saharan
Kiembu	429,000	Niger-Congo
Somali	420,000	Afro-Asiatic
Dawida	312,000	Niger-Congo
Luidakho-Luisukha-Lutirichi	306,000	Niger-Congo
Sabaot	279,000	Nilo-Saharan
Teso	279,000	Nilo-Saharan
Pökoot	264,000	Nilo-Saharan
Terik	262,000	Nilo-Saharan
Chiduruma	247,000	Niger-Congo
Chidigo	217,000	Niger-Congo
Lulogooli	197,000	Niger-Congo
Kuria	174,000	Niger-Congo
Samburu	174,000	Nilo-Saharan
Suba	174,000	Niger-Congo
Borana	162,000	Afro-Asiatic
Markweeta	161,000	Nilo-Saharan
Tugo	144,000	Nilo-Saharan
Kitharaka	139,000	Niger-Congo
Kiswahili	131,000	Niger-Congo
Chichonyi	121,000	Niger-Congo
Olunyole	120,000	Niger-Congo
Keiyo	111,000	Nilo-Saharan
Sagalla	110,000	Niger-Congo

Source: Extracted from <http://www.ethnologue.com>.

as Daholo. Although the last group is spread over wide territories, it includes few languages with as many as 100,000 speakers. Bantu speakers account for 66% of the country's population (Myers-Scotton 1993, 19).

Any information on language use must be considered in the light of a range of methodological and conceptual limitations, such as the language- and identity-awareness of speakers themselves. In the case of East Africa, there is also considerable variation in the classification of speech-groups as languages or dialects, with mutual intelligibility not necessarily being the deciding factor (Myers-Scotton 1993, 17). The above data nonetheless clearly indicate that Kenya, with a population of 38.5 million, has a degree of linguistic diversity higher than in most of central-southern Africa.

Crucial to this diversity, yet commonly overlooked in data-gathering, is the high level of multilingualism, with most speakers who have any regular contact with those outside their speech-community being fluent in at least one other language. Code-switching has been widely reported (for example, Myers-Scotton 1993). While the statistics indicate only 130,000 L1 speakers of Kiswahili, the language has wide vehicularity as a lingua franca. It is claimed to be spoken by some 70% of the population (Mazrui and Mazrui 1998), has had the status of national language since independence, and is one of the few indigenous languages with a considerable body of literature.[2] As few as 24,000 claim English as their L1, yet the language, used widely both inter- and intra-ethnically, is spoken by up to 45% of Kenyans (Mazrui and Mazrui 1998) and is the medium of nearly all education except at early elementary level.

English emerged as the language of government and education on independence in 1963. While an educational report published soon after the Second World War proposed using the vernaculars in the first four grades of primary school (before switching to Kiswahili medium, with English to be introduced as a subject in grade five and as the main medium of instruction for secondary education), the following decade saw a steady erosion of the status of Kiswahili. In 1953—the year UNESCO promulgated the importance of mother-tongue instruction—English was made a compulsory subject in the primary school-leaving exams. In 1955, the report of the East Africa Royal Commission (Dow Report) expressed support for English, reflecting a shift in British colonial policy in the last decade of empire to ensure that the postcolonial rulers would be favorable to British interests. In general, English education was widely supported by Africans as well (Hargreaves 1996, 252). However, the nation's first African leader, the Gikuyu-speaking Jomo Kenyatta, was well aware of the symbolic and nationalizing power of Kiswahili. He ended his first parliamentary speech in it in 1964, publicly

2 While writer Ngugi wa Thiong'o has gone to great lengths to encourage literacy in Gikuyu, the limited success of his efforts was clear when one of the authors bought a Gikuyu-language Bible for Nairobi friends. Despite being native speakers of the language, they had never seen the language written, and kept the gift as a novelty while preferring to read in English, and to a lesser extent, Kiswahili.

described it in 1969 as the national language, and planned, against the opposition of his Attorney-General, to give it priority in parliamentary debate (Mazrui and Mazrui 1996, 293). His Minister of Information, Robert Matano, once threatened to fire bureaucrats lacking proficiency in the language. However, President Moi, from one of the smaller, non-Bantu groups (Tugen), restored English for debate in 1979, and there were no ministerial-level commissions or major reforms until 1985, when an 8–4–4 (8 years primary, 4 years secondary and 4 years higher) education structure was established, emphasizing the vernacular of the local area for the first four years, followed by English. Kiswahili was made a compulsory examination subject from the first grade. Increased enrolment in Swahili-language courses at Nairobi and Kenyatta Universities has been reported, and there is some evidence that the national language's status has been rising, although it is not clear whether this has been at the expense of other vernaculars or English (Myers-Scotton 1993, 30).

While Kiswahili has made some inroads into the educational domain, it has had far less impact on the legal domain. Both Kiswahili and English are referred to as official languages. Article 53 (s.1) of the constitution states that the business of the National Assembly may be in English or Kiswahili, and s.34(c) requires candidates for the Assembly to be able to speak and read both languages. However, the constitution itself was drafted in English and as yet lacks an official translation in the national language. Laws and bills presented to parliament are in English.

The legal profession remains heavily anglicized, with legal training entirely in English, although the majority of lawyers now train in Kenya rather than the United Kingdom.[3] Half of Kenya's chief justices are foreign-born, and Ali and Alamnin Mazrui conclude that most Kenyans feel alienated from a judicial system that is "based on the assumption that many of the most senior judges might be completely illiterate in Kiswahili" (Mazrui and Mazrui 1998, 113). Lawyers routinely take oral depositions from clients in a vernacular, record it in English, explain what has been written, and then have them sign or thumb-print it.[4] Constitutional Article 77(2)(f) states that a person charged with a criminal offence is permitted to have the assistance of an interpreter at the state's expense, but there is no provision for the use of any language other than English in proceedings.

However, Kiswahili does have an important oral role. In the Nairobi High Court, signs are all in English, but some Kiswahili signs and notices can be found in the magistrates' courts. Cases are announced first in English and then in Kiswahili. Court documents are exclusively in English, and conversation among lawyers and judges predominantly so—much of it never being translated for the benefit of defendants or witnesses. Verdicts, given in English, are often interpreted into Kiswahili by court clerks. Some judges, especially in the lower courts, routinely explain parts of the proceedings to defendants in Kiswahili,[5] and the language

3 Ngunku Kibanya (attorney-at-law), personal interview, Nairobi, January 8, 2002.

4 Joseph Maloba (state counsel), personal interview, Nairobi, January 8, 2002.

5 Ngunku Kibanya (attorney-at-law), personal interview, Nairobi, January 8, 2002.

may be used in oral evidence without translation.[6] In general, oral examination tends to be in English in the High Court and for socially-higher ranking witnesses, but in Kiswahili in the lower courts and for less-educated witnesses. English was also used with socially higher-ranking witnesses in the Anwar case (see David 2003). Local-level police officers are required to be proficient in Kiswahili, but not English, and so defence lawyers often take advantage of them by insisting on questioning them in English when they give evidence in court.[7]

Sociolinguistic Context of Malaysian Law

Ethnologue.com lists 137 languages for Malaysia for a population of 26 million. Many of these are for speech communities of less than 20,000 speakers in rural areas of Borneo (see Table 11.2).

There are also large immigrant speech-communities, including the Rohingya, who number some 100,000. Standard Malay has been the national language since independence in 1957. An acrolectal form is taught in all schools, and is the main medium of instruction in state secondary schools. It is also used widely in meso- and basilectal varieties as a lingua franca between different ethnic communities. English is used for the teaching of some school subjects, and widely in tertiary education. It is an important lingua franca, especially in business and the professions. Bi- and tri-lingual code-switching is widely reported (for example, David et al. 2009).

Malaysia's language policies and language politics continue to attract wide academic interest, particularly with regard to the educational domain. While the 1957 Constitution declared Malay the national language, English remained the main medium of government and education for the first decade of independence. In the 1970s, Malay was gradually phased into elementary, secondary and finally tertiary education. While English-medium schools were eliminated from the public sector, however, Mandarin- and Tamil-medium elementary schools were provided at elementary level as alternatives to Malay schools for the Chinese and Indian population (see David and Govindasamy 2005 and David 2004 for details of the language policy and effects on the education system). A provision for the Pupils' Own Language to be taught as a school subject in areas with sufficient demand has also provided some support for languages such as Iban and Dusun. The policy of bringing Malay into the educational domain was reinforced by requiring high-school leaving qualifications in the language for anyone seeking government employment.

The subsequent rise in Malay proficiency across all ethnic groups has been accompanied, perhaps inevitably, by concerns about a decline in the standards of English, even though it has continued to be taught as a compulsory subject.

6 W. Kutete-Matimbai (attorney-at-law), personal interview, Nairobi, January 10, 2002.

7 Ibid.

Table 11.2 Malaysian languages with over 50,000 reported speakers

Malay	11,000,000	Austronesian
Hokkien	2,020,000	Sino-Tibetan
Tamil (may include Malayalam)	1,400,000	Dravidian
Hakka	1,090,000	Sino-Tibetan
Yue (Cantonese)	1,070,000	Sino-Tibetan
Banjar (E. Malaysia)	900,000	Sino-Tibetan
Iban (E. Malaysia)	658,000	Austronesian
Negeri Sembilan Malay (Minang)	508,000	Austronesian
Teochew	497,280	Sino-Tibetan
Mandarin	417,070	Sino-Tibetan
English	380,000	Indo-European
Javanese	300,000	Austronesian
Min Dong (Fuzhou)	252,000	Sino-Tibetan
Tausug (E. Malaysia)	150,000	Austronesian
Dusun, Central (E. Malaysia)	141,000	Austronesian
Hainanese	141,000	Sino-Tibetan
Bidayuh (3 groups in E. Malaysia with limited mutual intelligibility)	140,000	Austronesian
Southern Sama (E. Malaysia)	119,000	Austronesian
Melanau, Central (E. Malaysia)	113,000	Austronesian
Kadazan, Coastal (E. Malaysia)	60,000	Austronesian
Bajau	55,000	Austronesian
Brunei	51,000	Austronesian
Semai	44,000	Austronesian

Source: Extracted from <http://www.ethnologue.com>.

In the 1990s there was a return to greater use of English at university level in order to address some of these concerns, and in 2002 the decision was made to teach mathematics and science (as well as English itself) in English at school level. Attitudes to this controversial move have been complex. Many Chinese educationalists feared a decline in standards of mathematics, which had been taught successfully in Mandarin, and negotiated a compromise for teaching subjects in both Mandarin and English. Some Tamil groups have seen the policy as offering greater opportunities to young Indians, while others would prefer the continuance of Tamil at elementary level and Malay at secondary. Some Malays in urban areas welcomed the change, while many in rural areas opposed it. Faced with wide dissatisfaction, in 2009 the government initiated the process of returning to the teaching of maths and science in Malay.

Following the phasing of Malay into the educational and administrative domains, a series of language reforms was launched in the 1980s to bring it into the legal domain. Malay was installed as the language of the courts, and required for proceedings and for documentary submissions. However, provision was made for the continuation of English where its use was deemed in the "interests of justice" (Constitution, Art. 152, Rules of the High Court 1980), and the language could continue to be used in testimony without being translated. These reforms enabled a rapid shift in the lower courts, where fewer witnesses and defendants are proficient in English, toward the national language. New laws are drafted bilingually. No language other than Malay or English may be used in court without interpretation. The right to an interpreter is provided for defendants and witnesses in criminal cases under Article 152 of the Constitution and also Clause 270(1) of the Criminal Procedure Code.

The result of the policy to promote Malay while allowing the continuation of English is a legal system in which either language may be used for most proceedings in most courts. Malay is more common in lower courts and criminal cases, in routine applications, and where the presiding judge was appointed from government service rather than from the bar. However, English continues to be used widely in the higher courts, and exclusively in the Federal (Supreme) Court. Judges are especially likely to exercise their discretion to allow English in civil and commercial cases and where legal arguments rely on judicial precedents. It is very common to find both languages used in the same proceedings.

Language Alternation in Courtroom Interactions

Identification, classification and analysis of language alternation is fraught with methodological and conceptual difficulties, including the construct of code itself, the possibility of differentiating between code-switches and established loans (a vain pursuit, according to Eastman 1992, 1), and the distinction between code-switching and code-mixing. The environment of courtroom conversation compounds these difficulties because of the prevalence of technical terms (which may be in Latin or French), citation of authorities (which may be written in a language different from the one being used in oral argument) and style-switching (for example, between more and less formal registers). Matters are not helped by the fact that the literature on courtroom language alternation is relatively sparse; this might reflect the rarity of the phenomenon itself, but more probably results from its under-reporting, since evidence for it has been found in a number of common law jurisdictions, including Malaysia (David 1993; David 2003; Powell 2008b), Botswana (Thekiso 2001), the United States (Angermeyer 2003) and Sri Lanka (Powell 2008a).

For the purposes of this study, the general term "language alternation" is used to cover code-mixing (the insertion of single words from one language into speech acts predominantly in another), code-switching (alternation of languages at phrase or clause level, both intrasententially and intersententially), code-shifting (changing from one language to another when there is a change of interlocutor) and non-accommodating dialogue (when interlocutors exchange speech acts in different languages without the intervention of an interpreter). While it is accepted that distinguishing loans from mixes is in practice difficult, and on occasions impossible, the distinction is nevertheless held to be useful when the use of certain words appears marked by others involved in the discourse. Similarly, the concept of discrete codes is itself held to be an important one, even though they may not easily be separated out in practice. When language alternation is extensive or habitual, there seems to be some validity in Gibbons' (1987) concept of code-switching as a code in itself.

Code-mixing

Insertion of single nouns and short nominal phrases appears to be the most common pattern of language alternation in the Nairobi Magistrates' Court data (see Table 11.3 for the transcription key). There seems to be a slight preference for embedding English within Kiswahili, rather than the other way around. Many of these English lexemes are legal terms used frequently by all main parties:

Table 11.3 Transcription key

[1]	Example number
( )	Translation below original[8]
J	Justice (judge, registrar, magistrate)
C	Counsel (PC = Prosecutor; DC = Defence)
PO	Police Officer
W	Witness or Complainant
Ck	Court Clerk

8 Since Kiswahili and Malay syntax are generally similar to English, translation has been added mostly at word- or phrase-level, without giving a translation of the entire clause. Hence "*Kuna uwezekano* accused *kupotele*" is rendered "*Kuna* (there is) *uwezekano* (possibility) accused *kupotele* (disappear)," rather than "There is a possibility the accused will disappear." For clarity, however, some clauses have been translated en bloc instead of being broken down into components. The main syntactical differences between English and Kiswahili/Malay relevant to the data are that in the latter two, adjectives and possessive pronouns follow the nouns they modify (*jina lako* in Kiswahili and *nama kamu* in Malay, meaning "name your"). An important morphological aspect of Kiswahili is that complex verbs are written as single words with affixes representing person and tense. For example, *aliniambia* can be broken down into *a-li-ni-ambia* = [s/he] [past-tense] [me] [tell], that is, "he told me." This feature does not seem to inhibit the borrowing and integration of English verbs, however, especially in the urban patois known as Sheng, which produces forms such as "*nili*showup" = I showed up, and "*nilij*bring" = I brought myself.

[1] J[to C]: *Una* witness *yeyote*?
(Do you have) (any)

[2] J: *Una*prefer *upelekwe* remand *ama* police station?
(You prefer) (to be taken to) (or)
D: *Ndio*, police station *ni mzuri*.
(Yes) (is good)

[3] C: *Kesi yako itakuwa na* mention on 6/8/2009.
(Case) (your) (will have)

[4] D: Magistrate *alinipatia* bond of 50,000, but *singeweza kulipa*.
(gave me) (I could not) (pay)

Other common insertions, while not legal terms, have administrative connotations:

[5] C: *Wakati polisi walienda, gari yako, ilikuwa na* registration?
(When) (the police) (went) [to] (vehicle) (your), (it had)

[6] W: *Hakuna* authority *ya kutoa* anything *bila mwangi kupeana ruhusa*.
(There is no) (to remove) (without) (giving) (consent)

Quite often an English legalese code-mix precedes, and perhaps triggers, a clausal code-switch:

[7] PO: The accused *alienda kwa nyumba ya* complainant and took gas cylinder.
(went) (to) (house) (of)

Interestingly, a number of examples of embedding Kiswahili legalese within English prevent us from drawing simple—indeed, intuitive—conclusions about English being the default language of the law in Kenyan magistrates' courts:

[8] J: You, *mshukiwa*, do you have anything to say?
(accused)

[9] C: I'm applying for adjournment *kwa sababu mlalamishi*
(because) (complainant)
is in hospital after the tragic death of her father.

[10] Ck: Do you have any *pingamizi*?
(objection)
D: *Sina pingamizi* at this time.
(I don't have) (objection)

Further, a lesser but significant number of non-legalistic insertions found in the data draw attention to the prevalence of code-mixing in Kenyan society in general, not just in legal contexts. Again, nouns seem to be the most commonly inserted items:

[11] C: *Uliskia* *noise yeyote* *ndani ya hio ofisi*?'
(Did you hear) (any noise) (in the office)
W: *Alipoingia* *nilienda kuosha*
(When he entered) (I went to wash)
dirisha *za* floor *ingine* *kwa hio* building.
(windows) (on another floor) (in the)

But we also find a few examples of adjectives and adverbs:

[12] C: *Tuna* witness. *Uko* *tayari* *kuendelea*?
(We have) (Are you) (ready) (to proceed)
D: *Mazee*,[9] Your Honour, *siko* ready.
(Hey) (I'm not)

[13] C: *Hii* *mguu* *uliitoa* immediately?
(This) (tyre) (you removed)
W: *Tuliitoa* immediately.
(We removed it)

Very few English verbs appear embedded in Kiswahili in isolation. This raises the possibility of a grammatical inhibition on the code-mixing of verbs, given that they may need morphological changes in combination with auxiliaries. However, several witnesses and defendants, particularly those with a tendency to use Sheng patois, use English root-verbs embedded in Kiswahili morphology to indicate subject, object or tense:

[14] D: *Ulini*get *kwa* Administration Police Camp *ama*
(Did you find me) (at) (or)
nilijibring alone?
(did I bring myself)

[15] D: Your Honour, *na*plead for leniency.
(I am pleading)

9 This rather informal Sheng term (*mazee*) belies the idea that all conversation in court, or at least all utterances from defendants and witnesses, are constrained by the formality of the occasion.

[16] D: Your Honour, *naomba* *uni*consider.
(I pray) (you consider me)

This tendency is found much less among justices and advocates, who seem more likely to use English verbs as part of entire English clauses, but the following is an example from a prosecutor:

[17] C: It is alleged that *uli*disappear *na mzigo*.
(you disappeared) (with the baggage).

The counterpart to the paucity of English verbal mixes is a large number of Kiswahili verbs inserted into English. The possibility must be considered that speakers feel better able to express complex combinations of subject, object, tense and aspect in Kiswahili:

[18] Ck: *Unashtakiwa* that you failed to stop theft *iliotekea* Norfolk Towers,
(You are accused) (that occurred)

[19] J: Complainant *hajaonekana* for any hearing so I'm releasing you.
(has yet to appear)
D: Your Honour, *naweza* *rudishiwa* cash bail *yangu*?
(may I) (be returned) (my)

In Malaysia, code-mixing of English lexical items within a Malay matrix, or vice versa, is quite common, as in the following example from C:

[20] C: Now the fact that immediately prior to the police station he was assaulted by the public.
J: Prior to …
C: the *balai* my lord, the police station the accused was…
(police station)
J: Was?
C: Apprehended by the public.

(Noraini Ibrahim 2006, 47)

In other examples, Noraini Ibrahim shows that English still often dominates in the High Court despite the fact that Malay is the national language; yet there are frequent Malay insertions, including personal titles:

[21] C: Now *Tan Sri*, this constellation of factors,
(title conferred by the Sultan)
must they be related to that particular day?
W: *Habis* for this particular time
(finished)

C: No, no! My question is this constellation of factors, are they for this particular day?
W: For that particular day.

(Noraini Ibrahim 2006, 27)

[22] J: ... so I told your counsel whether this word, "under the influence of alcohol" includes a person on glass of brandy or whisky and 20 mg per 1000 of blood, do you also include him?
W: No *yang Arif.*
(Your Honour)

(Noraini Ibrahim 2006, 8)

The use of single lexical Malay words embedded in English text does not preclude the opposite from occurring, as shown in Ex. 23, where single lexical English items like "supervisor" and "deposit" are embedded in Malay-dominated discourse. Code-mixing has become habitual in multilingual Malaysia, as noted in the many examples provided:

[23] C: *Sebagai* supervisor *di* hotel, *apa prosedur kepada orang yang ingin menginap di* hotel?
(As a supervisor, what are the procedures for those who want to stay in the hotel?)
W: *Beri* IC *atau passport.*
(Need to provide IC or passport.)
C: *Beri kad pengenalan,* IC *dan bagi tujuan pendaftaran. Pendaftaran dibuat berdasarkan*
(Provide an idenitification card, IC for the purposes of registration. Registration is done based on:
IC *dan* passport *yang diberikan. Kemudian*?
(the given IC and passport. And then?
Ada deposit *diambil dari pelangan*?
Is any deposit taken from the guest?)
W: Deposit *seperti biasa. Seratus lima puluh ringgit.*
(We will take deposit as usual. RM150.)
J: *Seratus lima puluh ringgit, ya*?
(RM150, right?)
W: *Seratus lima puluh ringgit.*
(RM150.)
J: Deposit *satu ratus lima puluh ringgit.* [Saying out loud while writing into case record log book]
(Deposit of RM150.)
C: *Bagi* deposit, *ada bayaran resit diberikan*?
(For the deposit, any receipt of payment given?)

(High Court 2009)

Apart from it being habitual, code-mixing occurs sometimes due to a need for precision—that is, to ensure that the correct word is being used in order to convey the exact shade of meaning. The need to be specific and exact is vital in a court of law, and in Ex. 24 it is clear that despite using the correct word for "consume" in Malay, the judge feels the need to verify the use by asking what the word for "consume" is in Malay:

[24] J: *Perayu, Yap Choy, awak dibawa ke hadapan saya berdasarkan rayuan ke Mahkamah. Hukuman yang dijatuhkan oleh Majistret ke atas awak kerana kesalahan awak di bawah Seksyen 15(1)(a), mengatakan bahawa awak telah masukkan dadah ke tubuh badan awak. Di bawah Seksyen 15 tu, hukuman itu mengatakan bahawa sesiapa yang makan, consume..* "Consume" *dalam Bahasa apa?*
(Appelant Yap Choy, you have been brought in front of me on the basis of your appeal to the court against the sentence imposed on you by the magistrate for an offence under Section 15(1)(a), stating that you took drugs into your body. Under that Section 15, the sentence for anyone whoever has eaten, consumed.. What is "Consume" in Malay?)
C: *Makan. Guna.*
(Eat. Use.)

(High Court 2009)

Code-switching

Because of the complexity of Kiswahili verbs, which often indicate both subject and object, the distinction between code-mixes and code-switches in Kenya is often unclear, but the data for this study include numerous instances of language alternation that clearly goes beyond word- or phrase-level. This indicates a considerable degree of bilingual proficiency, and is found not only with the justices and advocates, but also with court officers, defendants and witnesses:

[25] J: *Utaskiza* instructions. *Halafu utatueleza* if it's true or not true.
(Listen to) (Then) (tell us)

[26] C: Your Honour, *kuna uwezekano* accused *kupotelea njiani*
(there is) (possibility) (disappear) (on the way)
because he has another case pending

[27] Ck: *Ukiskia jina lako,* you should respond.
(If you hear) (name) (your)
D: Sorry, *sikukusikia*.
(I didn't hear you)

[28] D: N*dio*, Your Honour, *aliniambia* he will be here today. *Sijui nini imetokea.*
(Yes) (he told me) (I don't know) (what) (happened)

Indeed, there are a number of extended exchanges where both justice and defendant switch back and forth between languages:

[29] J: *Unge sema* anything against the allegations?
(Would you) (say)
D: *Tangu* last year December I've been coming, Your Honour.
(From)
Lakini complainant *aonekani hadi leo.*
(but) (hasn't appeared) (till) (today)
J: Your complaints *zinaisha leo. Kwa nini ulitoroka na mzigo*?
(end) (today). (Why) (did you run away) (with the luggage)

[30] J: Application *ya* adjournment of this case has been filed.
(for)
Una pingamizi yeyote?
(You have) (objection) (any)
D: Your Honour, first time *nilianza hii kesi nili*showup in court.
(I started) (this) (case) (I appeared)
Lakini complainant *hajawahi fika mpaka leo* and I pray *hii* court
(But) (hasn't arrived) (up to) (today) (this)
itupilie mbali hii case.
(forget about) (this)
J: Mention *itakuwa* on 3rd 8 2009 at 10am
(will be)

In the Malaysian courtroom, even where Malay tends to be the matrix language, as is often the case in the lower courts, when it comes to legal terms there is a tendency to switch to English, as shown in the use of the term "rebuttal evidence" within the matrix language of English in Ex. 31. Such code-mixes often appear to be a trigger for the speaker to switch to English as he or she continues. The switch to dominant English is seen in "Hari ini my learned friend Encik Fairuz will do the questioning" with Malay "hari ini" embedded in the dominant English text. The single lexical item regular is soon followed by more English words.

[31] J: Waiting long? I hope I can do the case today as I'm not feeling too well.
C: *Dengan izin yang Arif,*
(With Your Honour's permission)
Hari ini kita memanggil saksi pendakwa untuk rebuttal evidence. *Hari ini* my learned friend Encik Fairuz will do the questioning.
(Today we will call the witness for the accused for…) (Today …)

J: Rebuttal witness number what?

(Noraini Ibrahim 2006, 1)

Code-switching can also be seen as a trigger to code-mixing, and in Ex. 32, C starts in dominant Malay then slips into the English lexical items for "register" and "front desk." The national language policy is being adhered to, but there are many examples of slippage to English:

[32] C: *Saya katakan bahawa* OKT *pertama*, Amri *tidak* register *sendiri di* front desk *itu*.
(I say that the 1st OKT, Amri didn't register by himself at that front desk)

(High Court 2009)

Verifying the correct time an incident occurred is often the responsibility of the lawyer. To ensure that he or she is clearly understood, the lawyer embeds an important phrase in English in his or her dominant Malay discourse. Words like "sixth November," "at that time" are embedded in the matrix language, Malay:

[33] C: *Laporan tersebut disimpan oleh* ASP Tonny?
(Was that report kept by ASP Tonny?)
W: *Benar*.
(Correct)
C: OK. *Pada hari 6hb 11 2006*, 6th November, 2:30 *petang, adakah kamu pada masa itu berada*
(On sixth November, at 2:30p.m, were you at that time
di IPK? *Dan* at that time *adakah seorang pegawai yang bernama* Sirul *berada di situ*?
(at IPK? And was one of your officers named Sirul there?)
C: *Kemudian*?
(Then?)

(*Altantuya* Case 2008)

[34] J: 4th May, *empat haribulan Mei* oral submission, morning? or maybe we
(4th May)
can start at *sepuluh pagi* for oral submission.
(ten o'clock in the morning)

(Sessions Court 2009)

[35] W: *Ya. Yang arif. Iaitu ASP Lim Meng Seah*.
(Yes, Your Honour, is ASP Lim Meng Seah)
C: *Adakah kamu tahu pukul berapa*? What time was it?
(Do you know what time was it?)

W: *Lebih kurang pukul 5.*
(Around 5 o'clock)

(*Altantuya* Case 2008)

[36] C: *ASP telah cam kamu di* ... (inaudible—Malay)?
(Did ASP recognise you at ...)
W: *Ya.*
(Yes)
C: Still around the same time, *pada waktu yang sama, adakah kamu berjumpa dengan seorang wanita yang bernama Burmaa*?
(... at the same time, did you met another women named Burmaa?)
J: *Di D9.*
(at D9)

(*Altantuya* Case 2008)

To determine the exact date and time when an incident occurs, both the lawyer and the judge code-switched from language to language in Exx. 33, 34, 35 and 36 to ensure they were understood. Such a mixed discourse appears common in the Malaysian courtroom, and is also noted in Ex. 37, where both speakers shift from language to language within the same utterance:

[37] C: *Kamu lihat gambar 17, lokasi tempat kejadian.* Left or right?
(Look at picture 17, this is the place the incident occured.)
W: Right side. *Sebelah kanan tempat kejadian.*
(Right side the incident occured)

(*Altantuya* Case 2008)

[38] C: *Kamu berhentikan persekolahan anak kamu supaya mereka terus jadi alat memuaskan*
(You stopped your children going to school so that they could just become tools to
nafsu seks kamu
(satisfy your sexual desires.)
... you disallowed them to go to school, stop their schooling to be ...
W: *Saya tak setuju, itu satu penipuan.*
(I do not agree, it is a lie)

(Sessions Court 2009)

Ex. 38 shows the prosecutor (C) code-switching and repeating the same facts so that he is understood.

Non-accommodation and Code-shifting

In contrast to the collaborative code-switching referred to above, there are few clear examples of interlocutors maintaining separate codes. One possible instance is Ex. 39, where "Yes" might have been expected rather than "*La*," but here there are at least code-mixes by each party ("Your Honour" is the only way in which magistrates are addressed in either language in the data). Another is Ex. 40, where the clerk, justice and second defendant show a preference for English while the first defendant prefers Kiswahili, while clearly understanding what he is being asked. In Ex. 41, we can see stronger evidence of differential code-preference. However, in all these examples, code-mixing and code-switching blur the picture:

[39] J: I observed that *mshtakiwa wa kwanza* is already serving a sentence.
(accused) (the first one)
Are you aware?
C: *La*, Your Honour.
(No)

[40] Ck: First accused, do you have any *pingamizi*?
(objection)
D1: *Ndio*, Your Honour, *Sikufanya na bado nakataa.*
(Yes) (I didn't do it) (and still) (I disagree)
D2: *Ndio*, Your Honour. *Nina* objection as I need more time
(I have)
for hospitalisation.
J: The matter *imekuwa* adjourned. *Mwende* Court 1 for allocation.
(has been) (Go to)

[41] W: Your Honour, *kampuni imeonelea kuwasamehe washukiwa.*
(the company) (has decided) (to forgive) (the accused)
J: Are you sure of this *kwa sababu* they will be released
(because)
because it means the case has been withdrawn.
W: *Ndio*, Your Honour.
(Yes)
J: Granted. The accused persons are free to go *na* cash bail *ilipiwe.*
(and) (be paid)

Non-reciprocal language use is noted in Ex. 42 in a sessions court in Malaysia, where W starts questioning in English and although J attempts to accommodate initially by responding in English shortly after, he shifts back to Malay, the national language and the language of the courts:

[42] W: Can I get the question again?
J: The question is this, *tadi kamu kata kamu bapa yang baik, jadi tiada sebab*
(just now you said you are a good father, so there is no reason)

anak-anak tuduh kamu.
(your children should accuse you)

(Sessions Court 2009)

While code-shifting between interlocutors has been widely reported in Kenya,[10] especially the tendency of advocates and judges to use English among themselves but shift to Kiswahili for witnesses, the only clear example in the current data is of a shift on the part of a witness:

[43] W [to C] *Ndio. nguo zake*
(Yes) (her clothes)
[to J] These are her clothes, I am sure.

In another example, the magistrate uses Kiswahili with a defendant and English with a clerk, but slides between the two by first switching to English with the defendant:

[44] J [to D]: *Nimesikia ushaidi uliotelewa mbele ya koti hii.*
(I've heard) (evidence) (that has been given) (before) (in this court)
If your lawyer doesn't arrive here *kabla* 10 o'clock I will give the
(before)
hearing date.
[to Ck] Some people aren't very observant with time. *Nitapeana* a date.
(I will give)

Shifting from one code to another also depends on who is speaking to whom. When speaking to a higher-educated person like a doctor (see Ex. 45), there is a tendency to use English, and usually there is a shift to Malay when speaking with a lower officer like a policeman:

[45] C: *Soalan akan diberi dalam Bahasa Inggeris. Dato* can you tell where are
(Question will be given in English)
you attached?
W: Currently I am attached to the Department of Psychiatry Hospital Kuala Lumpur.

(Noraini Ibrahim 2006, 1)

Similarly, in Ex. 46, when the DPP wants to speak to the judge, he shifts to English, but shifts back to Malay when speaking to a policeman:

10 W. Kutete-Matimbai (attorney-at-law), personal interview, Nairobi, January 10, 2002; Joseph Maloba (state counsel), personal interview, Nairobi, January 8, 2002.

[46] C: My Lord, positions are the same except Dev—he is doing a watching brief.
J: When is he watching? [laughter from the gallery]
C: My Lord, we have a new witness to call. May I call Professor Vincent Marks?
Datuk boleh tunjuk? [To policeman to direct the Prof.]
(Datuk can you show?)
W: [Affirms in English]

(Noraini Ibrahim 2006, 1)

Conclusion

Our data from two different geographical settings show that members of the legal fraternity in these two settings have no option but to be bilingual. Clarity and precision are essential prerequisites in a court of law, and the ultimate goal is to attain justice. Lawyers and judges have to shift from code to code to achieve their specific objectives. This mixed code varies and ranges from code-mixing to code-switching to code-shifting and to code-alternation. We argue that such a mixed code should not be stigmatized, and should not be viewed as a symptom of deficiency. The reality is that the use of a mixed code in this specific setting must be viewed positively as a means of exploiting codes to achieve professional objectives.

There is also evidence from both sites that language-alternation can be both a strategy to accommodate and support interlocutors (typically, friendly witnesses, but also hostile ones when politeness must be seen to be observed), and also to coerce interlocutors. Similarly, refusal to accommodate, for example by maintaining a differential code while understanding what is being asked without the need of interpretation, can be a strategy to resist coercion.

Language-alternation may occur not only where it is officially sanctioned (for example, in Malaysia through the legal loophole of the "interests of justice"), but also where bilingualism is hardly recognized at all (for example, in Kenya, where parties concerned are either monolingual in Kiswahili or bilingual in Kiswahili and English). It therefore seems likely that it will be found in many other common law jurisdictions functioning within multilingual settings, whatever the official language policy for the legal domain may be.

References

Angermeyer, P.S. (2003), "Lexical Cohesion as a Motivation for Codeswitching: Evidence from Spanish-English Bilingual Speech in Court Testimonies," in L. Sayahi (ed.), *Selected Proceedings of the First Workshop on Spanish*

Sociolinguistics, Somerville, MA: Cascadilla Proceedings Project, 112–22, <http://www.lingref.com/cpp/wss/1/abstract1014.html>.

David, M.K. (1993), "Language and Law: Communicative Strategies in a Court of Law—a Malaysian Experience," in L.T. Khaw (ed.), *Legal Education in Malaysia: Quo Vadis?*, Kuala Lumpur: University of Malaya, 111–16.

David, M.K. (2003), "Role and functions of code-switching in Malaysian courtrooms," *Multilingua*, 22, <http://www.deepdyve.com/lp/de-gruyter/role-and-functions-of-code-switching-in-malaysian-courtrooms-xP6bwIarIV>.

David, M.K. (2004), "Language Policies in a Multilingual Nation: Focus on Malaysia," in M.K. David (ed.), *Teaching of English in Second and Foreign Language Settings: Focus on Malaysia*, Frankfurt: Peter Lang, 1–15.

David, M.K. and Govindasamy, S. (2005), "The Construction of National Identity and Globalization in Multilingual Malaysia," in A. Tsui and J.W. Tollefson (eds.), *Language Policy, Culture, and Identity in Asian Contexts*, Hillsdale, NJ: Lawrence Erlbaum, 55–72.

David, M.K., McLellan, J., Rafik-Galea, S. and Abdullah, A.N. (2009), *Code-switching in Malaysia*, Duisburg Papers on Research in Language and Culture, vol. 77, Frankfurt: Peter Lang.

Eastman, C. (1992), "Codeswitching as an urban language contact phenomenon," *Journal of Multilingual and Multicultural Development*, 13, 1–17.

Ethnologue.com (2010),<http://www.ethnologue.com/show_country.asp?name=kenya>.

Fishman, J.A. (1972), "Domains and the Relationships between Micro- and Macro-sociolinguistics," in J.J. Gumperz and D. Hymes (eds.), *Directions in Sociolinguistics: The Ethnography of Communication*, New York: Holt, Rinehart and Winston, 435–53.

Gibbons, J. (1987), *Code-mixing and Code Choice: A Hong Kong Case Study*, Clevedon: Multilingual Matters.

Gumperz, J.J. (1992), "Contextualization and Understanding," in A. Duranti and C. Goodwin (eds.), *Rethinking Context*, New York: Cambridge University Press, 229–52.

Hargreaves, J.D. (1996), *Decolonisation in Africa*, Harlow. Addison Wesley Longman.

Noraini Ibrahim (2006), *Courtroom Discourse: Expert Witness Testimony in a Criminal Case in Malaysia*, Ph.D thesis, Faculty of Languages and Linguistics, University of Malaya.

Jacobson, R. (2001), "Aspects of Scholarly Language Use in Malaysia: Switching Codes in Formal Settings," in U. Ammon (ed.), *The Dominance of English as a Language of Science: Effects on Other Languages and Language Communities*, Berlin: Mouton de Gruyter, 177–92.

Labov, W. (1971), "The Notion of 'System' in Creole Language," in D. Hymes (ed.), *Pidginization and Creolization of Languages*, Cambridge: Cambridge University Press, 447–72.

Mazrui, AA. and Mazrui, A.M. (1996), "A Tale of Two Englishes: The Imperial Language in Post-colonial Kenya and Uganda," in J.A. Fishman, A.W. Conrad and A. Rubal-Lopez (eds.), *Post-imperial English: Status Change in Former British and American Colonies, 1940–1990*, Berlin and New York: Mouton de Gruyter.

Mazrui, A.A. and Mazrui, A.M. (1998), *The Power of Babel: Language and Governance in the African Experience*, Chicago, IL: University of Chicago Press.

Myers-Scotton, C. (1993), *Codeswitching: Evidence from Africa*, Oxford: Clarendon Press.

Myers-Scotton, C. (1999), "Explaining the role of norms and rationality in codeswitching," *Journal of Pragmatics*, 32, 1,259–71.

Poplack, S. (1981), "Syntactic Structure and Social Function of Codeswitching," in R.P. Durán (ed.), *Latino Language and Communicative Behavior*, Norwood, NJ: Ablex, 169–84.

Powell, R. (2008a), "Bilingual Courtrooms: In the Interests of Justice?", in J. Gibbons and M.T. Turrell (eds.), *Dimensions of Forensic Linguistics*, Amsterdam: John Benjamins, 131–59.

Powell, R. (2008b), *Motivations for Language Choice in Malaysian Courtrooms*, Kuala Lumpur: University of Malaya Press.

Thekiso, E. (2001), "Bilingualism in a courtroom," paper delivered at 34th Annual Baal (British Association of Applied Linguistics) Meeting, Reading, UK, 6–8 September 2001.

Utusan (2004), "Bahasa Melayu kian luntur—masyarikat bersikap tidak pekak gunakan bahasa rojak" ("Malay getting tarnished—society must not be deaf to mixed-up language") Muka Hadapan, Utusan Online, 27 April, <http://www.utusan.com.my/utusan/archive.asp?y=2004&dt=0428&pub=utusan_malaysia&sec=muka%5Fhadapan&pg=mh_01.htm&arc=hive>.

Chapter 12
The Place of Arbitration in Online Proceedings as a Simulacrum

Joanna Jemielniak

Introductory Remarks

Historical origins of arbitration are primeval and it is considered to be a most ancient form of dispute resolution based on adjudication (Varady et al. 2006). Still, for several ages its practical significance remained very limited in comparison with the dominating form of domestic litigation. In the last century, in the sphere of international trade disputes, this process has been reversed, however. The contemporary renaissance of popularity of international commercial arbitration has led this method to become a principal way of deciding controversies in this field (López Rodríguez 2003). As discussed in detail in this chapter, arbitration turned out to be a sufficiently flexible procedural form to meet the requirements and needs of the quickly growing global trade exchange. Efficiency, competence, neutrality and predictability are the factors frequently noticed in this context. As a result, arbitration evolved into the most successful alternative to commercial dispute resolution by the national courts. Kauffmann-Kohler (2006, 1) remarks that: "The last decades of the twentieth century have seen a phenomenal boom in arbitration, with all the hazards and vagaries that come with sudden success."

This process has been accompanied by a growing institutionalization, described as a transition from an informal "merchants' justice" towards professionalism, legalism and proceduralization (see Bühring-Uhle et al. 2006, 32). It is also sometimes criticized for a tendency towards excessive formalization, making it increasingly close to litigation.

As von Mehren and Jiménez de Aréchaga (1989, 194) observe:

> arbitration—unlike national-court adjudication—is a dispute resolution process whose venue is contingent and transitory so that the place of arbitration neither represents nor establishes a permanent geographical or governmental relationship with a given national legal system. … The days when national legal systems intervened, as England did through the case-stated system, with on-going arbitrations are largely past.

Thus, from the very beginning of present-day arbitration, it has been observed that determinacy of the geographically understood place of arbitration does not result in limitation of the proceedings to the regulatory framework of the domestic legal system connected with this place. The link between actual venue and *lex loci arbitri* has thus been made deliberately weak, so as to encourage parties coming from different legal traditions to seek a non-discriminatory, possibly most neutral forum. This link seems to be even further weakened in online proceedings. Its existence, character and legal as well as philosophical effects are the object of analysis in this chapter. It discusses the issues of practical importance and popularity of arbitration; the development of arbitral online proceedings; the role of *loci arbitri*, and the proposed interpretation of ontological and semiotic relevance of venue in virtual arbitration.

Significance of Arbitration

In the sphere of international trade relations, the evolution and rapid expansion of arbitration in recent decades turned out to be spectacular. According to López Rodríguez (2003), at the beginning of the twenty-first century, as much as around 95 percent of international commercial contracts contained an arbitration clause. López Rodríguez also notices, after Brækhus, that: "in the field of [international] commercial contracts the only disputes, falling under national courts concern less professional milieus, which conclude their deals under homemade or obsolete contract forms" (López Rodríguez 2003, 67).

As a consequence, arbitration, conventionally discussed as an alternative method of dispute resolution to the default adjudication by domestic courts, in the field of international commercial disputes has itself become the default technique (see Petsche 2005, 1). As early as 1987, Lalive observed that: "International arbitration is now known to be 'the' ordinary and normal method of settling disputes of international trade (Lalive 1987, 293).

The reasons for this global success can be attributed mainly to the essentially pragmatic and functional design of arbitration. Confidentiality, professionalism and time efficiency have traditionally been promoted as major advantages in the use of arbitration in international trade disputes. The global tendency towards increasing autonomy of arbitration, its independence from national legislation and institutions, as well as recognition of arbitral awards worldwide have added to the current renaissance of this method. The irreducibly international character of contracts, from which the disputes result, calls for a non-domestic procedural (and, in many cases, also substantive) regime, to be found in arbitration. The a-national character of this method of dispute resolution greatly enhances the neutrality of the forum—much needed in cross-border trade debates.

Another important factor, particularly relevant in the context of place of arbitration and its procedural role, is legal certainty and the predictability of results of the proceedings. In the area of international commercial contracts, in arbitration this certainty is evaluated as high when compared with international litigation before domestic courts (Carter 2003, 24). The reasons for this lie in a three-level mechanism of applying the law in resolution of a private international dispute. Firstly, rules of procedure (in litigation—the civil procedure of *lex fori*) govern the course of case examination and resolution. Secondly, conflict of laws regulations (private international law rules, again belonging to domestic legal orders of particular states) shall be construed in order to determine the rules to be applied to the substance of the dispute. Thirdly, *lex causae* (proper law), the substantive regulations which have been identified on the second level, are applied so that the decision on the merits of the controversy can be reached (see von Mehren and Gottschalk 2007).

A litigating party, especially before a foreign court, might find the results of interpretation and application of the law on each of those levels very difficult to predict. On the procedural level, familiarity with such factors as the status of participants, admissible evidence, oral/documentary orientation of the procedure or the course of a lawsuit might in practice lead to a lack of equal footing and balance between the positions of the parties. As there are remarkable differences between national private international law criteria used for determining proper substantive law for the same type of legal relationship, the outcomes of application of those rules might also be difficult to predict for the foreign parties and their counsels. Finally, proper law found by the court may contain provisions that have unexpected effects on the position of a party—potentially large ones (regarding, for example, the presence or absence of particular types of remedies).

In arbitration, the parties are able to reduce the risk of such unanticipated results of application of the law on all three levels. Commencement of arbitral proceedings and authority of the arbitrators is directly derivative from the will of the parties. However, common intent of the parties is, as a standard, decisive for the choice and/or drafting of the applicable rules of procedure, as well as for the determination of substantive law governing the contract. In case of the lack of such choices by the parties, when the dispute is to be resolved by an arbitral institution, its standard rules of procedure will be applied, which are accessible in advance to both parties. Whereas a judge is bound to apply conflict of laws rules belonging to the geographically and legislatively determined *lex fori*, an arbitrator is obligated to follow the domestic private international law regulations of *lex loci arbitri* to a far lesser degree. It is worth bearing in mind that in legislations based on UNCITRAL Model Law on International Commercial Arbitration (currently in force in nearly 70 states and territories[1]), arbitrators are granted wide discretionary power in selecting the conflict of laws rules to apply in order to determine proper substantive law.[2] Moreover, through an increasingly popular instrument of direct choice (*voie directe*), an arbitrator might be empowered to omit the application of conflict of laws standards and select substantive rules which he or she deems to be

1 As of March 31, 2010; see <http://www.uncitral.org/uncitral/en/uncitral_texts/arbitration/1985Model_arbitration_status.html>.

2 See, for example, UNCITRAL Model Law on International Commercial Arbitration, Art. 28(2); UNCITRAL Arbitration Rules, Art. 33(1).

proper, without any intermediary means.[3] The risks of abuse of this far-reaching competence are arguably reduced by a mandatory requirement to provide a rationale for an award (which shall also state sufficient grounds for the performed choice of substantive law—see López Rodríguez 2003, 77).

Another key factor, connected with the legal geography of arbitration and enhancing its state of weak embedment in local realities, is the awareness of the fact that the main consequences of an arbitral award will take place principally in the country where it will be enforced, not in the one where the arbitration took place. Therefore, the physical location of arbitration is secondary, and recognition of the effects of an award surpassing the limits of one particular domestic legal regime naturally supports adopting a more universal approach to shaping and interpreting the standards on all three levels of application of the law in a private international case: procedure, conflict of laws principles and substantive rules (including transnational, and not only domestic, regulations).

As a consequence, arbitration seems to be an attractive option for the parties seeking standard and uniform treatment that transgresses national particularities. It is also considered to be a method that minimizes the risk of court (forum) shopping, or competing efforts by the parties to commence the proceedings before the domestic court in expectation of a favorable decision (Bell 2003, 275ff.)—a practice which substantially increases the level of legal uncertainty in resolving a controversy.

As von Mehren and Jiménez de Aréchaga (1989) remark, as a result of a natural evolution of arbitration and the tendency to escape from under the restrictions of *lex loci arbitri*, most popular locations for major arbitral centers are in those states where the autonomy of this form of dispute resolution is firmly granted and where the possibility of court intervention in pending proceedings has been reduced to a minimum. A practical consequence of this autonomy is the undeniable substantial role of arbitration in formulating autonomous rules for international trade, both procedural and substantive (see, for example, De Ly 2000).

New Means of Communication: Online Proceedings

The evolution and popularization of international commercial arbitration (ICA) has recently been accompanied by the development of new technological means enabling efficient and instant communication at a distance. The possibility of using cyberspace in arbitral proceedings seemed a natural field of expansion for this method of dispute resolution, already regarded as to a large extent de-territorialized in comparison with domestic litigation. The use of electronic

3 See, for example, ICC Arbitration Rules, Art. 17.1; Arbitration Rules of the Arbitration Institute of the Stockholm Chamber of Commerce, Art. 22.1; 2006 Rules of Arbitration of the International Arbitration Centre of the Austrian Federal Economic Chamber (Vienna rules), Art. 24.2.

instruments of communication to conclude arbitration agreements, as well as to run the proceedings, started to be considered as a method for ICA in the 1990s (see Arsic 1997, 209), and their popularity has grown significantly since then.

Online virtual (Carrington 2000) or electronic (Cachard 2003) arbitration has been deemed a form particularly suited to those disputes that themselves have resulted from the use of Internet (such as e-commerce transactions and domain name controversies—see Morek 2007). The concept of "online resolution" being most appropriate for "online disputes" (Girsberger and Schramm 2002, 605) has been a powerful incentive for the development of relevant mechanisms of arbitration. However, these mechanisms and means turned out also to be functional and effective in the settlement of "traditional" or "offline" controversies, and their use in all types of disputes has increased rapidly. Accordingly, the term "online arbitration" might be defined *sensu stricto* as resolution through arbitration of (commercial) disputes that have arisen online by the means of electronic communication, or *sensu largo* as a resolution of any (commercial) dispute through arbitration by means of electronic communication (Morek 2007, 5ff.). In this chapter we will adopt the second, broader meaning of online arbitration. We will further assume, after Arsic (1997, 209), that "online arbitration" refers to arbitration in which all activities are conducted over the Internet. However, it is recognized that in general, the application of various instruments and forms of electronic communication—to varying extents and at different stages of the proceedings—definitely poses new challenges to the actors in arbitral proceedings. In all such cases, the method used shall still be defined as (a specific form of) arbitration, and its legal aspects accordingly considered under the legal framework of ICA (see Manevy 2002).

Indeed, the pre-existing body of international regulations (including the 1958 New York Convention on the Recognition and Enforcement of Foreign Arbitral Awards,[4] hereafter referred to as the New York Convention), soft law instruments (such as the United Nations Commission on International Trade Law Model Law on International Commercial Arbitration, hereafter referred to as UNCITRAL Model Law[5]) and domestic legislation can be characterized as providing a basis that promotes rather than hampers the implementation and development of online methods in arbitration. It has thus offered a non-intrusive legal environment to advance private initiatives among a variety of arbitral organizations and institutions which have decided to offer services for virtual resolution of disputes, and in some cases, introduced separate sets of rules for online arbitration to promote this form. These bodies include new, specialized institutions, but also large, long-established, general arbitral centers of global significance that have incorporated online arbitration into their range of services. Recognition of the practical importance of new technologies in arbitration, and of the issues resulting therefrom, has also

4 Available at <http://www.uncitral.org/pdf/07-87406_Ebook_ALL.pdf>.

5 Available at <http://www.uncitral.org/pdf/english/texts/arbitration/ml-arb/07-86998_Ebook.pdf>.

led to such endeavors as the creation of specialized panels, like the International Chamber of Commerce (ICC) Task Force on IT in Arbitration, dedicated to the study of legal aspects of this phenomenon and to proposing new solutions. In 2005, the ICC also introduced *NetCase*, a separate platform for conducting arbitral proceedings online, and has been developing it ever since.

This search for relevant forms and rules for expansion of the forms of dispute resolution by virtual means on offer will be examined further in the context of defining the place of arbitration.

Place of Arbitration: Legal Relevance and Regulatory Framework

As discussed above, the fact that international commercial arbitration is not endorsed by a particular state's authority is often indicated in the literature (see, for example, Lew et al. 2003; Drahozal and Naimark 2005) as facilitating conflicting parties' efforts to seek non-discriminatory treatment and awards. Additional procedural standards, such as limitations on deciding disputes by arbitrators of the same nationality as one of the parties,[6] protect the same value of detachment of ICA from the domestic background.

Arbitration is thus frequently identified as being a-national, delocalized, floating or drifting (see, for example, Park 1983; De Ly 1992). According to Carbonneau, it is an effect of a nearly complete privatization of the international arbitral process:

> By ratifying the New York Arbitration Convention, states abandon their sovereign authority over arbitration—legitimating the process with their sovereign legal authority initially, but thereafter allowing it to self-regulate. The proclaimed independence of arbitration from national law traditionally was expressed in terms of the autonomy of the procedure and the award. Progressively, a-national arbitration also gained expression through a statement of substantive arbitrator autonomy: international arbitrators were alleged to have the authority to apply a nonnational arbitral commercial law to the merits of disputes. (Carbonneau 1998, 6)

Still, in traditionally organized arbitration, even if the proceedings were based solely on a review of documentary evidence without summoning the parties and witnesses, the place of arbitration has always been, by definition, physically existent and specific. It has never been entirely legally irrelevant regarding such critical issues as application of *lex loci arbitri*, the possibility of recourse to the domestic court of a state, and enforcement of an award.

Some level of conventionality in ascertaining *locus arbitri* in the traditional "offline" disputes has generally been secured by UNCITRAL Model Law, as

6 See, for example, LCIA Arbitration Rules, Art. 6.

well as by the rules of arbitration of different institutions, which allow procedural acts (and, in practice, practically entire proceedings) to be physically performed outside the agreed place of arbitration. The default option is then frequently an indication that, in the absence of other choices by the parties, the seat of arbitration shall be the city where the arbitral institution is located.[7]

Another possibility, in cases where the parties have not agreed upon the determination of the seat, is to leave the decision to the discretion of the tribunal. Such a competence, seemingly unlimited under Article 14 of the ICC Rules of Arbitration, is moderated under Article 16.1 of the UNCITRAL Arbitration Rules (in use at the Hong Kong International Arbitration Centre, for instance) by the regard the tribunal must apply to the circumstances of the arbitration. According to the latter rules, it seems an obviously undesired solution to identify a seat of arbitration on an entirely free basis. Also, the provision of Article 16.4 of the UNCITRAL Arbitration Rules ("The award shall be made at the place of arbitration") sets up a further standard of required localization of arbitration. This approach has been assumed by the UNCITRAL Model Law, a soft law instrument, which has become a pattern for numerous domestic legislations on ICA. As it states in Article 20:

> Article 20. Place of arbitration
>
> (1) The parties are free to agree on the place of arbitration. Failing such agreement, the place of arbitration shall be determined by the arbitral tribunal having regard to the circumstances of the case, including the convenience of the parties.
>
> (2) Notwithstanding the provisions of paragraph (1) of this article, the arbitral tribunal may, unless otherwise agreed by the parties, meet at any place it considers appropriate for consultation among its members, for hearing witnesses, experts or the parties, or for inspection of goods, other property or documents.

The discretionary power of the tribunal in ascertaining the *situs* has thus been further limited by the mandatory regard for the convenience of the parties.

In both variants described above (*locus arbitri* being either predetermined or found by the tribunal), the link between the seat of arbitration and an actual place of performance is *prima facie* definite; it may be weakened through the conduct of particular proceedings, but this does not essentially influence its effects nor the legal embedment of arbitration and an award in a legal system of the seat. The formulation of Article 16.2 of the LCIA Arbitration Rules seems exemplary in this regard:

---

7 See, for example, International Arbitral Centre of the Austrian Federal Economic Chamber (VIAC) Rules of Arbitration 2006, Art. 2; London Court of International Arbitration (LCIA) Arbitration Rules, Art. 16.

> Art. 16.2
>
> The Arbitral Tribunal may hold hearings, meetings and deliberations at any convenient geographical place in its discretion; and if elsewhere than the seat of the arbitration, the arbitration shall be treated as an arbitration conducted at the seat of the arbitration and any award as an award made at the seat of the arbitration for all purposes.

Locus Arbitri in Online Proceedings

The legal consequences of the determination of the seat are the same in online arbitration as in traditional arbitration. However, in the former, the *locus arbitri* may frequently turn out to be purely conventional, as it is possible for not only the parties and witnesses, but also the arbitrators to participate in the proceedings remotely and from different locations. The currently available technological means—from various methods of electronic documentary creation and submission to video conferencing and other forms of instant communication and real-time interactions—are presumably just forerunners of future developments. The possibility of their implementation in particular proceedings is considered an aspect of the parties' freedom to shape the rules of procedure for their case inasmuch as it does not contradict mandatory regulations.

As discussed above, determination of the *situs* lies primarily within the scope of party autonomy. In the absence of choice by the parties, the methods of discovery of the seat of arbitration are to be found in relevant rules of procedure, be they mandatory provisions of the law or, in the case of institutional arbitration, the rules of the proper institution. The legal framework for declaring the place of online arbitration is thus already in existence, and it is not based on some novel concept. Accordingly, case law also expresses the view that the seat of arbitration can be a "strictly legal concept dependent on the will of the parties" (*Société Procédés de prefabrication pour le béton* v. *Lybie*—after Morek 2007, 35). The difference in comparison with traditional arbitration therefore lies in shifting the emphasis: whereas in offline proceedings the possible detachment of the seat from an actual location or locations in which the procedural acts are performed is merely an acceptable deviation from the classical doctrine of the *situs*, in online proceedings the *situs* is by nature conventional, for two reasons. Firstly, especially in the case of a fully electronic arbitration, there is no physically existent point at which the actors meet. The location declared as a seat of arbitration is therefore a purely virtual creation, not a geographical spot where an actual interaction takes place. Secondly, the limits of detachment of the place(s) of particular procedural acts from the *situs* are much more vague, as proceedings involving the use of electronic means of communication can be conducted either fully or partially in cyberspace (and, in the latter case, this involvement may be effective to a different extent).

The resulting observation that in online arbitration no identifiable seat can be indicated, as it "is not pertaining to any particular geographical territory" (Hörnle 2003, 9), is a statement of limited validity, however. It might be acknowledged as an expression of factual indeterminacy of a *situs*, formulated from the implied reductivist, materialist perspective. A consequent claim of parallel legal indeterminacy would be ungrounded, however, therefore the resulting postulate of restructuring arbitration in accordance with the delocalization theory (Yu and Nasir 2003, 473) seems debatable, for at least two reasons.

Firstly, as discussed above, the declarations of ICA being an a-national or non-national phenomenon refer primarily to the private character of this method of dispute resolution and its already well-established autonomy, understood as independence from states' intervention and administration of justice (observable, for example, in the international standards of recognition and enforcement of arbitral awards). Despite enjoying such an autonomy, and although its embedment in the national legal system is relatively weaker compared to litigation, arbitration, be it traditional or electronic, it is not completely free from the influence of the geographically attributable domestic legal regime. On the contrary, the current international legal framework for ICA, including the New York Convention and the UNCITRAL Model Law, is, as Morek (2007, 34) observes, essentially rooted in the territoriality principle regarding such key issues as the determination of jurisdiction and enforceability of an award. The statement of *situs* is therefore a concern of critical importance.

Secondly, legal actors facing the problem of determining the seat of arbitration are sufficiently equipped for this task, as the international regulations on ICA, as well as the rules of arbitral institutions and, to a large extent, the national acts offer adequate sets of criteria. These criteria, as analyzed above, are generally not based on any inquiry as to the material facts of simultaneous, physical presence of the participants to the proceedings in the same place. Application of such a test is thus much more a question of mental habits of an interpreter than a result of any mandatory requirement. The territoriality principle, as formulated in the current legal framework of ICA, shall be observed not necessarily by fulfillment in the sphere of material reality, but by the agreement of the parties, and failing that, by the relevant decision of the arbitrators. The possible considerations to be respected (circumstances of the case, convenience of the parties) do not imply a joint, physical presence of the actors on one spot either.

Locus Arbitri as a Simulacrum

The formal requirement of territoriality attribution can, and in online arbitration does, lead to the creation of an entirely conventional image of a place where the proceedings were declared to have been held—a simulacrum that "bears no relation to any reality whatever" (Baudrillard 1998, 170). It is not the occurrence in material reality that carries legal implications—it is a social construct, and the acts of determining *locus* in online arbitration have merely uncovered this. It is not a coincidence that Baudrillard chose for the explication of his theory of simulacra a Borges tale of cartographers who drew a map of the empire so detailed that it covered its entire territory, and became being confused with the real thing (Baudrillard 1998, 166ff.). The physical organization of space being depicted by an assembly of signs is a particularly persuasive vision. According to Baudrillard, the Borgesian narrative, in which the map imitates and then shuts out the territory, belongs to the second-order simulacra, where they mask and pervert a basic reality. But then:

> Abstraction today is no longer that of the map, the double, the mirror or the concept. Simulation is no longer that of a territory, a referential being or a substance. It is the generation by models of a real without origin or reality: a hyperreal. The territory no longer precedes the map, nor survives it. Henceforth, it is the map that precedes the territory. (Baudrillard 1998, 168)

The advancement of forms of simulacra up to the fourth stage, where the image is its own simulacrum, is based on the release from the demand of representation, a project of an "ideal coextensivity between the map and the territory" (Baudrillard 1998, 167). The fourth-order simulacra are not bound by this demand any more, as it is they that create, not portray, the reality.

This state can be found in the act of construction of place of arbitration in online proceedings. It is not meant to feign material reality in which a physical meeting of the actors takes place in a certain geographically determined location. Their conventional character is known from the very beginning; it is manifest in the nature of arbitration by electronic means that the indication of its seat as a material spot is an agreed-upon fiction. The consequences of adoption of this fiction are most far-reaching and authentic. Reality is created by the adopted simulacrum of the *situs*, and this is achieved by the means of the law, itself a conventional social construct.

Contrary to the views of proponents of deterritorialization theory, the act of stating the place of arbitration in online proceedings seems not to be a step into an entirely new realm, but rather an innovative exploration of possibilities already granted by the existing legal skeleton. Such a practice remains in deep accordance with the very foundations of the recent development of ICA, as from the ontological perspective, contemporary promotion of arbitration can be perceived as an outcome of postmodern pragmatism (see Dickstein 1998). International commercial arbitration owes its intensive development to a grassroots movement of businesspeople seeking an efficient alternative to state-regulated and formalized litigation. It serves the needs of transnational global trade while being based on local and individual legitimizing grounds derived directly from the will of the parties. In its development, it has circumvented the limitations of traditionally perceived administration of justice rather than openly opposing it. The principle of party autonomy has been used in this process as a means of putting a foot in the door, and the way in which this traditional instrument has been used has been unprecedented, not only due to the scale of its use, but also to its practical and qualitative effects. Determination of seat of arbitration in online proceedings seems to be a facet of this exploratory approach, and yet another example of the creative use of the existing legal framework in arbitration.

References

Arsic, J. (1997), "International commercial arbitration on the Internet: Has the future come too early?", *Journal of International Arbitration*, 14, 209.

Baudrillard, J. (1998), "Simulacra and Simulations," in M. Poster (ed.), *Jean Baudrillard, Selected Writings*, Palo Alto, CA: Stanford University Press, 166–84.

Bell, A.S. (2003), *Forum Shopping and Venue in Transnational Litigation*, Oxford Private International Law series, Oxford: Oxford University Press.

Bühring-Uhle, C., Kirchhoff, L. and Scherer, G. (2006), *Arbitration and Mediation in International Business*, 2nd edn., International Arbitration Law Library, Alphen aan den Rijn, the Netherlands: Kluwer Law International.

Cachard, O. (2003), *International Commercial Arbitration: Electronic Arbitration*, New York: United Nations Conference on Trade and Development, <http://www.unctad.org/en/docs/edmmisc232add20_en.pdf>.

Carbonneau, T.E. (1998), "The Remaking of Arbitration: Design and Destiny," in T.E. Carbonneau (ed.), *Lex Mercatoria and Arbitration: A Discussion of the New Law Merchant*, Boston, MA: Kluwer Law International.

Carrington, P. (2000), "Virtual arbitration," *Ohio State Journal on Dispute Resolution*, 15, 669.

Carter, J.H. (2003), "Dispute Resolution and International Agreements," in T. Varady, J.J. Barceló and A.T. von Mehren (eds.), *International Commercial Arbitration: A Transnational Perspective*, St. Paul, MN: Thomson West.

De Ly, F. (1992), *International Business Law and Lex Mercatoria*, Amsterdam and New York: North-Holland, TMC Asser Instituut).

—— (2000), "Lex mercatoria (new law merchant): Globalization and international self-regulation," *Diritto del Commercio Internazionale*, 14(3), 555–90.

Dickstein, M. (ed.) (1998), *The Revival of Pragmatism: New Essays on Social Thought, Law and Culture*, Durham, NC: Duke University Press.

Drahozal, C.R. and Naimark, R.W. (2005), *Towards a Science of International Arbitration: Collected Empirical Research*, International Arbitration Law Library, The Hague and Frederick, MD: Kluwer Law International.

Girsberger, D. and Schramm, D. (2002), "Cyber-arbitration," *European Business Organization Law Review*, 3, 605.

Hörnle, J. (2003), "Online Dispute Resolution: More than the Emperor's New Clothes," in E. Katsh and D. Choi (eds.), *Online Dispute Resolution (ODR):*

Technology as the "Fourth Party." Papers and Proceedings of the 2003 United Nations Forum on ODR, 9.

Kauffmann-Kohler, G. (2006), "Foreword," in W.W. Park (ed.), *Arbitration of International Business Disputes: Studies in Law and Practice*, Oxford: Oxford University Press.

Lalive, P. (1987), "Transnational (or Truly International) Public Policy and International Arbitration," in P. Sanders (ed.), *Comparative Arbitration Practice and Public Policy in Arbitration*, ICCA Congress Series 3, Boston, MA: Kluwer Law and Taxation Publishers.

Lew, J.D.M., Mistelis, L.A. and Kröll, S. (2003), *Comparative International Commercial Arbitration*, The Hague and Frederick, MD: Kluwer Law International.

López Rodríguez, A.M. (ed.) (2003), *Lex Mercatoria and Harmonization of Contract Law in the EU*, Copenhagen: Djøf Publishing.

Manevy, I. (2002), *Online Dispute Resolution: What Future?*, <http://www.ombuds.org/cyberweek2002/manevy_odr01.pdf>.

Morek, R. (2007), *Regulation of Online Dispute Resolution: Between Law and Technology*, ODR Working Papers, <http://www.odr.info/papers.php>.

Park, W.W. (1983), "The lex loci arbitri and international commercial arbitration," *International and Comparative Law Quarterly*, 32(1), 21–52.

Petsche, M.A. (2005), *The Growing Autonomy of International Commercial Arbitration*, Beitrage zum internationalen Wirtschaftsrecht, vol. 3, Munich: Sellier European Law Publishers.

Varady, T., Barceló J.J. and von Mehren, A.T. (2006), *International Commercial Arbitration: A Transnational Perspective*, 3rd edn., American Casebook Series, St. Paul, MN: Thomson West.

von Mehren, A.T. and Gottschalk, E. (2007), *Adjudicatory Authority in Private International Law: A Comparative Study*, Hague Academy of International Law Monographs 5, Leiden and Boston, MA: Martinus Nijhoff.

von Mehren, A.T. and Jiménez de Aréchaga, E. (1989), "Final report on arbitration between states and foreign enterprises," *Annuaire de l'Institut de Droit International*, 63(2), 194.

Yu, H. and Nasir, M. (2003), "Can online arbitration exist within the traditional arbitration framework?", *Journal of International Arbitration*, 20.

Index

FSC
www.fsc.org
MIX
Papier | Fördert gute Waldnutzung
FSC® C083411

Kolibri 360 GmbH
Ferdinand-Jühlke-Straße 7
99095 Erfurt, Deutschland
produktsicherheit@kolibri360.de